A Guide to
CONTEMPORARY SOUTHWEST INDIANS

Written by Bernard L. Fontana

Southwest Parks and Monuments Association
Tucson, Arizona

Library of Congress Cataloging-in-Publication Data
Fontana, Bernard L.
A guide to contemporary Southwest Indians/
Bernard L. Fontana.
    p. cm.
    ISBN 1–877856–77–0
    1. Indian reservations—Southwest, New—Guidebooks.
    2. Indians of North America—Southwest, New—Material
        culture—Guidebooks.
    3. Southwest, New—Description and travel—Guidebooks.
    I. Title.
    E78.S7F583 1998

917.904'33—dc21   98–24657
                              CIP

Published by Southwest Parks
and Monuments Association
221 N. Court
Tucson, AZ 85701
www.spma.org

The net proceeds from SPMA publications
support educational and research programs
in your national parks.

Editorial by Derek Gallagher
Copy editing by Melanie Mallon
Design by Mo Martin
Electronic prepress preparation by Color Masters
Printing by Imago

Printed in Singapore

Front cover: *Santa Clara Pueblo basket dancer
by John Running, background: dunes in Monument Valley,
Navajo Reservation, Arizona by Jack Dykinga*

Title page: *Cellición Traditional Zuni dancers
by John Annerino*

CONTENTS

▼▼▼

	Hunting	Fishing	RV and/or Camping	Boating	Snow Skiing	Water Skiing/ Tubing	Swimming	Rafting	Museum	Arts & Crafts
Acoma			✓						✓	✓
Ak-Chin							✓		✓	✓
Chemehuevi	✓	✓ P	✓	✓		✓			✓	✓
Cochiti		✓ P	✓ P	✓		✓	✓			✓
Cocopah	✓ P	✓ P	✓	✓			✓		✓	✓
Colorado River	✓ P	✓ P	✓	✓		✓			✓	✓
Fort McDowell Mojave-Apache			✓ P							
Fort Mojave	✓ P	✓ P		✓		✓			✓	✓
Gila River									✓	✓
Hualapai	✓ P	✓ P	✓	✓ P				✓		✓
Havasupai			✓						✓	✓
Hopi										✓
Isleta		✓ P	✓ P	✓ P					✓	✓
Jemez	✓ P	✓ P				✓ P			✓	✓
Jicarilla Apache	✓ P	✓ P	✓ P	✓ P	✓ P				✓	✓
Kaibab Paiute			✓							✓
Laguna		✓ P							✓	✓
Mescalero Apache	✓ P	✓ P	✓	✓	✓				✓	✓
Nambe		✓ P	✓ P						✓	✓
Navajo	✓ P	✓ P	✓ P	✓ P					✓	✓
Pascua Yaqui										✓
Picuris		✓ P							✓	✓
Pojoaque				✓ P		✓			✓	✓
Quechan (Fort Yuma)		✓ P	✓	✓					✓	✓
Salt River Pima Maricopa			✓							✓
San Carlos Apache	✓ P	✓ P	✓ P	✓ P		✓		✓ P	✓	✓
Sandia		✓ P								✓
San Felipe										
San Ildefons									✓	✓
San Juan		✓ P	✓ P	✓ P						✓
San Juan Southern Paiute			✓ P							✓
Santa Ana										✓
Santa Clara		✓ P	✓ P							✓
Santo Domingo									✓	✓
Southern Ute		✓ P	✓ P	✓ P					✓	✓
Taos									✓	✓
Tesuque		✓ P	✓ P							✓
Tohono O'odham									✓	✓
Tonto Apache			✓ P							✓
Tortugas										
Ute Mountain Ute										✓
White Mountain Apache	✓ P	✓ P	✓ P	✓ P	✓ P	✓ P		✓ P	✓	✓
Yavapai-Apache	✓	✓	✓ P				✓			✓
Yavapai-Prescott			✓							
Ysleta del Sur									✓	
Zia		✓ P								✓
Zuni	✓ P	✓ P	✓ P						✓	✓

Casino	Bingo	Golf	Tennis	Hiking	Horse Riding	Rodeo	Photos	Alcohol	Tours	Tribal Events	Historic Sites
	●			● P			● P		● P	● P	● P
$										●	
$				●				●	●		
	●	●		● P						● P	● P
$	●	●	●						●	●	
$	●				● P	★		●		●	●
$	●								●	●	
$								●		●	
$	●					★			●	●	
				● P						● P	
				● P	● P		●			● P	
				● P					● P	● P	
$	●	●						●		● P	
				●	● P				●	●	● P
				●		★	● P	●	●	●	●
$									●	● P	●
							● P			● P	● P
$		●	●		● P	★	● P			● P	● P
							● P		●	●	● P
	●				● P	★			● P	●	●
$	●									●	
							● P			● P	● P
$	●									●	
$		●								●	
						★				●	
$	●					★		●		●	
$	●				● P					● P	
$										● P	
							● P		● P	● P	● P
$							● P			●	
		●								●	
$								●		● P	● P
							● P		●	● P	● P
			●							● P	● P
$	●					★		●		●	
			● P			★ P		●	●	● P	
$	●						● P		●	● P	● P
$	●					★				● P	●
$	●					★				●	●
										●	
$	●				●	★			●	●	●
$	●				● P	★		●	●	●	●
$									●	●	●
	●							●		●	
	●							●		●	●
										● P	
							● P			● P	● P

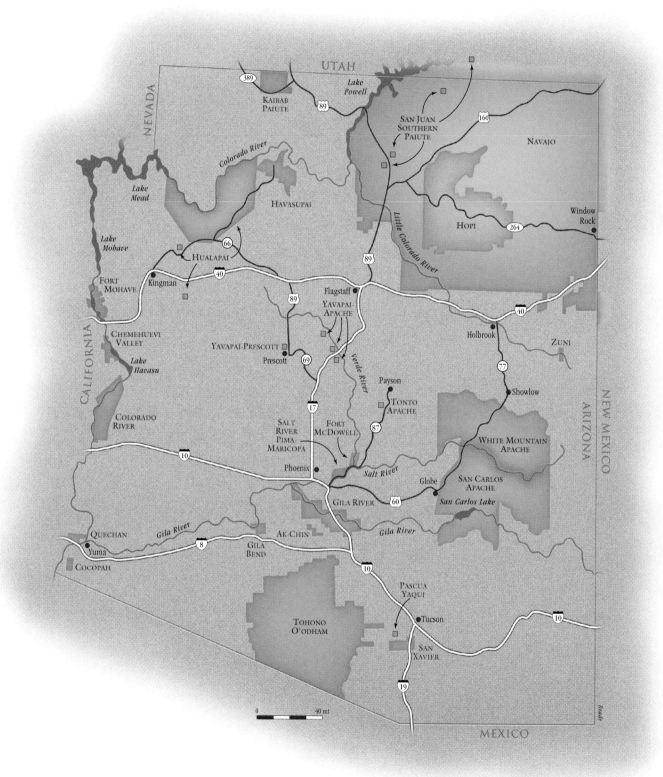

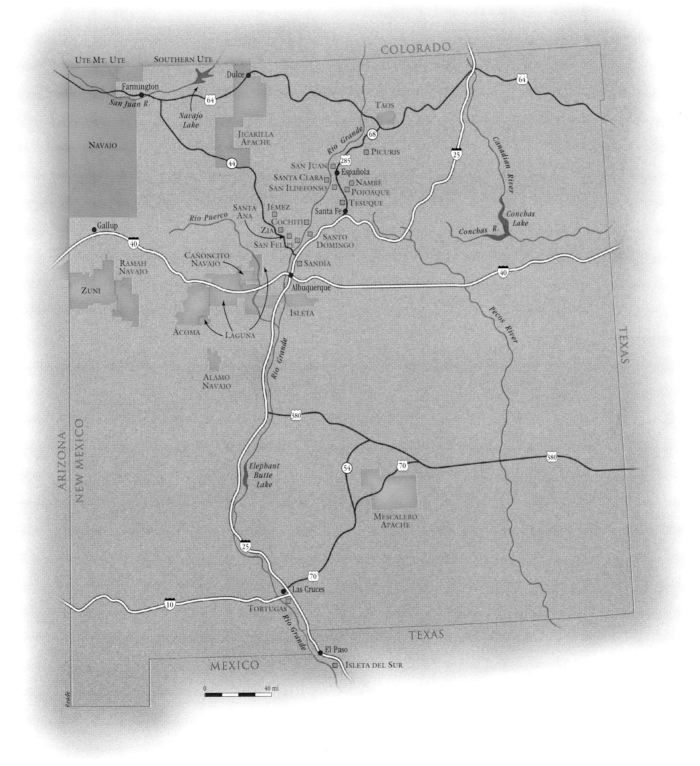

COLORADO

UTE MT. UTE   SOUTHERN UTE

Dulce

Farmington

San Juan R.

Navajo Lake

64

Taos

64

NAVAJO

JICARILLA APACHE

Rio Grande

68

44

PICURIS

25

Canadian River

SAN JUAN

285

Española

SANTA CLARA

NAMBÉ

SAN ILDEFONSO

POJOAQUE

TESUQUE

Conchas Lake

Gallup

SANTA ANA

JÉMEZ

COCHITI

Santa Fe

Conchas R.

40

Rio Puerco

ZIA

SAN FELIPE

SANTO DOMINGO

CAÑONCITO NAVAJO

SANDÍA

RAMAH NAVAJO

Albuquerque

40

Pecos River

ZUNI

ISLETA

ÁCOMA   LAGUNA

Rio Grande

ALAMO NAVAJO

TEXAS

380

Elephant Butte Lake

54

70

380

MESCALERO APACHE

ARIZONA

NEW MEXICO

25

70

Las Cruces

10

TORTUGAS

Rio Grande

TEXAS

El Paso

MEXICO

ISLETA DEL SUR

Reade

0   40 mi

It was the summer of 1949. Three fellow college students and I drove east across Hoover Dam in our 1936 Ford sedan headed toward the red cliffs and turquoise skies of the Colorado Plateau. None of us had been to the Southwest before and we were on a camping trip and voyage of discovery. We hoped to explore scenic wonders like the Grand Canyon, to look in awe over endless vistas toward mountain ranges rising from great plateaus, and, of course, to meet aboriginal Americans in their native surroundings.

Our first Indian sighting took place in a service station in Seligman where we'd stopped to gas up. There was no self-service in 1949, and the attendant who came to wait on us had brown skin, brown eyes, and black hair.

Unable to contain my excitement, I asked him if he was an Indian. He smiled, nodded in the affirmative, and that was the end of it. Except that now, nearly half a century later, I shudder with embarrassment when I recall the event. He was, after all, a person, not some kind of exotic animal on public display.

Indians loom large in the American psyche. They have become the convenient "other" onto which we non-Indians have projected our own images, both positive and negative. The result has been an endless series of cardboard cutouts: Savage; Noble Savage; Drunken Indian; Virtuous Maiden; Promiscuous Squaw; Environmentalist; Dumb Indian; Spiritualist; Trickster; Healer; Stoic;

Activist; Keeper of Wisdom; Warrior; Militant Red Man; Disappearing Indian; Defender of Tradition; and similar forms created out of the anxieties, fears, hopes, and dreams of those among us who would define away the world's complexities and bury our secret past.

So has the Indian image attained monumental proportions in the fantasies of Europeans and Asians. Whether because of their exposure to pulp fiction or "Spaghetti Westerns" and other popular movie and television projections of the American West, many foreigners arrive in the Southwest hoping to see red men in loin cloths carrying bows and arrows or, at the very least, performing exotic masked dances and living in tepees. The tepee, totem pole, birch bark canoe, tomahawk, two-headed drum (an Old World invention), and Plains Indian headdress have become symbols of some kind of universal "Indian" identity, and except that the drum and tepee remain in occasional ceremonial use among a handful of Southwest tribes, the other elements are missing from the region.

The "Indian" was born out of the meeting of Old World and New World cultures beginning in the late fifteenth century, a product of the mistaken notion by Europeans that they had sailed their westward course to outliers of India. Thus, thousands of separate and distinct indigenous cultures were soon defined out of existence, lumped together by conquering outsiders under a single label. While the term has never been a good one, attempts to replace it with such concepts as "Amerindian" or, more recently, "Native

American," have not achieved universal acceptance. Throughout North and South America, the term "Indian," or *indio* in Spanish, continues to stereotype everyone directly descended from peoples resident in the New World before Columbus arrived in the Caribbean in 1492.

In the Southwest, where most indigenous peoples continue to occupy portions of the same land their ancestors controlled in the sixteenth century and where tribal entities have remained intact, there truly are few "Indians." There remain instead people called Chemehuevi, Chiricahua, Cocopah, Eastern Keres, Havasupai, Hopi, Hualapai, Jémez, Jicarilla, Maricopa, Mescalero, Mohave, Navajo, Piman, Quechan, Southern Paiute, Tewa, Tiwa (or Tigua), Ute, Western Apache, Western Keres, Yavapai, Zuni, and, since the late nineteenth century, Yaqui. Their spoken words derive from presumably totally unrelated language families classified by linguists as Athapaskan, Yuman, Kiowa-Tanoan, Uto-Aztecan, Keres, and Zuni.

Apache includes, besides Arizona's Western Apache

(who are themselves now divided into the San Carlos, Tonto, and White Mountain Apaches), New Mexico's Jicarilla, Chiricahua, and Mescalero. The Puebloans are Arizona's Hopi and New Mexico's Zuni; Western Keresan of Ácoma and Laguna pueblos; Eastern Keresan of Cochiti, San Felipe, Santa Ana, Santo Domingo, and Zia pueblos; Northern Tiwa of Picuris and Taos pueblos; Southern Tiwa of Isleta and Sandia pueblos; Towa-speaking people of Jémez Pueblo; and Tewa of Nambé, Pojoaque, San Ildefonso, San Juan, Santa Clara, and Tesuque pueblos. The Tigua of Ysleta del Sur are within the city limits of El Paso, Texas.

Arizona's Pimans are the Pimas, Tohono O'odham, and Hia Ced O'odham (Sand Papago); southern Colorado's Utes include the Southern Ute and Ute Mountain Ute; and Arizona's Southern Paiute are divided into the San Juan and Kaibab tribes. The Chemehuevi are a Southern Paiute group whose reservation is in California.

All these people, whose histories, languages, and other aspects of culture are as varied as are those, say, of the people of Europe, have land bases called "reservations" where the seats of tribal governments are located. By no means, however, does everyone who qualifies live permanently on a reservation. A great many people, if not the majority, have chosen to seek employment opportunities elsewhere, especially in urban centers in Arizona and New Mexico, as well as throughout the United States. Nearly all of the Southwest's reservations are in a distinctly rural setting, and as elsewhere in the industrial world, rural dwellers find it increasingly difficult to forge for themselves a life they deem to be satisfactory. In the Southwest, tourism and other forms of visitation by outsiders are emerging as a major source of income for people otherwise hard-pressed to make ends meet in their traditional surroundings.

A GLIMPSE OF THE PAST
Prehistoric Times
Men, women, and children have lived in what today is the southwestern United States for at least eleven to twelve thousand years. A few

archaeologists believe, and there is some evidence to support their assertions, that human beings first entered this region as many as thirty thousand or more years ago.

The majority of archaeologists would argue that the earliest humans to come into the region were primarily hunters, people seeking Late Pleistocene game animals like the elephant paleontologists call the Colombian mammoth as well as now-extinct species of tapir, bison, jaguar, antelope, and horse. These early hunters, or Paleo-Indians, as they've been labeled, were succeeded by "Archaic" peoples whose primary means of survival lay in collecting edible and other useful parts of wild plants and by hunting small game, especially rabbits, rodents, and reptiles.

About thirty-five hundred years ago, beginnings were made toward improvement in a gathering/hunting lifestyle. Tiny cobs of domesticated corn made their way into the Southwest, probably from Mesoamerica, and a New World version of the Neolithic Revolution—but a slow "revolution" indeed—got underway. By around two thousand years ago, many Southwesterners were raising crops of corn, squash, beans, and, occasionally, cotton—all domestic plants over whose output people exercised at least nominal control. Added to the yield from hunting and gathering, domestic crops enabled people to acquire food surpluses and to live in more sedentary communities. Other developments came with horticulture. To fairly simple tools of stone, bone, wood, fiber, and antlers were added new forms made of these same materials intended for specialized tasks. For the first time, too, earthenware clay was fired into pottery, some of it elaborately painted in beautiful designs.

Throughout the Southwest, about fifteen hundred or more years before the arrival of Europeans, regional cultures developed whose people raised crops and fashioned ceramic vessels. Based on similarities in their material remains, they have

been labelled by archaeologists with such terms as Hohokam, Anasazi, Mogollon, Hakataya, Patayan, Sinagua, and Fremont.

In the fourteenth and fifteenth centuries, before Europeans reached the New World, these regional cultures suffered great population declines and dispersals for reasons archeologists continue to research. Scientists are confident that many contemporary Indians in the Southwest descended from these ancient cultures.

Indians on the Eve of European Conquest
Outsiders to the Southwest are often surprised to discover that much of it remains Indian Country. People live here in reduced acreages of the same areas utilized by their ancestors more than 450 years ago. In 1539, for example, Indians had authority over 100 percent of the lands now in Arizona. In 1997, their descendants controlled some 27 percent of these same lands, or more than a fourth of Arizona's real estate. Moreover, Southwestern Indians have not been dispersed; rather they have seen their domains compressed into reservations. Nearly all continue to live within some portion of their aboriginal territories.

A few groups, like the Piros, Tompiros, and Jumanos of New Mexico and the Soba, Sobaipuri, Opa, Comaricopa, Halchidhoma, Halyikwamai, Kaveltcadom, and Kohuana of Arizona are no longer extant as distinct tribes as they were perceived by Spaniards to have been in the sixteenth, seventeenth, and eighteenth centuries. Nor are the Comanches of eastern New Mexico and southern Colorado any longer there. But most of these people, other than the Comanches, who were eventually settled elsewhere, seem to have become amalgamated among their linguistic brethren. Sobas and Sobaipuris were absorbed by their fellow O'odham, and "Maricopas" were born of a fusion of Kohuana, Kaveltcadom, Opa, Comaricopa, Halyikwamai, and Halchidhoma. What became of the Piro, Tompiro, and Jumano peoples is more problematical, but even they may have found a path to cultural extinction through intermarriage with other peoples, Spanish-speaking mexicanos included. Some

Hispanic Americans like to point out that half of their ancestors began arriving in the New World a little more than five centuries ago, while the other half have been here for thousands of years.

At the time of first contact with Europeans, Southwestern Indians exhibited great variety of lifestyles. These have been classified into four major groups: ranchería peoples; village peoples; band peoples; and non-horticultural band peoples. Except for the latter, all were involved in varying degrees in horticulture, that is, in the raising of corn, squash, beans, and, to a lesser extent, cotton. All, however, depended largely on hunting and gathering for their subsistence as well as for their clothing, shelter, and other everyday needs.

The village peoples were those who lived in concentrated and permanent settlements Spaniards called pueblos. In Arizona, these were the Hopi towns. The others lived in New Mexico in many dozens of pueblos that by 1999 had dwindled to nineteen, or to twenty if one counts Ysleta del Sur in southwestern Texas.

Band peoples were those whose settlements had no fixed locations and whose primary food sources were hunted and gathered rather than grown. In Arizona and New Mexico these are primarily the Navajos, other Apaches, the Utes, Paiutes, and related Chemehuevi.

What may have been a majority of people in the Southwest—all the Piman and Yuman speakers—lived in settlements that Spaniards called rancherías. These consisted of communities of scattered houses, the houses themselves being made of easily collected impermanent materials, principally wood and grass. Many rancherías shifted locations seasonally and could be rebuilt without too much labor or abandoned without serious loss. Ranchería peoples balanced an economy of food collecting and hunting with one of horticulture.

What is perhaps most important to remember concerning Indians on the eve of their conquest by Europeans is that over centuries they had adapted to their regional environments in mountains, deserts, and plateaus to fashion a living that was generally satisfactory to them. Each group became essentially self sufficient and self reliant, and while there was trade, most goods traded—with the possible exception of salt—were not essential. People enjoyed their independence, a status quickly threatened after Europeans came into view.

The Spanish and Mexican Eras

Early Spanish colonists in New Mexico viewed the entire Colorado Plateau as belonging to their administration, including the lands of Hopi and Navajo peoples in what since 1863 has been northern Arizona. Spaniards made no direct impact on Indians in southern Arizona until the arrival in 1687 in northern Sonora, as southern Arizona was then regarded, of a Jesuit missionary named Eusebio Kino. Father Kino's founding of missions among the O'odham (Piman Indians) of the region marked the beginning of a non-Indian presence there that has continued unabated.

Spaniards were responsible for setting in motion a whole series of irreversible changes in the cultures of respective Southwestern Indian groups, changes that penetrated virtually every aspect of life. It would be wrong, however, to assume that

▼▼

all these changes were forced on the native populations. The introduction of epidemic diseases was unintended. And many of the other changes resulted from the Indians' own desires to claim for themselves Old World products: tools, technology, domestic plants and animals, and even various aspects of Christianity and European social and political organization.

Spain's rule in the Southwest came to an end in 1821 when Mexico successfully concluded its revolution against the mother country. Between 1821 and 1848, the Southwest—actually Mexico's far Northwest—was under the political and military sway of the Republic of Mexico. The Mexican government recognized no special "Indian" status for any of its people. On paper, at least, everyone was a Mexican citizen with equal rights. All persons were to be politically and economically incorporated within the new nation. New Mexico and northern Sonora, however, were so remote from Mexico City and the centers of power that Indians, or "indígenes," as they were called, were left largely to their own devices. Indeed, Apaches involved in continuous cycles of raiding and warfare were a serious military threat to the continued presence of Mexicans in much of the region, especially in Sonora. Northern Pimans were also militarily troublesome to Mexicans in Sonora in the late 1830s and early 1840s.

Mexican rule came to an end in most of the northern half of its territory in 1848 as a result of the Treaty of Guadalupe Hidalgo signed at the conclusion of the United States' war with Mexico. Additional northern Mexican lands were added to the United States with the Gadsden Purchase ratified in 1854. The stage was set for what had been the Northwest to become the Southwest, the southwestern United States, with a whole new set of Indian policies and cultural attitudes.

Southwestern Indians and the United States
When the United States acquired its new Southwest in the mid-nineteenth century, the Territory of New Mexico reached westward to

include what in 1863 was severed to become the separate Territory of Arizona. By this time, earlier United States' Indian policies, like those of relocating Indians to Indian Territory in Oklahoma and of prolific treaty making, had all but come to an end. What had taken their place in the middle of the 1800s was what might be called the "reservation policy," the practice of withdrawing lands from the public domain and reserving them for the exclusive use and occupancy of designated Indian tribes. The initial Navajo Indian Reservation resulted from an 1864 treaty. All other reservations in New Mexico, Arizona, southeastern California, southern Utah, and southern Colorado, however, were created either by executive order of the President of the United States or by Act of Congress. Neither

Taos Pueblo, New Mexico

treaties nor executive orders can any longer be used in establishing reservations. Only congressional legislation applies. Since passage of federal legislation in 1927, all reservations in the Southwest, regardless of their legal origins, have been treated the same under United States law.

Counting reservations is not a simple matter. Many reservations include non-contiguous units that historically have been called "reservations." The Papago Indian Reservation, for example, the home of the Tohono O'odham Nation, consists of the San Xavier Indian Reservation with one political district; the Gila Bend Reservation with one political district; the Sells Reservation with nine political districts; and a small community at Florence, Arizona. Similarly, the Cocopah Reservation is made up of the so-called East Cocopah Reservation, West Cocopah Reservation, and North Cocopah Reservation.

Laying aside this confusion in land units and counting only tribal jurisdictions, there are twenty-one reservations in Arizona and twenty-five reservations in New Mexico. Arizona includes the main Navajo Reservation, which is the largest in the United States and which sprawls from northeastern Arizona into southeastern Utah and northwestern New Mexico.

Conceptualized in this guide as part of the Southwest are the Southern Ute and Ute Mountain Ute reservations of southwestern Colorado (the Ute Mountain Utes also own land in New Mexico); the Ysleta del Sur Reservation of El Paso, Texas; and the Chemehuevi Reservation along the lower Colorado River in Southern California. The Fort Yuma, Colorado River, and Fort Mojave reservations have lands in both California and Arizona, and the Fort Mojave people have land in southern Nevada as well.

Most reservation lands in the Southwest are tribally owned. That is, they are lands held in common by tribal political entities. In 1887, however, Congress passed a law providing that reservation lands be divided and allotted among individual tribal mem-bers. Some Southwest reservations, in addition to tribal lands, have individually allotted lands that belong to single persons

or, far more commonly, to members of particular families. The further allotment of tribal lands was stopped by congressional action in 1934, but the legacy of the earlier allotments remains.

Reservation lands, both tribal and allotted, are held in trust by the federal government, a fact which makes reservation property—but not the people or business operations on leased Indian lands—exempt from state or local taxes other than those that might be levied by the tribes themselves. The federal agency responsible for administration of the trust is the Bureau of Indian Affairs, a branch of the United States Department of the Interior.

Indian tribes, or "nations" as some groups prefer to be called, enjoy sovereignty to the extent it has not been constrained by federal law and federal court decisions. Each reservation bears a large responsibility for its own governance. The

laws of the states, counties, and other local jurisdictions do not apply on reservations except as specifically provided for in federal law or as worked out in mutual agreements between tribes and off-reservation governmental entities. Such matters, however, are constantly in a state of flux, forever being challenged in federal courts or altered by Congress.

This confusion—unique among inter-ethnic relationships in the United States—results from a decision by non-Indians early in the history of the country to deal with Indian tribes as if they were sovereign nations, even though some of those groups may have had only a few members. In its early years the United States reserved to the central government all dealings with Indians to prevent non-Indians from engaging in private, territorial, or state actions that might inflame Indians and provoke uprisings requiring federal action to subdue them. The legacy remains, and while military conflict is no longer a credible threat, relations between tribes and immediately neighboring jurisdictions occasionally become contentious and lead to various kinds of public protests. Travelers in Indian Country need to know when they are on reservations they must observe reservation laws, a simple matter if one obeys posted signs and observes universal rules of common sense, decency, and respect.

It was only in 1924 that Congress bestowed American citizenship on all Indians. Even at that, until 1948 in Arizona and New Mexico, Indians were prevented by state laws from voting in state, county, city, or other non-reservation elections.

In 1999, Indians who are enrolled members of specific tribes—and one cannot be enrolled in more than one tribe—to enjoy a kind of dual citizenship. They have rights that are exclusive to tribal members even as they have all the rights of any American citizen.

Each reservation has its own tribal government. Elected officials go

by such titles as president, chairman, vice chairman, chairperson, vice chairperson, governor, or lieutenant governor. These officers, as well as treasurers, secretaries, and, occasionally, comptrollers, are backed by council members who serve as legislative bodies and who often oversee various appointments. Depending on the particular tribe, there may be various tribal judges as well as chiefs of police and other law enforcement officers. On some reservations Bureau of Indian Affairs personnel provide law enforcement.

Since the 1850s when the federal government began to administer Southwest Indian affairs, the status of Indians has been one of increased integration with and dependence upon non-Indian society. Subsistence economies that had characterized Indian tribes from prehistoric times to near the end of the nineteenth century yielded to a national, and now international, cash economy. Indians, like other citizens of the United States, have come to depend, not directly on the products of their own labor, but on the larger society to supply life's necessities, not to mention luxuries.

Although the native languages spoken at one time by all members of these tribes were many and varied, the fact is that today English has become the first language for most Southwest Indians, particularly among the younger generations. It is a sad fact that many younger people have become monolingual speakers of English, having lost their native language altogether. The situation varies from reservation to reservation, and it would be a mistake to think that native languages have become extinct. On many reservations there are tribal programs and programs in schools working to ensure the survival of native tongues.

Navajo Whirling Log sand painting

Betatakin at Navajo National Monument, Arizona

VISITING RESERVATIONS— SOME GENERAL OBSERVATIONS

With some exceptions, visitors who are respectful and well behaved are welcomed in Indian communities. This is especially the case in communities whose people have become accustomed to outsiders and who have products or services available for sale. More isolated communities and some others, like a few Hopi and New Mexico pueblos, may be more inclined to value their privacy above uninvited intrusions by complete strangers.

No one enjoys being regarded as an object of curiosity. Many of us, however, respond in a positive way to those who seem to have a genuine empathetic interest in our particular lifestyle, and we are willing to share our time and knowledge with people whose goal is furthering their own understanding. This does not, however, mean we are prepared to share with others our innermost religious and personal beliefs and practices, nor should we be expected to do so. All of us, Indians included, live in public and private worlds. It is when others try to invade our private precincts that we rebel.

In general, American Indians, unlike many non-Indians, consider it impolite to establish direct eye contact when talking with someone. Indians are usually more comfortable looking at the ground or away from the speaker when they are listening. Similarly, speaking loudly or talking too much are discouraged among traditional Indians from childhood. To be loud or garrulous is to be obnoxious. Paradoxical as it may seem, silence is itself a form of communication among Indians. And neither do most Indians share the proclivities of outsiders to embrace or to give firm handshakes. Most prefer a handshake to be light.

Indians don't get acquainted with such direct questions as, "What is your name?" or, "Where are you from?" or, "How many children do you have?" These kinds of questions are likely to be regarded as impertinent, akin to asking people how much money they make, how old they are, or what religious or political preference they have.

Perhaps the question most often asked by visitors to Indian communities is whether or not it is permissible to take photographs. Still cameras and movie and video cameras have become standard equipment among the touring public, but pointed without permission at people and their activities, their dwellings, or religious shrines, cameras can—and often do—provoke strong negative reactions. The general rule is that you should not take photos of persons without their permission. Some communities, most notably among the Pueblos, prohibit photography altogether. Still other groups require permission before photos can be taken of public religious ceremonies, and some, such as the Yaquis during their Easter season ceremonies, don't allow photography, tape recording, note-taking, or sketching under any circumstances. Some Indians will ask to be paid to allow their picture to be taken. When it comes to landscape photography on reservations, taking pictures of scenic vistas, there are usually no problems—although Puebloan peoples object to having their communities photographed from a distance with powerful telephoto lenses. This is an undue violation of their right to privacy.

Because casino operators are protective of the anonymity of their patrons, photographing casinos, even on the outside, is also discouraged.

Photography may be allowed at occasional public events, such as powwows and rodeos, but even here, in order to avoid embarrassment, ask in advance.

Collectively, Southwest Indian reservations offer opportunities for all kinds of outdoor recreation: golfing, boating, river rafting, fishing, hunting, camping, horseback riding, mountain climbing, hiking, and skiing. Most now have gambling casinos; a few have museums or culture centers; many sponsor annual rodeos, fairs, and powwows; many sponsor public religious dramas that may be native or Christian in origin or a blend of the two. The guide that follows makes every effort to provide up-to-date information about these facilities. Visitors, though, should know that the one constant on Indian reservations is change. People planning to visit reservations are advised to call ahead if they have any doubts about current facilities. The telephone numbers of tribal offices are listed for each tribe.

COCOPAH TRIBE

In the nineteenth century, nearly all Cocopahs—a Yuman-speaking people—lived south of the International Boundary in Sonora and Baja California Norte. Between 1900 and 1910, some Cocopah families moved north to live near Somerton, Arizona. In 1917, by executive order, these people were given two reservations with a total of 1,772 acres, the East Reservation and West Reservation. In 1985, Congress gave Cocopahs additional lands, including a north reservation of some 600 acres. All three reservations are administered by the Cocopah Tribe whose headquarters are on the West Reservation. Near Somerton, Arizona, these reservations are some thirteen miles south of Yuma, Arizona, and five miles north of San Luis, Sonora, Mexico.

This southwestern corner of Arizona lies within the Sonoran Desert. It joins with the Quechan, Colorado River, Ft. Mohave, and Chemehuevi reservations in being among the hottest places in Arizona and California. This warmth has made the region an ideal winter resort and recreation area, but most tourists will want to avoid it during the summer, especially from June through August.

Recreational Opportunities
Hunting and fishing are permitted. Fishing is in the Colorado River and most hunting is for game birds. Tribal permits are required and can be obtained either at the Cocopah Tribal Police Department on the West Reservation between 8:00 a.m. and 5:00 p.m. Monday through Friday (or call 520/627-8857 ext. 8858), or at the Cocopah-Easy Corner convenience market, 15126 S. Avenue B, Yuma, AZ 85364 (phone 520/344-4814). Although Arizona hunting and fishing permits are not required on the reservation, the Cocopah Tribe has adopted the State of Arizona seasonal hunting and fishing regulations that must be observed. Additionally, no shooting is allowed within 300 feet of any buildings or thoroughfare and can take place only between a half hour before sunrise and noon.

The Cocopahs operate the Cocopah Casino as well as a bingo hall. Both are located near Somerton at Highway 95 and County Road 15. The casino is open 24 hours a day Thursday through Sunday but is closed between 2:00 a.m. and 6:00 a.m. Monday through Wednesday. The casino includes a snack bar.

The Cocopah Bend RV & Golf Resort on the North Reservation, operated as a seasonal adult park by Resorts West, Inc., features an eighteen-hole, par seventy golf course; pro-shop; lighted driving range; snack bar; laundry; showers; tennis courts; heated swimming pool; ballroom; billiards; card rooms; exercise room; crafts; library; shuffleboard; horseshoes; jacuzzi; fishing; pet area; and barber and beauty shop.

The Yuma Valley Railway operates an excursion train along the Colorado River through parts of the Cocopah Reservation either on Saturdays or Sundays of each weekend between November and May. It is a 22-mile round trip that allows excursionists to view the surrounding desert, wildlife, and produce being grown in large quantities adjacent to the river. Regular runs last about two hours, while meal runs require three hours for the round trip. For full particulars, call or write the Yuma Valley Railway, P.O. Box 10305, Yuma, AZ 85366 (520/783-3456).

The Cocopahs hold an annual powwow on grounds adjacent to the Cocopah Casino on the East Reservation. It is normally held the second week in February, but call first: 520/627-2102. The public is also invited to Indian Recognition Day, normally held the last Friday in September. Again, call first.

Tribal Museum: The Cocopahs operate a tribal museum adjacent to tribal headquarters on the West Reservation. Because Cocopahs, like other Yuman peoples, traditionally cremate their dead along with all of the deceased's personal possessions, there are few heirloom pieces on display. Cocopah elders sell traditional fry bread and beaded jewelry. For museum hours and additional information, call 520/627-2102.

Cocopah Tribe
Ave. G & Co. fifteenth, Somerton, AZ 85350
Phone 520/627-2061; Fax 520/627-1617
Population: 799
Acreage: 6,009

QUECHAN TRIBE

The Quechans, who until the second half of the twentieth century were generally known to outsiders as the Yuma, have been in their present location since "time immemorial," another way of saying they have been here since some unknown time in the remote prehistoric past. Europeans visited Quechan ancestors as early as 1540 when sailor Hernando de Alarcón, in a futile effort to bring supplies to the Vásquez de Coronado expedition making its way north from Mexico overland to New Mexico, got two boats up the Colorado River to the vicinity of modern Yuma, Arizona. In 1604, Governor Juan de Oñate of New Mexico led an expedition nearly all the way to the mouth of the Colorado passing through Quechan lands both going south and on his northward return to New Mexico. Spaniards attempted to plant a combination mission and colony among these Indians in 1780, but the following year the Quechans rebelled and killed four Franciscan missionaries as well as a hundred additional Spaniards, sparing only some of the women, children, and a few men. The action is one that effectively closed this important crossing of the Colorado River to outsiders for nearly the next seven decades. Portions of the region in California and north of the Gila River became part of the United States in 1848 thanks to the Treaty of Guadalupe Hidalgo between the United States and Mexico. Southwesternmost Arizona became part of the United States in 1854 with ratification of the

Gadsden Purchase, by which time U.S. troops fighting Mexico and both Mexican and Yankee Forty Niners en route to California's gold fields had poured unimpeded across the river through Quechan territory.

Because of the meandering of the Colorado River, the Fort Yuma Reservation, the official name of the Quechans' reservation established in 1884, lies in both California and Arizona. The Quechans, although most of their lands are in California and their tribal headquarters are on Indian Hill in Winterhaven, California, use a Yuma, Arizona, address and are one of Arizona's federally recognized tribes.

Recreational Opportunities

The Quechan Tribe coordinates with the State of California concerning seasonal hunting and fishing, and California regulations must be honored. However, a state license is not required to hunt or fish on the reservation.

Most reservation lands are allotted to individual families, meaning owners of these lands must grant permission before entry and hunting—principally for game birds—are allowed. Detailed regulations, as well as permits, are available in the tribal offices as well as at the Laguna Dam R.V. Park, Ft. Yuma Quechan Museum, and at Sleepy Hollow. For information, call 760/572-0544.

The reservation's San Pasqual High School sponsors an annual powwow, usually in March. Indians in ceremonial regalia from throughout the United States and Canada compete with one another in bird singing and dancing and in gourd dancing. Also, invited groups, such as Mescalero Apache Mountain Spirit Dancers, perform along with other singing groups. There is a nominal admission charge. For information, call 760/572-0222.

An Indian Days celebration is usually held the last weekend of each September in the stomp grounds near the base of Indian Hill. There are traditional dances; traditional food, including fry bread, is available; and Quechan traditional beadwork and other items of Indian manufacture are for sale. For information, call 760/572-0213.

The Colorado River here, as is the case for other reservations on the river, offers opportunities for water sports, including boating, water skiing, and tubing.

Sleepy Hollow, the tribe's R.V. park next to Andrade, California, and a few yards from the international boundary at Algodones, Baja California, has enclosed recreational facilities as well as facilities for shuffleboard and horseshoes.

The tribe operates the Quechan Paradise Casino in a modern facility next to Indian Hill just below tribal headquarters. Free shuttle services connect the casino and several of the larger motels, hotels, R.V. parks, and shopping centers in the Yuma and Winterhaven areas.

Tribal Museum: The Ft. Yuma Quechan museum is housed on Indian Hill in the oldest building of the former Fort Yuma U.S. military post. Refurbished by Quechan vocational trainees, in the mid-nineteenth century the museum was the commanding officer's kitchen. It later became a school for Indian children and is now a museum displaying historical artifacts and housing historical records, photographs, and archaeological items. It also displays Quechan arts and crafts including intricate beadwork. Although no photos are allowed inside the museum, it has a small gift shop with items for sale. Hours are 8:00 a.m. to 5:00 p.m. weekdays and 10:00 a.m. to 4:00 p.m. Saturdays. It is closed on Sundays and holidays. The museum's phone number is 619/572-0661.

Fort Yuma-Quechan Tribe
P.O. Box 11352, Yuma, AZ 85366
Phone 760/572-0213; Fax 760/572-2102
Population: 2,502
Acreage: 43,589
(includes California and Arizona)

COLORADO RIVER TRIBES

Long before Europeans arrived on the scene, and no one can say precisely how many centuries or millennia ago that may have been, ancestors of the Mohave Indians occupied lands along the Colorado River within and beyond the boundaries of today's Colorado River and Fort Mojave reservations. The first Europeans likely to have encountered the Mohaves were members of New Mexico Governor Juan de Oñate's 1604 expedition through the region. Oñate's people and later Spaniards referred to the Mohave as the "Amacava," a variation of the term Mohaves used for themselves *(hàmakhá·v)*. Direct Spanish influence on the Mohaves was minimal, but in the early nineteenth century beaver trappers began to penetrate their territory. In 1851, three years after Mohave lands had been incorporated within the boundaries of the United States, Captain Lorenzo Sitgreaves of the U.S. Topographical Engineers led a reconnaissance party to the Colorado River in Mohave territory and thereby became the vanguard of American expansion into the region.

In 1859 in the aftermath of military defeat at the hands of the U.S. Army, an influential Mohave chief named Irretaba persuaded a large group of Mohaves to move south from their homelands in the Mohave Valley to the Colorado River Valley where some of their ancestors had resided as early as the sixteenth century. The Colorado River Reservation was created by an Act of Congress in 1865 "for the Indians of said river and its tributaries," the Congressman who introduced the bill not having the slightest idea that the Colorado's tributaries included virtually the whole of the Southwest west of the Continental Divide.

In 1874 the reservation's boundaries were extended to the west side of the Colorado River so that Chemehuevis, with whom the Mohave had been fighting as recently as 1871, would also be within the reservation's boundaries. Peaceful removals of Chemehuevis to the Colorado River Reservation occurred through the years, but it was only late in the 1800s and early twentieth century that some Chemehuevis agreed to reside there permanently. In 1945, relying on the "tributaries" clause in the law that established the reservation and on an ordinance approved by the Colorado River Tribes, Hopi and Navajo colonists began moving onto the land. By 1951 there were 148 families of such colonists. Colonization by other Indians has ceased, but today's reservation is now home for Mohaves, Chemehuevis, Hopis, and Navajos. Mohaves remain in the numerical majority.

The economy of the Colorado River Reservation is supported by agriculture, recreation, government, and light industry. The tribes also lease land on a long-term basis to outsiders who have developed R.V. parks and other riverside communities for vacationers and retirees.

Recreational Opportunities:
The Colorado River provides outstanding recreational and scenic attraction. Lake Moovalya, which has formed behind Headgate Rock Dam less than one and a half miles north of Parker, Arizona, is considered to be among the choice water skiing lakes of the Southwest. Various R.V. parks and resorts boast stretches of sandy beach and concrete launching ramps in addition to dining, drinking, dancing, and accommodations.

Hunting and fishing are allowed on the reservation with tribal hunting and fishing permits. Everyone must honor tribal fishing and hunting regulations as well as all state and federal game and fish laws. Hunting and fishing permits can be obtained at the tribal offices (phone 520/669-9285) or at several sporting goods stores in Parker and other nearby communities. There are excellent dove and quail hunting areas. Flocks of waterfowl, including Canadian Geese, offer a challenge for hunters. Some sixty miles of Colorado River open waters and associated backwaters and sloughs as well as 250 miles of irrigation canals are available to fishermen. Channel catfish, trout, largemouth and smallmouth bass, bluegill, and crappie are among the popular species of fish, and during fall through spring large numbers of rainbow trout are stocked on the reservation.

The Colorado River Tribes operate the Blue Water Casino in Parker (520/669-7777), which offers slot machines and live keno, bingo, and poker.

The Colorado River Tribes hold an annual Fourth of July celebration that is open to the public in Manataba Park just north of the tribal museum and library on the reservation. Featured are Miss, Junior Miss, and Little Miss Colorado River Indian Tribes pageants. For information and precise dates, call 520/669-9652. Also at Manataba Park, on the

last weekend of each September there are a National Indian Days Celebration and Miss Indian Arizona pageant. Information is available at 520/669-9211.

An All Indian Rodeo takes place the first weekend of each December on the reservation's Indian Rodeo Grounds, Rodeo Sub-division. For information, call 520/669-2121.

Tribal Museum: The Colorado River Indian Tribes Museum and Tribal Public Library/Archives are housed in a handsome building on the reservation at Second Avenue and Mohave Road. The address is Route 1, Box 23-b, Parker, AZ 85344 (phone 520/669-9211 ext. 335 for museum; 520/669-9211 ext. 330, 331, or 332 for library). The museum, closed from noon to 1:00 p.m., is open 8:00 a.m. to 5:00 p.m. Monday through Friday and from 10:00 a.m. to 3:00 p.m. on Saturday. It is closed on Sunday and holidays. In addition to excellent displays of traditional arts and crafts, there is a small gift shop where one can purchase items of local manufacture, including Mohave beadwork and pottery, Navajo silver jewelry, and Hopi kachina dolls.

The library, which is open from 8:00 a.m. to 5:00 p.m. daily and closed on weekends, serves tribal members as well as the general public. Begun in 1958, the Colorado River Tribes Public Library/Archives is an accredited general library providing periodicals, texts, paperbacks and reference works. The archives is a research center for persons wanting to study the culture and history of the four tribes on the reservation. The archive contains original written documents, photocopies of documents, microfilm, photographs, videotape, and audiotape. Personal correspondence, government documents, and the writings of historians and anthropologists are included. These materials are available to tribal members. Non-tribal members must apply to use them and agree to abide by the rules governing their use and dissemination.

Through the museum, the tribes maintain two sites on the National Register of Historic Places. Open to the public, these are the old Mohave Presbyterian Mission dating from 1912 and the old Arizona frontier community, now essentially an archaeological ruin, of La Paz, Arizona. La Paz, a half dozen miles north of Ehrenberg at the Interstate 10 crossing of the Colorado River, was an 1860s mining town and Colorado River port, a jumping-off place for persons headed to mining fields in interior Arizona.

Colorado River Indian Tribes
Route 1, Box 23-B, Parker, AZ 85344
Phone 520/669-9211; Fax 520/669-5675
Population: 3,104
Acreage: 268,691
(includes California and Arizona)

CHEMEHUEVI TRIBE

"Chemehuevi" is not a name these people used for themselves in their own language. It seems to be a term applied to them by Yuman-speaking peoples, such as Mohaves, with whom they were in contact from very early times. Chemehuevis are a subgroup of a larger cultural and linguistic entity known as the Southern Paiute. Like the related Southern Paiute and Ute languages, Chemehuevi is part of the larger Aztec-Tanoan linguistic family whereas the Yuman languages spoken by other tribes on the Lower Colorado River belong in the Hokan linguistic family. The Chemehuevi are the southernmost of sixteen groups of Southern Paiute, and their culture has been strongly influenced by that of the neighboring Mohave.

In the middle and late 1860s, Chemehuevis were engaged in warfare against the Mohaves. After the conflict was settled in 1871, some Chemehuevis were included within the expanded boundaries of the Colorado River Indian Reservation. Others continued to live in traditional California locations near Blythe, Needles, Beaver Lake, and in Chemehuevi Valley. Some Chemehuevis took refuge among the Cahuilla near Banning, California, and among the Serrano at Twenty-Nine Palms, also in California. After 1911, the Indian population at Twenty-Nine Palms was consolidated with that near Banning on Southern California's Morongo Indian Reservation.

In 1907 the Chemehuevi Indian Reservation was created to protect Chemehuevis' land in the Chemehuevi Valley. The Chemehuevis who remained enjoyed limited success with cattle raising until 1939 when completion of Parker Dam on the Colorado River flooded most of their lands. Although few Chemehuevis elected to remain on their isolated reservation, many of those who had left wanted to return. In 1965 they shared with other Southern Paiutes in federal monetary compensation for loss of their aboriginal lands, and in 1970 the tribe adopted a new constitution. By extending their tribal rolls to include people with one-sixteenth Chemehuevi blood, they were able to attract enough people to repopulate their reservation. Today most of them live in Chemehuevi Village just south of Catfish Bay on the west banks of the Colorado River. The reservation is reached either by boat from Arizona's Lake Havasu City or via a 17-mile paved road from the west that connects with U.S. Highway 95 between Vidal Junction and Needles.

Recreational Opportunities:

Hunting (waterfowl) and fishing regulations on the reservation conform with those of the State of California. A tribal trespass permit is required as are tribal licenses. Boating on the Colorado, whether for fishing or sightseeing, is a pleasurable pastime here. There is a 38-mile shoreline along the reservation's edge that includes some of the most popular bays, fishing coves, and campsites on Lake Havasu, the enormous body of water formed behind Parker Dam. Water activities include water skiing, jet skiing, and wind surfing. The marina has boat rental slips, three launch ramps, and a gas dock. The boat house sells fishing tackle, bait, boating accessories, water toys, and various convenience items.

Havasu Landing Resort includes a main casino, lounge casino, bar, and restaurant as well as beaches for swimming and sun bathing. It also offers an unobstructed view of Lake Havasu City sprawling upward from the lake on the opposite shore in Arizona. The Colorado River Express provides boat tours between Havasu Landing and the English Village at Havasu City on a regular schedule seven days a week (call 760/858-4593 for details). The reservation keeps its time in conformity with Arizona time, which means that when California goes on daylight savings time, the reservation, like Arizona, does not.

The northern part of the reservation consists of the Chemehuevi Wildlife Refuge and Wilderness Area. For more information about this region, contact the tribal offices at 760/858-4531.

Tribal Museum: There is a small museum and Indian arts store next to the marina. Chemehuevis are noted for their exceptionally fine basketry and for their beadwork.

Chemehuevi Indian Tribe
P.O. Box 1976, Chemehuevi Valley, CA 92362
Phone 760/858-4301; Fax 760/858-4818
Population: 675
Acreage: 30,654

FORT MOHAVE TRIBE

Many Mohaves elected to remain in the Mohave Valley after Chief Irrateba, with a large Mohave contingent, moved south in 1859 to the Colorado River Valley. Their leader was the conservative Homosequahote ("good star," also known as Sickahoot). Since 1859, the Mohaves have remained divided into two communities, one on the Colorado River Reservation and another on the Fort Mohave Reservation. There is, however, regular communication between the two groups as well as some intermarriage.

In 1858, Mohaves in the Mohave Valley attacked a wagon train of emigrants headed toward California as they reached the crossing on the Colorado River. The upshot was that the U.S. Army established a military post, Fort Mohave, in the valley on the east side of the river in 1859 and brought the Mohaves under permanent subjugation. An executive order created the Fort Mohave Reservation in 1880 and another executive order enlarged it in 1910. The fort was abandoned by the military in 1890 and turned over to the Indian Service for use as an Indian boarding school. The Indian Service closed the school in 1935 and the buildings were destroyed by wrecking bars in 1942.

The area of the reservation was "checkerboarded," with alternate sections of land given to railroads to sell to finance construction. The other alternate sections, which had remained in federal ownership, were given to the Mohaves in the 1910 extension to the reservation. Nearly all the checkerboarded lands are in Arizona, with those in California and Nevada generally comprising large contiguous blocks of land. All lands are tribally owned; allotment never took place here.

In 1988 the Fort Mohave Tribe signed an intergovernmental agreement with the State of Nevada which places tribal gaming activities under regulation of the Nevada State Gaming Commission. The agreement is one that opened the door to the tribe's construction and operation of the Avi Hotel & Casino, a Las Vegas–style gambling operation that is the centerpiece for a planned four-thousand-acre development, Aha Macav. Aha Macav is projected eventually to grow into a city of some twenty thousand houses, a town center, eleven riverside casino-resorts, schools, parks, and all the necessary infrastructure. The tribe is the master developer for this master-planned community, but development is expected to occur primarily through long-term leasing.

Many of the reservation's acres are in farmland. Most of them are under lease but a comparatively few are being farmed by Mohaves who raise principally cotton and alfalfa.

Recreational Opportunities:

Seventeen miles of the Colorado River flow through the reservation. Fishing, water skiing, jetboating, and other water sports are popular recreation activities. There is also hunting for ducks, geese, and doves. Both fishing and hunting permits must be obtained from the tribal offices. Arizona hunting and fishing regulations apply on the reservation.

The Avi Casino and Hotel, 10,000 Aha Macav Parkway, Laughlin, NV 98028-7011, features slot machines, video poker, keno, 21, roulette, craps, Caribbean stud poker, and "let it ride"—amusing in view of the fact that gambling used to be absolutely forbidden on the reservation. One tribal elder reminisced with me how as a child he used to sit as lookout on a levee watching for the approach of tribal police as Mohave men played gambling games next to the river. The irony of sanctioned modern casino gambling on the reservation was not lost on him.

Live music and comedy are featured in the hotel's Arrowweed Lounge and in the Coyote Club throughout the day and night. There are also a gift shop, five restaurants, video arcade, swimming pool and spa, and banquet and conference facilities. A marina and boat launch are in the planning stages.

A special tribal event open to the public each October is Ft. Mohave Indian Days with its Miss Fort Mohave Pageant and Fort Mojave Spirit Run. For information concerning the exact day of this annual celebration, one that includes a powwow and parade in Needles, call the tribal offices at 760/326-4591.

Tribal Museum: The Fort Mohave Mini Museum is located in the tribal offices at 500 Merriman Avenue, Needles, CA 92363 (760/326-2371) where a few crafts of Mohave manufacture are on display.

Fort Mohave Indian Tribe
500 Merriman Avenue, Needles, CA 92363
Phone 760/326-4591; Fax 760/326-2468
Population: 997
Acreage: 41,884
(including Arizona, California, and Nevada)

*A wikieup
at dawn on the
Hualapai
Reservation,
Arizona*

PRENTICE

HUALAPAI TRIBE

Pronounced "Walapai," and often spelled that way, the Hualapais, a Yuman-speaking people, may have occupied the area where their reservation is now located—and beyond—since the middle part of the seventh century A.D. The aboriginal territory of these people, whose name means "Pine Tree People" in their own language, extended at least from the Colorado River on the north to the south at Bill Williams River and from the Black Mountains and eastern boundary of Mohave territory on the west eastward to at least the western boundary of today's Havasupai Reservation. In 1776 Father Francisco Garcés, a Spanish Franciscan missionary, became the first European to make direct contact with the Hualapais, but the contact was only fleeting. Permanent involvement with non-Indians began in the mid-nineteenth century with the arrival in Hualapai territory of U.S. government exploring and surveying expeditions. Non-Indian prospectors rushed into northwestern Arizona when gold was discovered near Prescott in 1863.

This gold rush led to inevitable conflicts between outsiders and native peoples, and in 1866, Anglos killed Wauba Yuma, a respected Hualapai leader. Full-scale warfare between the Hualapais and the U.S. Army ensued until the Hualapais were defeated in 1869. In 1874 the defeated Indians were removed to the southern portion of the Colorado River Indian Reservation, but the following year they fled to return to their homeland. During the interim, Anglo settlers had appropriated the best Hualapai lands and springs and had put herds of cattle on the best grasslands. Finally, executive orders of 1883 and 1911 set aside nearly a million acres for the Hualapai Reservation within a small portion of their aboriginal territory, thereby foreclosing the prospect that the Indians might get their former lands returned to them.

Because of the unproductive nature of reservation lands, most Hualapais sought employment off-reservation. It wasn't until federal relief and development programs were instituted on the reservation during the Great Depression era of the 1930s, also a time when a tribal government was formed, that significant numbers of Hualapais returned. Since then, many Hualapais have become successful cattle ranchers. Timber sales have also been some help in improving economic circumstances. The tribe is working to expand and improve opportunities for trophy game hunting on the reservation and to develop its other outdoor recreational attractions, most notably taking advantage of the fact that a 108-mile stretch of the lower Grand Canyon forms its northern boundary.

Peach Springs, the only town on the entire reservation, is headquarters for tribal operations.

Recreational Opportunities

The Hualapai Reservation is known throughout the world to trophy hunters for its desert bighorn sheep and elk. Lion and turkey hunting are also permitted. Hunting on the reservation is controlled so that only limited numbers of hunters are allowed each year. Indian guides, one per hunter, are required for elk, bighorn sheep, and lion hunts. The guides are well equipped with a back country vehicle and camping gear. They are also excellent cooks. Lodging and three meals daily are provided in cabins at Frazier Wells. Desert bighorn hunting takes place along a 108-mile length of the South Rim of the Grand Canyon. A tribal brochure warns, "You must be in top physical condition to hunt the sheep, as the expeditions include miles of backpacking in the rugged canyon."

There are only two annual week-long hunts on the reservation. The first is normally the last week of September with the second following in the first week of October. Half the persons successful in acquiring tags from the tribe are included in each hunt. Full details, including costs, are available from the Hualapai Wildlife Conservation Project, P.O. Box 249, Peach Springs, AZ 86434 (phone 520/769-2227).

The Hualapai River Runners, the only Indian owned and operated raft company in the Southwest, conducts one and two-day Colorado River trips in the Grand Canyon's Lower Granite Gorge between Diamond Creek and Pierce Ferry on Lake Mead

Falls in Travertine Canyon

Delmar Honga, a Hualapai guide

from May through September. The boats, made of neoprene and with compartmentalized air chambers for safety, are powered by 25 hp-35 hp outboard motors. Each holds a maximum of ten passengers. Clients who choose to do so can be picked up at Peach Springs at 7:00 a.m. Monday, Wednesday, and Friday for the one-hour drive to Diamond Creek. Peach Springs departures for the two-day trip starting Saturday are at 8:00 a.m. Those who pay for motel accommodations as part of the tour package are picked up in front of the Holiday Inn in Kingman, Arizona. Pickups in Kingman are at 6:00 a.m. Monday, Wednesday, and Friday for one-day trips and at 9:00 a.m. Saturday for the two-day trip. The accommodations package includes two nights' stay at the Holiday Inn in Kingman, one before the trip and one afterwards. The rafts hit eight major Grand Canyon style rapids, making a stop at Travertine Rapids and Travertine Falls where participants take a short hike up the canyon to look at the rock formation caused by Travertine Falls. Children eight years and younger are not allowed.

To make reservations or for further details, including costs, contact the Hualapai River Runners, P.O. Box 246, Peach Springs, AZ 86434 (phone 520/769-2210 or 2219; out-of-state, call toll free at 800/622-4409).

The Hualapais are working toward development of Grand Canyon West as an attraction for tourists. A remote and scenic area on the south rim of the Grand Canyon in the northwestern corner of the reservation, Grand Canyon West can presently be reached only by unpaved, graded roads either from State Highway 66 out of Peach Springs or from the Pierce Ferry Highway off U.S. Highway 93 between Las Vegas, Nevada, and Kingman, Arizona. This trip requires payment of a fee that includes admission, a sightseeing permit, a 4.6-mile guided tour on a school bus along the rim of the Grand Canyon, and a barbecue lunch. The guides are Hualapai with a thorough knowledge of the region. For further information, including times and cost, call 520/769-2210.

Persons wanting simply to tour reservation back country in their own vehicles need to get a sightseeing permit at the tribal offices.

Each June the Hualapais have a powwow that includes a fun run, food booths, and an arts and crafts sale. It is held in Peach Springs, For further information and dates, call the tribal office at 520/769-2216.

Although there is no museum on the Hualapai Reservation, there is a tribal store as well as Mrs. K's Curios & Trading Post at 880 Highway 66 across the street from the tribal complex in Peach Springs.

Hualapai Tribe
P.O. Box 179, Peach Springs, AZ 86434-0179
Phone 520/769-2216; Fax 520/769-2343
Population: 1,500
Acreage: 992,463

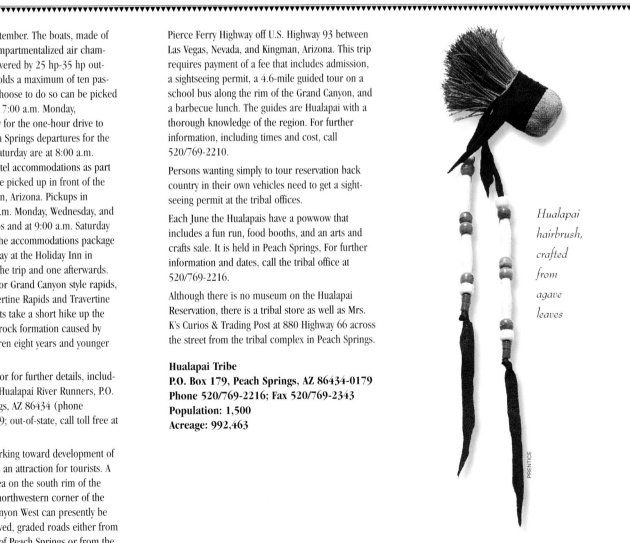

Hualapai hairbrush, crafted from agave leaves

19

*Havasu Falls,
Havasupai Indian
Reservation,
Arizona*

HAVASUPAI TRIBE

The Havsuw 'Baaja:, or People of the Blue-Green Water, live in what arguably is one of the most romantic settings in Arizona. Their community of Supai, 3,200 feet above sea level, lies just below Cataract Creek on both sides of Havasu Creek, a Colorado River tributary whose mouth is fewer than ten miles north of Supai in the depths of the lower Grand Canyon. The dark red cliffs surrounding the area are spectacular, and within two miles downstream from Supai are three great waterfalls: Navajo, Havasu, and Mooney.

The Havasupai and Hualapai are so closely related in language and traditional culture that some scholars have argued they are essentially one people, the Pai, who became divided into two tribes only in the nineteenth century when non-Indians imposed those definitions on them. Other students of Indian history, however, insist the distinction is at least centuries old and that the Havasupai occupied their own aboriginal territory distinct from that of the Hualapai. Those lands spread south from the Grand Canyon and the Colorado River to the vicinity of today's Williams, Arizona. The Aubrey Cliffs demarcated the western boundary while a long stretch of the Little Colorado River formed the eastern limit. Both Hualapai and Havasupai traditionally hunted and gathered wild plants and animals on the Coconino Plateau during the winter and farmed fields down in the canyon tributaries of the

Colorado River in the spring and summer. Native crops, raised with the help of irrigation ditches, consisted of corn, beans, and squash—the great triumvirate of domestic plants for all Southwest Indians who practiced horticulture.

There were sporadic contacts between Havasupais and Europeans beginning perhaps as early as 1540 when García López de Cardenas, a member of the Vásquez de Coronado expedition into the Southwest, at least made mention of wandering tribes in the area later certainly occupied by Havasupai. Franciscan missionary Francisco Garcés paid a brief and pleasant visit to Havasu Canyon in 1776, and in the first half of the 1800s, Havasupais witnessed the comings and goings of non-Indian European beaver trappers and U.S. military surveyors and explorers. It was in these times that horses, cattle, peaches, sunflowers, apricots, watermelons, and figs were absorbed by Havasupai culture.

*Red sandstone formations,
Havasupai Indian Reservation,
Arizona*

In the late nineteenth century, white cattle ranchers began to encroach in ever-growing numbers on Havasupai lands on the plateau and prospectors became interested in the mineral potential of Cataract and Havasu canyons. To afford the Indians at least some protection, executive orders were issued in 1880 and 1882 that set aside a paltry 518 acres in the canyon itself. The Bureau of Indian Affairs established a day school and sub-agency at Supai in 1895. Families were encouraged to remain in the canyon year round while preemption of their plateau lands continued unabated. By the 1940s, virtually no one made the seasonal trek to the plateau to hunt and gather.

Although the Havasupais were later issued grazing permits on 286,000 acres of plateau land by the National Forest Service and National Park Service on a year-to-year basis, it wasn't until congressional legislation was approved in 1975 that the reservation's boundaries were enlarged from 518 acres to 188,077 acres. The Havasupais had gotten enough of their lands back to graze horses and cattle on the plateau without permits, something that had been denied them for nearly a century.

Although involved to some extent in cattle raising, Havasupais living on the reservation today are highly dependent on income from tourism for their livelihoods. In 1965, a Havasupai packer who accompanied me as we rode horseback out of the canyon asked if I would send him packets of watermelon seeds after I got home. "You must eat a lot of watermelons down here," I said. "Oh, no," he

Navajo Falls in Havasu Canyon

HOPKINS

Supai Village church

NEILSEN

replied. "We raise a lot of them, but we can't afford them. People come down here in the summertime thinking it's going to be cool, but it's blazing hot. And they'll pay anything for a watermelon!"

Recreational Opportunities:

Supai, the scenic heart of the Havasupai Indian Reservation, can be reached by foot or horseback after a drop in elevation of some two thousand feet via the eight-mile Hualapai Trail beginning at the Hualapai Hilltop parking lot on the plateau. Hualapai Hilltop is at the end of paved Indian Highway 18 which leaves U.S. Highway 66 seven miles east of Peach Springs on the Hualapai Reservation. The 62-mile stretch is over a good road, but advance inquiry concerning winter weather conditions is always a good idea (check with the Bureau of Indian Affairs agency in Valentine, Arizona, at 520/769-2279). Persons in good condition can backpack in and out of the canyon from the parking lot, while others may prefer to hire a Havasupai packer who will provide horse transportation both ways. The first mile on the trail into the canyon from Hualapai Hilltop is practically straight down, which means the last mile climbing out of the canyon is practically straight up.

It is also possible to fly round trip into Supai via a twenty- to thirty-minute helicopter ride from the Grand Canyon Airport at Tusayan, Arizona. One of the principal carriers is Papillon Grand Canyon Helicopters, P.O. Box 455, Grand Canyon, AZ 86023 (phone 520/638-2419 or 800/528-2418; Fax 638-9349). The reservation heliport is in the heart of Supai, and flying in and out offers passengers spectacular views of the colored cliffs and canyons rimming the village.

All visitors to Supai need to make advance reservations by phone (520/448-2731) or mail (P.O. Box 10, Supai, AZ 86435) regardless of mode of transportation into the canyon. Lodging and camping space are limited and the tribe strictly controls the number of people who may stay in the canyon at one time. Persons without reservations hiking into the canyon may be required to hike out again on the same day, an exhausting 16-mile prospect. All visitors, including those not staying overnight, are charged a daily fee simply to be in the canyon.

Hiking, sightseeing, and photography provide the chief recreation, just as they do at the neighboring Grand Canyon National Park. In January there is a Land Day celebration commemorating the Havasupais' 1975 re-acquisition of more tribal lands (phone 520/448-2731). There are also a Health Fair in March (phone 520/448-2641); an annual Easter celebration (phone 520/448-2731); a Peach Festival the second week of each August (phone 520/448-2731); and an Indian Day observance each September (phone 520/448-2901). The Peach Festival is the modern version of a traditional harvest festival that formerly attracted Hualapais, Hopis, and Navajos to come to the canyon for a few days of eating, gambling, dancing, singing, horse racing, and trading. Now, as then, a good time is had by all.

Supai has a general store, cafe with outdoor seating area, cultural center, and post office. The post office is the last in the United States to be served by pack trains of horses, mules, and burros. Most supplies come into the canyon the same way, although helicopters bring items in as well.

Tribal Museum: There is a modest tribal museum in Supai that displays traditional Havasupai crafts, especially basketry, and photos, maps, and text providing some of the tribe's history. T-shirts silk-screened in Supai are offered for sale as are other Indian arts and crafts. There is a small admission charge to visit the museum.

Havasupai Tribe
P.O. Box 10, Supai, AZ 85435
Phone 520/448-2731; Fax 520/448-2551
Population: 634
Acreage: 188,077

Yavapai country, Prescott National Forest, Arizona

YAVAPAI- PRESCOTT TRIBE

The Yavapais are a Yuman-speaking people whose language is a dialect of that spoken by the Hualapai and Havasupai. Aboriginally they were divided into four groups: Tolkapaya (Western Yavapai), Kewevkapaya (Southeastern Yavapai), Wipukpaya (Northeastern Yavapai), and Yavape (Central Yavapai), the latter two sometimes regarded collectively as the Northeastern Yavapai. Their lands stretched from the Bill Williams River and the vicinity of Ash Fork and Flagstaff on the north to areas just north of the Gila and Salt rivers on the south. Their western range stopped east of the valleys along the Lower Colorado River, and their eastern boundary coincided with the western boundary of Western Apaches on a line running from Flagstaff to Globe.

Although visited earlier by Spanish missionaries, non-Indian fur trappers, and U.S. exploring parties, Yavapai territory remained relatively untouched by outsiders until the 1860s when large numbers of Americans, drawn there by mineral finds and attracted by ranching possibilities, poured into the region. Inevitably, conflicts grew between Yavapais and the miners and settlers who were invading their lands. Unable or unwilling to distinguish Yavapais from Apaches, non-Indians lumped them together as enemies and the U.S. Army was given the task of resolving the problem. In 1871 General George C. Crook rounded up "roving" Yavapais and put them on the Rio Verde Reservation in the middle Verde Valley. By 1875, all the Yavapais had been militarily defeated and they were forced—along with many groups of the Western Apaches whose language they did not speak and with whom they had previously had no significant cultural ties— to move onto the San Carlos Reservation. A few managed to remain behind or to escape during the forced walk to San Carlos. Some of these returned to the Prescott area where they settled near Fort Whipple.

In the late 1880s and 1890s, by which time the Apache wars had come to an end, Yavapais who chose to do so were allowed to leave the San Carlos Reservation. Although many remained at San Carlos where they intermarried with Apaches and integrated themselves into the San Carlos communities, most Yavapais went back to their homelands where they became wage laborers and domestic servants for Anglos who by then had usurped all of their lands. The Prescott Yavapais were fortunate in appointing as their chief a man who had been born in captivity on the San Carlos Reservation, Sam Jimulla. He and his wife, Viola, who had also been born at San Carlos, built cultural bridges into the non-Indian community of Prescott that won for the Yavapais the support of influential Anglos in their drive to improve their living conditions. Such Great Depression programs as the Civil Works Administration and Works Progress Administration replaced make-shift Yavapai houses with homes built of stone, and dirt lanes in the Indian community became new roads. In 1935, Congress passed a law transferring seventy-five acres of land in Prescott from the Veterans Administration, then operating Fort Whipple, to the Department of the Interior, with the title to remain in the United States in trust for the Yavapai Indians. In 1955, to accommodate the growing numbers of Yavapai cattle, 1,320 acres were added to the reservation. By the late 1980s, the Yavapais had taken advantage of the fact that they were an integral part of the fast-growing city of Prescott and had leased some of their lands for lucrative commercial development.

Recreational Opportunities:
The only public recreational opportunities on the reservation are those provided by the Prescott Resort Conference Center and Casino, 1500 Highway 69, Prescott, AZ 86301 (phone 520/776-1666). The resort sponsors various promotions throughout the year such as a celebrity pumpkin carving contest in October and an annual New Year's Eve Extravaganza. Bucky's Casino & Lounge (520/771-8319) has more than three hundred slot and poker machines as well as a restaurant, lounge, and children's arcade. There is an additional gaming center (phone 520/445-5767) as part of the casino complex. Live music is often provided in the Eagle's Nest Lounge, and the Thumb Butte Room is a full service restaurant. The Yavapai Bingo Hall, at Highway 69 and Highway 89 (520/445-0286), is a high stakes bingo parlor with some individual games paying as high as $25,000 to winners.

There are plans for an outdoor amphitheater near the resort hotel.

Tribal Museum: A tribal museum, one likely to feature the fine baskets for which Yavapais are justly renowned, is in the planning stages.

Yavapai-Prescott Indian Tribe
530 E. Merritt, Prescott, AZ 86301
Phone 520/445-8790; Fax 520/778-9445
Population: 143
Acreage: 1,390

ANNERINO

Yavapai Arleigh Banaha, top rodeo bullfighter

Montezuma Well at Montezuma Castle National Monument, Arizona

HUEY

YAVAPAI-
APACHE TRIBE

The hyphenated name of this tribe reflects the fact that intermarriage occurred between Yavapais and Western Apaches when a period of their mutual internment began in 1871. The Yavapai-Apache Tribe is spread over six small reservations between Clarkdale and Camp Verde along the middle Verde River south of Flagstaff in central Arizona. These are the Clarkdale Indian Reservation, the Middle Verde Indian Reservation, the Lower Verde Indian Reservation, the Rimrock Indian Reservation, and two non-contiguous units of the Camp Verde Indian Reservation. The western unit of the Camp Verde Indian Reservation—also known as the Interstate 17 Visitor Activity Complex—is just east of Interstate 17 at the turnoff to Montezuma Castle National Monument. The eastern unit is on the eastern side of the Verde River one mile east of the town of Camp Verde. The Lower Verde Indian Reservation is in the town of Camp Verde; the Middle Verde Indian Reservation is reached via an extension of the Montezuma Castle Highway that runs west of Interstate 17 and is a little more than a mile from the interstate highway; the tiny Rimrock Indian Reservation is north of McGuireville on Interstate 17 about 1.4 miles on Beaver Creek Road that leads to Montezuma Well; and the Clarkdale Indian Reservation is in Clarkdale (Indian Village, Clarkdale, AZ 86324). Tribal headquarters are located on the Middle Verde Reservation.

The people who live on these reservations share much of the same history as the Yavapais who live in Prescott and the Tonto Apaches at Payson.

Although the Rio Verde Indian Reservation was established for Yavapais and Tonto Apaches in 1871, most people were unable to subsist there and raiding against non-Indian intruders continued. After suffering disastrous military defeats in 1872, Yavapais, as well as Tonto Apaches, were forced to live on the Rio Verde Reservation regardless of epidemics and the terrible living conditions that characterized the place. In 1875, the reservation was abolished and its residents—or those who were unable to escape or otherwise hide—were force-marched to the Western Apaches' San Carlos Reservation. At least 115 Indians died during the 150-mile February walk in freezing weather. When they were released from San Carlos in the late 1880s and 1890s, many Yavapais returned to their former lands along the middle Verde River where most went to work for Verde Valley farmers. Between 1910 and 1916, the Yavapais and Apaches with whom they had intermarried were given small reservations on the Verde River. In 1969, when the Phelps Dodge Corporation shut down its copper mining operation in Clarkdale, the company deeded sixty acres of land to the Department of the Interior as a land base for the community of Yavapais that had sprung up when they moved there to work in the mines and smelter.

Recreational Opportunities

The Cliff Castle Casino and Best Western Lodge, 353 Middle Verde Road (P.O. Box 4677), Camp Verde, AZ 86322 (phone 520/567-9186) are located on the east side of Interstate Highway 17 at the turnout to Montezuma Castle National Monument on the west unit of the Camp Verde Indian Reservation. The casino has 370 slot machines, a poker bar, video keno, and video poker. Blazing Trails, Inc., next to the lodge and casino, offers trail rides of the Verde Valley on "horses matched to your skills and adventures matched to your imagination."

Licensed by the U.S. Forest Service, Blazing Trails Stable conducts its rides in the Coconino and Prescott National Forests. Children must be at least six years of age. For complete information and reservations, call between 8:00 a.m. and 7:00 p.m. at 520/567-6611 or 800/524-6343.

The Yavapai-Apache Tribe shares with the off-reservation community several historic and scenic attractions that draw visitors to the area. These include prehistoric ruins at three national monuments: Montezuma Castle, Montezuma Well, and Tuzigoot. Fort Verde State Historic Park in Camp Verde preserves four of this nineteenth-century military post's original adobe buildings as a museum. Various reservations are within easy reach of the colorful and historic mining town of Jerome and scenic Sedona and Oak Creek Canyon. Fishing and hunting are plentiful in the Verde Valley.

Tribal Museum: There is no tribal museum, but there are outlets for Indian arts and crafts in Camp Verde at Yavapai-Apache Arts and Crafts (phone 520/567-3533) and Wiki Up Studios (phone 520/567-4922) and in the Clarkdale village at Mocasques Navajo Sand Painting (phone 520/567-6528).

Yavapai-Apache Tribe
3435 Shaw Avenue, P.O. Box 1188,
Camp Verde, AZ 86322
Phone 520/567-3649; Fax 520/567-3994
Population: 1,399
Acreage: 636 (Middle Verde, 458;
Camp Verde, 40; Clarkdale, 58.5;
Rimrock, 3.75; Interstate 17 Visitor
Activity Complex, 74.84)

TONTO
APACHE TRIBE

The Tonto Apache Reservation is on State Highway 87 immediately south of Payson in mountains that are about a mile above sea level. Before 1972, when Congress approved legislation giving them a small reservation, the Tonto Apaches—a group of Western Apaches—were, ironically enough, regarded by the U.S. Forest Service as "squatters" on the Tonto National Forest. Although they had returned to a part of their aboriginal homelands, their community was not given legal recognition by the federal government when they wandered back to the region after their involuntary internment on the San Carlos Reservation. The Tontos had been militarily defeated by the United States in 1872, and in 1874, along with Yavapais, Chiricahuas, and other Western Apache groups, they were confined to the San Carlos Reservation. In the late 1880s, by which time the Apache wars were over, the White Mountain, Cibecue, and Tonto groups of Western Apaches were allowed to leave San Carlos. It was after that that a handful of them arrived in the forest on the outskirts of Payson.

By the mid-nineteenth century there were five groups of Western Apaches who made use of and occupied as many contiguous tracts of land within the larger territory. These were the Northern Tonto, Southern Tonto, Cibecue, White Mountain, and San Carlos groups. Except that there was no dialect distinction in the language spoken by Northern and Southern Tontos, there were slightly different dialects spoken among the Tonto, Cibecue, White Mountain, and San Carlos peoples.

Precisely when the Apaches, including the Apachean-speaking Navajos, moved into the Southwest remains a matter of conjecture and debate. Apache is in the Athapaskan family of languages that is spoken by different tribes all the way into Alaska and northern Canada. It is generally believed, at least among non-Indian scholars, that Apaches began moving into the Southwest from the Great Plains either shortly before or about the time of the arrival of Spaniards in the region in the early sixteenth century. It was after that, possibly in the seventeenth century, that some of these people—who were seminomadic hunters and gatherers—moved into what today is Arizona and began developing the cultural characteristics that would distinguish them as Western Apaches.

Until the nineteenth century, European contact with Western Apaches in their mountain homelands was sporadic and fleeting at best. As early as the 1740s Apaches blocked efforts of Jesuit missionaries to travel north of the Gila River to reach Hopis among whom they wished to spread the tenets of

Christianity. However, by the eighteenth century, not only had Western Apaches become small scale-horticulturalists, having learned about planting, cultivating, and harvesting corn, squash, and beans from Puebloan and other Indians, but they had acquired horses either directly or indirectly from the Spaniards. This gave them tremendous mobility and enabled them to extend their hunting and gathering range beyond their territory.

Unfortunately for Apaches' foreign relations, they extended their cultural predilections for hunting and gathering to European domestic crops and livestock—grain, cattle, and horses—that belonged either to Spaniards or to such Indians as the O'odham (Pimans) of the southern desert country. The latter took exception to such Apache raiding and, when they could, killed or captured Apache raiders. That, in turn, triggered the Apaches' felt need to mount large-scale revenge attacks. A bloody cycle of raiding and revenge warfare was unleashed that came to an end only in 1886 with the final capture of Geronimo and his small band of Chiricahua Apaches.

Given the failure of Spaniards ever to Christianize Apaches or to bring them under direct military

Tonto Creek

Tonto Apache basket

PLACE

HUEY

control, it is ironic that, as one anthropologist has observed, "contact with Spaniards more completely revolutionized the life of Apaches than it did any other Southwestern people." Raiding, thanks to Spanish horses, cattle, and crops, became a major means of Apache subsistence beginning in the eighteenth century. This new economic activity was destined to earn for them the reputation as the most fierce and warlike of all Southwest Indians.

By the late eighteenth century, Western Apache territory extended from Flagstaff southward to the south end of the Santa Catalina and Galiuro mountains. A line drawn from Flagstaff down the crest of the Santa Catalinas passing near Payson and Superior was roughly the western limit while the eastern border lay in the mountains along the present Arizona and New Mexico boundary. In all, it was a land of some 90,000 square miles. Most of it was mountainous, but it included deep canyons as well as arid desert little more than two thousand feet above sea level.

It was the discovery of gold in 1863 near Prescott that brought Anglo-Americans into direct conflict with Tonto Apaches, Yavapais, and Hualapais. In 1864 the United States Army established Camp Goodwin just south of the Gila River near today's Geronimo on U.S. Highway 70. This was in White Mountain territory, and Camp Goodwin's establishment marked the beginning of the permanent direct involvement of non-Indians in the lives of Western Apaches.

Little known is the fact that a wristwatch that bore the face of U.S. Vice President Spiro Agnew, an obvious disparagement based on the Mickey Mouse wristwatch, is what led ultimately to the Tonto

Apaches' securing land in federal trust. Vice President Agnew had not given his permission to the manufacturer to use his likeness on a watch, but he agreed he would not press the issue were a certain percentage of the profits from its sale to go to the Save the Children Federation. The Save the Children Federation elected to invest the money in an effort to upgrade the living conditions in the Payson Tonto Apache community. Eventually, with help from a sympathetic field worker in the Indian Health Service, two anthropology students and an architect and architecture students from the University of Arizona, and from other persons sympathetic to their cause, Payson's Tonto Apaches were able to secure congressional legislation and presidential approval that gave them new lands closer to Payson where they built a modern community of their own design. Theirs is a remarkable success story that continues to the present.

Recreational Opportunities

"Hot times in the cool pines!" is the Tonto Apaches' boast concerning their Mazatzal Casino on State Highway 87 at the south edge of Payson (phone 800/552-0938). Slot machines, keno, high stakes bingo, and a card room are part of the action. The casino also houses the Cedar Ridge Restaurant, the Apache Spirits Sports Bar, an arcade for children, and the Dream Catcher Gift Shop, one specializing

in Indian arts and crafts. The casino, a half mile south of Payson on the Beeline Highway, is open twenty-four hours a day.

The Tonto Apache Reservation shares with the town of Payson many nearby tourist attractions, including Tonto Natural Bridge, the largest travertine bridge in the world, Roosevelt Lake, and many fishing streams. The people in Payson tout their community, a summertime retreat for people living in southern Arizona's desert country, as the "Festival Capital of Arizona." A Classic Auto Show and Swap Meet are held in May; an Old Timers Rodeo and a country music festival take place in June; the State Championship Loggers/Sawdust is featured in July; and there are a rodeo and rodeo parade in August. The State Champion Fiddlers' Contest wraps up the festival season in September.

Tonto Apache Tribe
#30 Tonto Apache Reservation,
Payson, AZ 85541
Phone 520/474-5000; Fax 520/474-9125
Population: 102
Acreage: 85

The Upper Salt River flows through Tonto Apache country, Arizona

Blessing Goklish, White Mountain Apache, in regalia

WHITE MOUNTAIN APACHE TRIBE

The home of the White Mountain Apache Tribe is the Fort Apache Indian Reservation in the heart of Arizona's mountain country. The White Mountain Apaches, like the Tonto Apaches and Apaches who live on the San Carlos Reservation adjoining to the south, are members of a larger cultural and linguistic entity known as the Western Apaches. Large numbers of White Mountain and Cibecue Apaches agreed to keep peace with the United States, and they made no resistance when Camp Ord, which in 1879 became the Fort Apache famed in western fiction and Hollywood movies, was established in the mountains on the White River in 1870. In November of 1871, an executive order officially set aside the White Mountain Reservation at what was then known as Camp Apache. The southern San Carlos Division was added by executive order toward the end of 1872. In 1871, at the behest of General George Crook, many White Mountain and Cibecue men agreed to serve as U.S. Army scouts in helping to defeat Tonto and Chiricahua Apaches, a fact that even today causes some Chiricahuas to harbor resentment toward Western Apaches.

After having experimented by establishing other reservations for various groups of Apaches, in 1874 the Department of the Interior began a "removal" program meant to consolidate many Western Apache, Chiricahua, and Yavapai peoples on a single tract of land, the San Carlos division of the Fort Apache Reservation. There were inevitable conflicts among these disparate groups of Indians, and the Chiricahuas in particular resented being confined at San Carlos. Some Indians fled and there were more military battles and skirmishes, but by 1884 peace had been re-established and Geronimo, the Chiricahua Apache leader best known to non-Indians, and his immediate kinsmen were taken to Fort Apache. The next year he and 133 of his followers fled the reservation, but in 1886 he surrendered for the final time, was shipped to Fort Marion in Florida, and the Apache wars ended.

In 1897, an Act of Congress provided that the portion of the White Mountain or San Carlos Reservation north of the Salt or Black River should be known as the Fort Apache Reservation. Since then, most Western Apaches have resided either on the Fort Apache or San Carlos reservations where they have maintained separate tribal governments since the 1930s.

Members of the White Mountain Apache Tribe have been largely dependent on cattle raising and the timber industry for their economic well being. The tribe owns its own sawmills in Whiteriver and Cibecue. In recent years, however, various forms of tourism as well as income from a gambling casino have played an ever-growing role in the tribal economy.

Recreational Opportunities

With twenty-six lakes; 420 miles of clear streams; more than a thousand campsites with picnic tables, fireplaces, and sanitary facilities; many miles of cross country skiing and hiking trails; and an abundance of rainbow, brown, brook, cutthroat, and Apache brown trout as well as such game animals as elk, bear, mountain lion, javelina, antelope, turkey, quail, and migratory waterfowl, the Fort Apache Reservation is an outdoor sports paradise. Like the Hualapai Reservation, the Fort Apache Reservation is well known for its annual trophy elk hunts. These are limited to three 6½-day hunt periods in September and October. The hunting of white-tailed and mule deer as well as of blue grouse is limited to tribal members. Hunting of desert bighorn sheep is not allowed on the reservation.

The tribe operates a thoroughly professional Game and Fish Department that helps it set strict limits and other regulations to insure the future of the reservation's fish and wildlife resources. That department—which distributes hunting and fishing regulations as well as general information—can be contacted at P.O. Box 220, Whiteriver, AZ 85941 (phone 520/338-4385 or 338-4386; Fax 520/338-1712). The hunting of some game requires that the hunter be accompanied by a registered reservation guide. A list of these guides is available through the Game and Fish Department.

*Drummers,
singers, and
gaan mountain
spirits*

ANNERINO

The U.S. Fish & Wildlife Service operates fish hatcheries at Williams Creek and at Alchesay Springs to insure a year-round plentiful supply of trout. Tribal permits are required to hunt, fish, or camp on the reservation for persons ten years or older. Children must be accompanied by an adult with a valid permit, with no state permits necessary. Fishing permits issued by either the White Mountain Apache Tribe or by the San Carlos Apache Tribe are honored on either bank of the Black or Salt rivers separating the two reservations.

During the spring snowmelt, usually in April and May, rafters and kayakers are invited to test their mettle on the fast waters and challenging rapids of the Black and White rivers. Backpackers are also invited to enjoy the spectacular mountain scenery of the back country. Both whitewater adventures and backpacking require special use permits.

The permit system allows the tribe to strictly control the numbers of people taking advantage of the reservation's outdoor recreational opportunities. It also allows the tribe to educate the public concerning rules and regulations and the reasons for them. The emphasis is on quality—and preservation of the ecosystem—rather than on quantity. The tribe is determined to avoid overcrowding and ensure that visitors will enjoy a positive experience.

One large area on the eastern side of the reservation shares with the surrounding Apache/Sitgreaves National Forest portions of the Mount Baldy Wilderness Area. This portion of the reservation is closed to fishing, hunting, and trespass of any kind. It encompasses the reservation's highest point, 11,403-foot Baldy Peak, a mountain sacred to Western Apaches. Although one can hike the Baldy trail from the off-reservation trailhead at Sheep's Crossing some ten miles southeast of State Highway

260 on State Highway 273 on the road to Big Lake, the last mile of trail to the top of Baldy is on the reservation and is forbidden to outsiders.

Winter sports on the reservation, provided there is sufficient snow, are as popular as those during the spring, summer, and fall. A cross-country ski touring area is open on part of the reservation, one with numerous trails. Winter fishing, especially ice fishing on lakes, has also become popular with anglers.

The jewel in the reservation's winter recreation crown, however, is the tribally owned and operated Sunrise Park Resort, P.O. Box 217, McNary, AZ 85930 (phone 520/735-7335 or 7600). Sunrise has a dozen lifts—including chair lifts, T-bars, and beginner tows—leading to sixty-five runs on three interconnected mountains. Four of these lifts take novices to beginners' slopes, while eight of them carry experienced skiers.

The lodge at the base of the mountains is at 9,200 feet of elevation, while summits of the peaks to which skiers can ride lifts are at 10,700 feet (Sunrise Peak), 11,000 feet (Apache Peak), and 10,700 feet (Cyclone Circle). Snowboarding, cross country and telemark skiing, snowmobiling, and weekend night skiing is offered as are skiing instruction. Child care is available for infants and toddlers. The Sunrise Ski School can be reached at 520/735-7518.

During the skiing season, there are special events nearly every weekend, including racing, equipment demonstrations, and festivals. The Southwest Holiday Festival during Christmas and New Year's features strolling Mexican mariachis providing south-of-the-border music for guests.

Sunrise Park Resort is open year round, and during the summer visitors can take advantage of hiking

and mountain biking at the ski area. There are also sailing and fishing at Sunrise Lake, horseback riding, in-line skating, archery tournaments, and volleyball. Frontier Days is celebrated at Sunrise in June of each year; in July there is a Fourth of July celebration complete with fireworks, lift rides, an archery tournament, and an old-fashioned barbecue; a Blue Grass Festival is in August; and mountain bike races are held in all three summer months. The White Mountain Native American Arts Festival takes place in July.

Each Labor Day weekend the fairgrounds at Whiteriver are the site of the Tribal Fair and All Indian Rodeo (phone 520/338-4346). There is also a children's Headstart Rodeo and Parade in Whiteriver in May (520/338-4938), and there is an All Indian Rodeo in July at Canyon Day (520/338-1764). A junior rodeo takes place in May at Cibecue (520/332-2488). Also in Cibecue, there is an August Old Timers Junior Rodeo, a Southwest Indian Rodeo Association sanctioned event (520/332-2535).

During the months of April through September, Sunrise Dance ceremonies are held in various locations on the reservation. These are "coming out" ceremonies for Apache girls celebrating their passage into womanhood. Many such Sunrise Dances are open to the public. For further information, contact the Tribal Council Secretary at 520/338-4346.

The reservation abounds in prehistoric pueblo ruins. Disturbing these sites or removing artifacts from them—as it is on all reservation, federal, and state lands—is strictly prohibited by law. To ignore the law is to destroy history and to invite severe penalties.

Mount Baldy Wilderness Area, adjacent to Fort Apache Indian Reservation, Arizona

Whiteriver basket weaver Mildred Goklish

One site, however, can be viewed and photographed by visitors. This is the large ruin of Kinishba, a National Historic Landmark, located seven miles west of Whiteriver north off State Highway 73. Spread out on both sides of an arroyo, half the site has been left unexcavated. A quarter of the remainder was archaeologically excavated and left uncovered in that condition, while the adjoining quarter was once restored. However, the restored portion is now falling into ruins.

Built between A.D. 1250-1350 by peoples whom archaeologists have labelled "Mogollon," the village once had as many as four hundred to five hundred ground-floor rooms standing two to three stories high. There may have been a peak of a thousand occupants. For unknown reasons, Kinishba was abandoned in the late fourteenth and early fifteenth centuries before the arrival of Europeans in the New World. Persons wishing to visit the site should first contact the tribe's Office of Tourism at 520/338-1230.

Visitors with a taste for gambling will enjoy the tribally owned and operated Hon-Dah Casino south of Pinetop at the junction of state highways 260 and 73. Open 24 hours a day and seven days a week, the Hon Dah Casino has slot machines, video blackjack, video keno, and video poker as well as live keno games with a $25,000 limit called every seven minutes. There are also a full service restaurant, bar, and lounge. The casino's phone number is 520/369-0299; Fax 520/369-0382.

Boats can be rented at Hawley Lake (520/335-7511), Horseshoe Cienega (seasonal; 520/338-4417), Reservation Lake (seasonal; 520/338-4417), and Sunrise Lake Boat Dock (520/735-7335). Sunrise is the only reservation lake where gasoline-powered outboard motors are permitted. Various local communities offer convenience stores, supermarkets, auto repair, gasoline, restaurants, liquor stores, and other conveniences.

Surrounding, off-reservation, areas in Arizona's White Mountains offer additional abundant recreational opportunities. In July, the White Mountain Native American Art Festival, for example, is held in nearby Pinetop (call 520/367-4290).

For further information, visitors are encouraged to contact Apache-Sitgreaves National Forests, Box 640, Springerville, AZ 85938 (520/333-4301); Pinetop-Lakeside Chamber of Commerce, 592 W. White Mountain Blvd., Lakeside, AZ 85929 (520/367-4290); Round Valley Chamber of Commerce, P.O. Box 31, Springerville, AZ 85938 (520/333-2123); St. Johns Regional Chamber of Commerce, P.O. Box 178, St. Johns, AZ 85936 (520/337-2000); Show Low Chamber of Commerce, P.O. Box 1083, Show Low, AZ 85901 (520/537-2326); and the Snowflake/Taylor Chamber of Commerce, P.O. Box 776, Snowflake, AZ 85937 (520/4331).

Tribal Museum: The White Mountain Apache Tribe owns and operates the Fort Apache Historical Park and White Mountain Apache Culture Center in Fort Apache. The address is P.O. Box 700, Ft. Apache, AZ 85926 (phone 520/338-4625). They are operated under the auspices of the tribe's Office of Tourism, P.O. Box 710, Fort Apache, AZ 85926 (phone 520/338-1230; Fax 520/338-1514). Inquiries concerning historical tours, cultural shows, and crafts demonstrations should be directed to the latter office.

Fort Apache Historical Park, a 288-acre historic site, was listed on the National Register of Historic Places in 1976. It has several buildings remaining from the period of the Apache Wars and from the period immediately following in the late nineteenth century. Premier among them is the log cabin that served as commanding officer's quarters beginning about 1871. The oldest surviving structure on the post, it may have been quarters for General George Crook, Commander of the Military Department of Arizona from 1871 to 1873 and from 1882 to 1886, when he visited the post on his first tour of duty in Arizona. It may also have been used as the post surgeon's quarters and provided shelter for Doctor Walter Reed and his family when he was stationed at Fort Apache. The Office of Tourism has available a Visitors Guide to the Fort Apache Park, one filled with historical information and excellent for self-guided walking tours of the area.

At the base of the cliffs beneath Fort Apache, a replica of a traditional Apache village has been constructed. This area is used for living history and culture demonstrations. Persons interested in these should call the Office of Tourism at 520/338-1230.

Indian arts and crafts, including basketry and beadwork for which Western Apaches are well known, are available in the museum at Fort Apache as well as in Whiteriver at Goseyun's, Whiteriver Commercial Center (variety store), Odette's, Jack's Trading Post, and the Whiteriver Restaurant. They can also be found in Cibecue at the Cibecue Trading Post and at the Cibecue Variety Store and in Forestdale (eight miles south of Show Low) at the Forestdale Trading Post.

Fort Apache Indian Reservation
P.O. Box 700, Whiteriver, AZ 85941
Phone 520/338-4346 or 338-4872;
Fax 520/338-1514
Population: 10,000
Acreage: 1,664,874

Western Apache
Gaan dancers from
the San Carlos
Reservation, Arizona

SAN CARLOS APACHE TRIBE

The San Carlos division of what was then called the White Mountain Reservation was added to the reservation by executive order in December of 1872. An Act of Congress of June 7, 1897, made two reservations out of one, the San Carlos and Fort Apache reservations, with a dividing line at the Black and Salt rivers. After that, the trust affairs of each reservation were administered separately by the Bureau of Indian Affairs, and in the 1930s the Western Apaches living on both reservations formally established their own tribal governments, San Carlos in 1936 and Fort Apache in 1938. Members of the San Carlos and White Mountain groups predominated at San Carlos.

The principal settlements on the San Carlos Reservation are at San Carlos, where the tribal headquarters are located, and Bylas. There are smaller communities at Peridot, Cutter, Calva, and Eight Mile Wash. Interestingly enough, today's principal population centers, rather than being at upper elevations in the mountains, are situated in fingers of the Sonoran Desert at lower elevations parallel to the Gila River.

Cattle, timber, the mining of peridot (also called olivine), a yellowish-green gemstone, and, most recently, gambling revenue are the reservation's chief sources of income. San Carlos Apaches are sometimes referred to as the "Cowboy Indians of the West," and typical male dress is often that of the cowboy.

As elsewhere in Southwest Indian country, increasing amounts of money are derived from temporary visitors to the reservation, including fishers, hunters, campers, tourists, and gamblers.

Recreational Opportunities

Fishing and hunting are two of the reservation's most popular recreational activities. Fishing is allowed year round, but a tribal fishing permit is required. A special permit is needed to fish on the Black and Salt rivers, the boundary separating the San Carlos and Fort Apache reservations. Hunters must obtain the appropriate tribal permits for all species as well as tags for elk, antelope, bighorn sheep, deer, javelina, mountain lion, bear, and turkey. Permits are also necessary for boating and outdoor recreation. Permits, tags, regulations, and general information can be obtained from the San Carlos Apache Tribe, Recreation and Wildlife Department, P.O. Box 97, San Carlos, AZ 85550 (phone 520/475-2343). The Recreation and Wildlife Department also has available a list of permit vendors in other reservation locations as well as in Globe and Miami, Safford, Mesa, and Winkelman.

Although roads are paved into San Carlos Lake and Seneca Lake and partially paved into Talkalai Lake, other good fishing spots are reached via unpaved roads that may require pickups or four-wheel drive vehicles, especially during the summer rainy reason in July and August and after snowfalls in higher elevations.

San Carlos Lake is open to anglers, boaters, and sightseers. Formed on the Gila River behind the waters of Coolidge Dam at 2,500 feet above sea level, it is well supplied with bass, crappie, and catfish. When the lake is at its highest level, which, unfortunately, is not very often because of releases

for downstream irrigation, there are 19,500 feet of surface water and 158 miles of shoreline. There are boat docks and a marina, store (phone 520/475-2756), toilets, and ramadas. Sailing, windsurfing, and waterskiing are also favorite pastimes here. San Carlos Lake has yielded a 65-pound flathead catfish and a record-setting 4-pound 10-ounce black crappie.

Talkalai Lake north of San Carlos is on the San Carlos River behind Elgo Dam. It is a five hundred-acre lake and is a great source of largemouth bass, bluegill, crappie, flathead catfish, and channel catfish. Arizona's biggest largemouth bass, a sixteen-pounder that was taken here, failed to make it into the record books because the tribal member who caught it in 1988 weighed it on scales that were not state certified and then cooked and ate it. Talkalai Lake, which has ramadas, picnic tables and benches, and privies, is reached from the town of San Carlos north via White Mountain Avenue to a sign that says "Talkalai Lake." From there it is about a mile to the lake on a dirt road.

Both the Black and Salt rivers are excellent for fishing. The Black River—good for smallmouth bass, rainbow and brown trout, and sunfish—is accessible only via a network of interconnected primitive roads. In many cases, the roads are very primitive. Entering this area from either the Fort Apache or San Carlos reservations requires a tribal special use permit. These permits, which allow fishing, are honored on both reservations. Special use permits are available at various locations both off and on the reservation.

ANNERINO

A Western Apache woman during her Sunrise ceremony on the San Carlos Reservation

The Salt River starts at the junction of the Black and White rivers. It harbors smallmouth bass, Gila trout, catfish, bluegill, bullhead, largemouth bass, and rough fish. During spring runoff or during summer rain storms, the fast moving waters of the river afford great challenges to whitewater enthusiasts, both rafters and kayakers. The rafting season starts in April or May. Many boats put in on the reservation at the U.S. Highway 60 crossing between Globe and Show Low.

There are innumerable stock ponds, or "tanks," on the reservation. Those at higher elevations have bass and trout while those in the lower, warmer elevations have catfish and bass. A map showing the locations of the best fishing ponds is distributed by the Recreation and Wildlife Department.

There are many miles of streams on the San Carlos Reservation, and these, too, are available to anglers, picnickers, and sightseers.

Both small and large game are hunted on the reservation, but only by special tribal permit. The state's largest game animal, elk, are numerous in the mountain areas. Bighorn sheep, mule deer, antelope, bear, mountain lion, turkey, white-tailed deer, and javelina (peccary) can also be hunted, as can such small game as rabbit, squirrel, and Gambel's, Mearns', and scaled quail. Migratory game birds include mourning and white-winged dove, band-tailed pigeon, ducks, and geese.

Some areas of the southern portion of the reservation are closed to hunting and fishing, and in some instances, hunters must be accompanied by a tribal guide.

Hiking, picnicking, touring, and taking part in similar outdoor recreational activities on the reservation require a tribal permit.

During a four-day period each November over the Veterans' Day weekend there is the San Carlos Apache Tribe Veterans Rodeo and Fair held in San Carlos at the rodeo grounds. Among the many events are a Veterans Memorial parade, a 10K run, all Indian junior and old timers' rodeos, the Miss San Carlos Apache Pageant, a pow-wow, and a gourd dance. There are demonstrations by Indian artists and craftspeople who offer their arts and crafts for sale to the public. Pottery, jewelry, baskets, and clothing are among the individually crafted items. Food booths offer such traditional foods as Indian fry bread, a universal—if fattening—favorite in the Southwest. For information, call or write the San Carlos Apache Tribe, P.O. Box "O," San Carlos, AZ 85550 (520/475-2361).

At Bylas, on U.S. Highway 70 on the east side of the reservation, there is a Mount Turnbull Celebration each April. There are also a June 18 celebration and an annual spring roundup rodeo in San Carlos (call 520/475-2361 for details).

The most popular public ceremony traditionally held on the reservation consists of the Western Apaches' Sunrise ceremony. Held to mark the coming of age of Apache girls and to entrust the spirits to help them lead long and happy lives, these ceremonial dances—which feature masked figures called Gaan dancers—are usually held on weekends during June, July, and August in or near San Carlos. For information, call the tribal office in San Carlos at 520/475-2361.

In nearby Globe and Miami, the off-reservation communities nearest to the reservation on its west side, a yearly October Apache Jii Day features the display and sale of Apache artwork, jewelry, dolls, pottery, baskets, and beadwork as well as Apache food. Masked Apache Gaan Dancers (also known as Crown Dancers) perform throughout the day. Cameras and video recorders are welcome. For information, contact the Globe-Miami Chamber of Commerce, 1360 N. Broad St., Box 2539, Globe, AZ 85502 (phone 520/425-4495 or 800/804-5623).

Gamblers can take their chances at the Apache Gold Casino Resort located about five miles east of Globe on U.S. Highway 70 (520/425-7800). There are slot machines, poker, live bingo, $50,000 keno, two restaurants, and a cabaret with live entertainment nightly.

Tribal Museum: The San Carlos Apache Cultural Center, which opened in September of 1995, is located at mile post 272 across the road from the Rodeo Grounds on U.S. Highway 70 in Peridot. In addition to excellent displays concerning Western Apache history and culture, the center has space for an arts and crafts studio as well as a sales outlet for Apache arts and crafts. It is operated as part of the Tribal History Program. For further information call either the Cultural Center at 520/475-2894 or the History Program at 520/475-2293.

In addition to the Culture Center, Apache arts and crafts are regularly on sale in Peridot at Nolines Country Store and in San Carlos at the R & S Market.

San Carlos Apache Tribe
P.O. Box "O," San Carlos, AZ 85550
Phone 520/475-2361; Fax 520/475-2567
Population: 10,500
Acreage: 1,877,216

Cottonwood trees line the banks of the Verde River not far from the Fort McDowell-Mohave-Apache Community

HUEY

The southwestern two-thirds of Arizona and a part of adjoining southeastern California comprise the northern portion of the Sonoran Desert. The Sonoran Desert includes the Lower Colorado River and lands that were the aboriginal domain of the Cocopahs and Quechans, but the permanently flowing waters of the Southwest's mightiest river give that part of the northern Sonoran Desert a unique environmental aspect. Most of the Sonoran Desert lies to the south of the U.S.-Mexico boundary in the State of Sonora and in the peninsula of Baja California, but two of its half dozen vegetation subdivisions—those labelled by botanists "Lower Colorado River Valley" and "Arizona Upland"—are situated largely north of the border. The former, exclusive of the Colorado River itself, includes some of the hottest and driest areas in North America. Its dominant vegetation consists of small-leafed plants like the creosote bush and bursage. Arizona Upland vegetation, on the other hand, is characterized by such stem succulent plants as the palo verde and saguaros and other columnar cacti. First time visitors in the Arizona Upland are surprised to find a desert seemingly so green and lush for much of the year. Not only do these aridity-adapted plants often occur in dense stands, but their trunks and stems are evergreen.

For Indians who had an intimate knowledge of the Sonoran Desert, the environs were a cornucopia. If one understood sufficiently the yearly habits of the region's plants and animals, it was possible to provide one's family with food, clothing, and shelter and to have time left over for leisure pur-

suits. In the non-riverine areas of the Lower Colorado River Valley, people had to rely almost exclusively on hunting and gathering. But in the Arizona Upland, both ephemeral and semi-permanent streams made small-scale farming an added option.

The early residents of the northern Sonoran Desert were principally the ancestors of today's Pima and Tohono O'odham, now occupants of the Tohono O'odham Nation (Papago Indian Reservation), the Ak-Chin Reservation, the Gila River Indian Reservation, and the Salt River Reservation. Other aboriginal dwellers in the Sonoran Desert were members of the Southeastern (Kewevkapaya) sub-tribe of Yavapais. Their descendants live on the Ft. McDowell Reservation on the lower Verde River near its junction with the Salt River.

In historic times, ancestors of today's Maricopa Indians were forced by their Indian neighbors from their homelands in the Lower Colorado River Valley, ultimately settling next to the Pima on what are now the Gila River and Salt River reservations.

The final group of people with reservation lands in the Sonoran Desert are the Yaquis, Indians whose aboriginal territory is far to the south in southern Sonora but whose members began migrating to southern Arizona in significant numbers early in the twentieth century, much of this movement having been prompted by the Mexican Revolution of 1910.

FORT MCDOWELL MOHAVE- APACHE COMMUNITY

The Fort McDowell Indian Reservation is easily reached via the Beeline Highway (Arizona Highway 87) about twenty-three miles northeast of Phoenix, the state's capital. Its southern boundary abuts the northern boundary of the Salt River Indian Reservation.

Nearly all residents of the Fort McDowell Indian Reservation, the "Mohave-Apache" label notwithstanding, are neither Mohaves nor Apaches, but are Yavapais whose ancestors were members primarily of the southeastern sub-tribe called Kewevkapaya. It was this group among all of Arizona's Indians that suffered the most horrendous massacre at the hands of the U.S. Army. In December of 1872, large numbers of these people were shot to death by American soldiers in the Salt River Canyon inside of what came to be known, with good reason, as Skeleton Cave. Surviving Kewevkapaya, along with other Yavapais, were settled involuntarily on the short-lived Rio Verde Reservation before being forced to move again, this time to San Carlos to live near Western Apaches. During the 1880s and '90s, most Yavapais were allowed to return to their homelands where they became wage laborers for non-Indians who by then had preempted most of their lands. The Kewevkapayas, along with Yavapais of other sub-tribes, tried in the late nineteenth and early twentieth centuries to resettle within their old homelands on the abandoned Fort McDowell military reservation, but they found the arable lands there occupied by non-Indian squatters, some of whom were farmers but others who were land speculators. Fort McDowell, named for Major

General Irvin McDowell, had been established in 1865 and abandoned by the U.S. Army in 1890.

With the help of sympathetic non-Indians, a Yavapai delegation went to Washington, D.C., where a favorable hearing led to a September 15, 1903 executive order setting aside a portion of the Fort McDowell military reservation for "Mohave-Apache" Indians, as these Yavapais had been labelled. For many years afterward, Yavapais at Fort McDowell had to struggle to maintain their land and water rights, an effort in which they were aided by one of their own, Dr. Carlos Montezuma, a Yavapai captive who had been purchased when he was a child by an Italian photographer and painter who saw to it that his charge obtained a formal education. Carlos Montezuma eventually earned a medical degree and subsequently became a national proponent of Indians' rights. He died on the Fort McDowell Reservation in 1923 when he was about fifty-seven years old and was buried in the Fort McDowell cemetery where his remains continue to lie in a well-marked grave.

In 1948 it was proposed that a dam be constructed on the Verde River that would have flooded a large portion of the reservation. After a prolonged contest between opponents and proponents of Orme Dam, as it was to have been called, the opponents, which included the vast majority of reservation residents, won out—in part because the dam would have destroyed habitat for nesting pairs of bald eagles.

Recreational Opportunities

Although the tree-lined Verde River that spans the entire length of the reservation formerly provided popular recreation for fishers, boaters, picnickers, bird watchers, and people who enjoy floating downstream in inner tubes, the river's shores along the reservation were closed to the public beginning July, 1997. This was because irresponsible visitors scattered trash throughout the area and otherwise vandalized the environment. The cost of cleanup far outweighed income received from selling use permits.

A similar situation prevailed on the Salt River Reservation, forcing the Salt River Pima-Maricopa Community to close access to the river on its reservation as well.

The tribally operated Fort McDowell Adventures offers trail horseback riding on the reservation. For details, call 602/816-1513 or send a letter of inquiry to 14832 Hiawatha Hood Road, Fountain Hills, AZ 85268.

The Fort McDowell Mohave-Apache Community operates the highly successful Fort McDowell Gaming Center (602/837-1424). Located on Fort McDowell Road, it offers bingo, slot machines, and card games. There are two separate dining facilities in the center, including the Red Rock Cafe.

Although not a tribal enterprise, the Out of Africa Wildlife Park on North Fort McDowell Road (phone 602/837-7779) is situated on leased reservation lands. The park, which features wildlife shows with African tigers, is open daily except Mondays during the winter and except Mondays and Tuesdays in the summer.

The first or second week each November there is a festival on the reservation called the "Orme Dam Recognition Days Celebration" which commemorates the fact that the tribe, with the help of conservationists anxious to save the habitat of breeding eagles, successfully resisted construction of the Orme Dam on the Verde River that would have inundated large areas of the reservation. The gala occasion includes a powwow. Call 602/837-7235 for particulars.

Fort McDowell Mohave-Apache
Indian Community
P.O. Box 17779, Fountain Hills, AZ 85269
Phone 602/837-5121; Fax 602/837-1630
Population: 816
Acreage: 24,680

Pima basket

SALT RIVER PIMA- MARICOPA COMMUNITY

By mid-1872, some three hundred Pima and Maricopa Indians had left their homes on the Gila River Indian Reservation to farm the lower Salt River. They moved because in 1868 non-Indian farmers had begun building irrigation canals on the Gila upstream from the reservation and a once-prosperous Pima and Maricopa agricultural enterprise was left without sufficient water. Confronted by economic ruin and even possible starvation, some Pima and Maricopa families took matters into their own hands by moving onto vacant land where the Salt River continued to supply a reliable flow of water. The United States formally recognized their use and occupation of this land in 1879 when an executive order created the Salt River Indian Reservation. Executive orders issued in 1910 and 1911 added more land to the reservation. When the reservation took its final form in the early twentieth century, it was regarded as being in a remote desert location. Since then, however, it has found itself

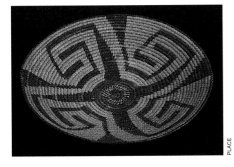

PLACE

next to one of the most rapidly growing population centers in the United States, and its lands now abut the affluent non-Indian community of Scottsdale.

The Pima Indian members of the Salt River Pima-Maricopa Community belong to a people who have lived in the northern Sonoran Desert since "time immemorial." This is another way of saying they

were here when Europeans first encountered them in the late seventeenth century, but how much earlier than that remains a matter of speculation and debate. In their own language they refer to themselves as the O'odham, "People," or, more specifically, the Akimel O'odham (also spelled Au-Authm), or "River People." This distinguishes them from their southern neighbors and close linguistic and cultural kinsmen, the Tohono O'odham, "Desert People," formerly known as the "Papago."

The Maricopas, on the other hand, are an amalgam of Yuman-speaking peoples who were driven from the lower Colorado River by other Yuman groups beginning at least as early as the eighteenth century. The Yumans forced from the Colorado River ultimately sought and were granted asylum on Pima lands on the middle Gila River. These migrations and resettlements had already occurred by the mid-nineteenth century when the United States acquired the territory from Mexico. Today's Maricopas refer to themselves as the Pe Pash (or Pi Posh or Pee Posh) in their own language.

Most Maricopas who live on the Salt River Indian Reservation are presumably descended primarily from the Halchidhoma, one of the groups of Colorado River refugees. Most Maricopas on the Salt River Indian Reservation live at Lehi or in its immediate vicinity.

Recreational Opportunities

The lowest part of the Verde River lies on the reservation where it empties into the Salt River. The Salt, in turn, flows along the reservation's southern boundary. Unfortunately, vandalism by thoughtless visitors forced tribal authorities to close access to the Verde River area in 1997. The large numbers of weekend visitors also reduced the area's wildlife population.

One of the more unusual recreational facilities on the reservation is the Red Mountain Trap and Skeet range where shotgun enthusiasts can improve their shooting skills. The range is located just north of the Beeline Highway between the highway and the Arizona Canal opposite Gilbert Road.

The Cypress Golf Course boasts two nine-hole courses and a driving range. Located near the junction of McDowell Road and the Beeline Highway in the southwestern quadrant of the reservation, the facility is open daily (phone 602/946-5155).

Native Hands Arts and Crafts, 8806 E. McDowell Road, Scottsdale, (phone 602/675-9443), is situated just northeast of the junction of McDowell and Pima roads. It offers authentic Indian arts and crafts for sale and has a restaurant as well.

Annual events on the reservation open to the public include New Year's "Chicken Scratch" (polka-schottische-two step) dance and the men's New Year's Invitational Basketball Tournament; the February or March Native American Indian Rodeo Days and the Valentine Classic Basketball Tournament; May's Senior Citizens' Bazaar; October's Miss Salt River and Junior Miss Salt River pageant; and November's Red Mountain Eagle Pow Wow. The Pima/Maricopa Basket Dancers perform at various times throughout the year. For further information concerning these events, call the Community Relations Department at 602/874-8056.

Tribal Museum: A nominal fee is charged to visit the tribes' Hoo-hoogam Ki Museum located at the intersection of Osborne Road and Longmore at 10,000 East Osborne Road in the reservation's tribal complex where administrative and other tribal buildings are located. Showcasing the traditional lifestyles, history, and culture of the Pima and Maricopa, the museum is constructed of adobe and wood from desert plants. There are exhibits of prehistoric Hohokam artifacts as well as displays of photos, basketry, and pottery of the Pima and Maricopa. Pima basketmakers and Maricopa potters occasionally demonstrate their crafts in the museum, and these and other authentic products are for sale. Enjoy traditional Indian foods from the museum's restaurant in the outdoor dining area. To check on the museum's hours, which vary in summer and winter, call 602/874-8190.

Salt River Pima-Maricopa Indian Community
Route 1, Box 216, Scottsdale, AZ 85256
Phone 602/941-7277; Fax 602/874-8014
Population: 5,704
Acreage: 46,619

GILA RIVER INDIAN COMMUNITY

In 1854 the United States acquired lands from Mexico in today's southern Arizona south of the Gila River. Its policies for dealing with Indian tribes soon extended into the region. In the mid-nineteenth century, the keystone of those policies was the creation of reservations for the exclusive use and occupancy of specified tribes. On the last day of February 1859, Congress approved legislation requiring the president to survey and mark the boundaries of lands then occupied by the confederated Pima and Maricopa tribes and to set those lands aside as a reservation. It was this way that the Gila River Indian Reservation, sometimes popularly referred to as the Pima Reservation, became

Arizona's first Indian reservation—although in 1859 the region was a part of New Mexico Territory (Arizona did not become a separate territory of the United States until 1863). Later additions were made to the 1859 reservation by executive orders in 1876, 1882, 1883, 1911, and 1913.

Located both north and south of the Gila River on both sides of U.S. Interstate Highway 10, the reservation is divided into seven political districts. Tribal administrative offices are in Sacaton, the largest community on the reservation.

The Maricopas—or Pee Posh ("People")—on the reservation were largely descended from Yuman migrant groups with such names as Halchidhoma, Halyikwamai, Kohuana, and Kaveltcadom. Many of the Halchidhoma later moved to the Salt River while the others remained at the Gila River in their own "Maricopa Colony" near Laveen. The Pimas, or O'odham ("People"), on the other hand, were living in their villages on the Gila when first seen and described by Europeans in the 1690s and had been there since the prehistoric past.

The Pimas and Maricopas were great farmers, and they quickly learned the advantages of growing European-introduced wheat, a winter crop. Until upstream non-Indian farmers siphoned off the Gila's reliable flow beginning in the late 1860s, the reservation's Indian residents were in the highly successful business of supplying wheat for flour for most people living in southern Arizona as well as in northern Sonora. There was a long period, however, when uncertain water rights and water shortages threatened to end farming as a reservation enterprise.

With water rights subsequently established and with the aid of drilling technology, agriculture again plays a major role in the reservation's economy. Such crops as cotton, wheat, millet, alfalfa, barley, melons, pistachios, olives, citrus, and vegetables now provide the mainstay. There are additionally a cotton gin and grain storage facilities as well as a facility providing chemical fertilizer. The Gila River Indian Community also leases land for three industrial parks, and in more recent times the amalgamated tribes have realized profits from casino operations on the reservation.

Recreational Opportunities

There are two casinos on the reservation, a mile-and-a-half apart on Maricopa Road on either side of Interstate 10 south of Phoenix and north of the Gila River. These are the Gila River Casino at Firebird (I-10 & Maricopa Road, exit 162A) and the Gila River Casino at Lone Butte Industrial Park (I-10 At Maricopa Road, exit 162B, one mile south of Chandler Boulevard; phone 800/946-4452 for information concerning both). Slot machines, bingo, and live keno are among the featured attractions twenty-four hours a day, seven days a week at these facilities. Deli foods are available in both places.

Near the casinos are popular enterprises operating on leased reservation lands. The complex leasing arrangements perhaps typify those in effect on many reservations in the Southwest. In 1972-73, the Gila River Indian Community, using federal grants from the Economic Development

Administration, constructed Firebird Lake and Sun Valley Marina. The tribal government then formed a corporation that leased the property from the community. The Indian corporation, in turn, subleased part of the property to a non-Indian partnership called Firebird International Raceway Park. Firebird further subleased some of its subleased lands close to Chandler for a large amphitheater for the performing arts—principally performances by musicians staging rock, rap, country and western, Tejano, or other kinds of concerts intended to attract large audiences.

The end result of these arrangements is Firebird Lake at 20,000 Maricopa Road on the west side of U.S. Interstate Highway 10 (exit 162A) that is used for professional drag boat racing, including Unlimited Hydroplanes (phone 602/268-0200); the immediately adjoining Firebird International Raceway, a driver training facility, track, and dragstrip for automobile racing (phone 602/268-0200); and Compton Terrace (exit 162B), where periodically there are major popular music concerts in this amphitheater setting (phone 602/796-0511).

Reservation visitors wanting to enjoy authentic Pima foods—including Indian fry bread and large wheat-flour tortillas—can do so in the restaurant located in the Gila Indian Center just to the west of I-10 at Casa Blanca Road at exit 175 (phone 520/315-3411). More standard fare is also on the menu.

Annual events at the Gila Indian Center open to the public include the Thanksgiving Celebration held the weekend following Thanksgiving Day, a celebration complete with Indian dancers and Indian craft demonstrations and sales. A similar event is held the third weekend each March. These affairs are staged in an open-air patio capable of seating five hundred people.

The annual Indian Rodeo and Tribal Fair, or Mul-Chu-Tha, with its parade, Indian dances, all Indian rodeo, food sales, and arts and crafts exhibits and sales occurs the second weekend in February at the rodeo grounds in Sacaton. This is followed on the third Saturday in February by the Ira Hayes Memorial Day observance to honor the memory of the Pima Indian and United States Marine who was one of the men to raise the American flag on top of Mount Suribachi on Iwo Jima during World War II. The ceremonies take place in Sacaton in the Ira Hayes Memorial Park.

The St. John's Indian Mission Festival is held annually on the first Sunday in March in Laveen and features Indian foods, dances, and arts and crafts demonstrations and sales (call 520/550-2400 for further information).

Hunting and fishing are not permitted on the reservation, nor are tourists encouraged to enter reservation communities except at times when there are celebrations open to the general public. Off-road travel is not allowed. Many of the reservation's lands are allotted to individual families and are therefore private rather than tribally owned.

Tribal Museum: The Gila Indian Center includes the Gila River Arts and Crafts Center and Heritage Park. The former has an excellent (and free) museum with displays of artifacts and photographs representing the region's prehistoric Hohokam culture as well as the historic Pima and Maricopa cultures. One of the Southwest's better Indian arts and crafts stores is located next to the museum in the same building. Featured are basketry, pottery (including excellent Maricopa pottery), jewelry, and paintings by noted Indian artists. Crafts from some twenty tribes are available for sale. There is also a selection of books about Native Americans.

Next to the museum and restaurant is Heritage Park, an outdoor museum—also free of charge— where visitors can view traditional native architecture characteristic of the prehistoric Hohokam, Maricopa, Pima, Tohono O'odham (formerly known as the Papago), and Western Apache. Traditional houses, cooking enclosures, and shades (ramadas) have been arranged in "villages" and have been constructed using desert plants and with great attention to authentic detail. Heritage Park is the only place in the Southwest where you can see these structures—most of which are no longer in daily use in Indian communities. Signs and a small booklet make Heritage Park an ideal location for self-guided tours.

Gila River Indian Community
P.O. Box 97, Sacaton, AZ 85247
Phone 520/562-3311
(Phoenix local 963-4323); Fax 520/562-3422
Population: 11,550
Acreage: 371,929

AK-CHIN INDIAN COMMUNITY

On many older maps, and even on a few maps published in the 1990s, the land that is home for the Ak-Chin Indian Community is labelled the "Maricopa Indian Reservation" or, sometimes, the "Maricopa Ak Chin Indian Reservation." The "Maricopa" name derives from the fact that the non-Indian settlement nearest the reservation is the community of Maricopa, a town created in 1879 as a station on the Southern Pacific's transcontinental line through southern Arizona. There are no Maricopa Indians on the Ak-Chin Reservation, but rather O'odham. Most of the reservation's residents

PLACE

are believed to be descended from Papagos (Tohono O'odham) who lived in the desert country to the south but who migrated seasonally to the Gila River. Some reservation residents also have Pima (Akimel O'odham) ancestors and relatives.

An executive order of May 28, 1912 set apart lands in Pinal County for "the Maricopa band of Papago Indians," which presumably meant Papago Indians living in the proximity of Maricopa, Arizona.

The reservation is situated south of Phoenix and northwest of Casa Grande on both sides of Arizona State Highway 347 (Maricopa Road) immediately south of Maricopa and the intersection of state highways 238 and 347. The only settlement on the reservation is Ak-Chin Village. It is located on Farrell Road 1.8 miles west of Maricopa Road (Highway 347; turn west at the Ak-Chin fire station).

The reservation's economy, casino income aside, is dependent on large-scale agriculture. The reservation has a guarantee of water from the Colorado River delivered via the Central Arizona Project, and the result has been that Ak-Chin Farms, Inc., a tribal enterprise, has been able to use some 16,500 acres of previously uncultivated land on the reservation for agriculture. The Ak-Chin Community operates a cotton gin and has developed an industrial park on which non-Indian tenants have leased space for their operations.

Recreational Opportunities
The greatest attraction for visitors to the reservation is Harrah's Phoenix Ak-Chin Casino located on Maricopa Road (Highway 347) south of Maricopa just beyond Farrell Road. This modern building, constructed and operated via a leasing arrangement with the Ak-Chin Community, looks like a miniature Las Vegas gambling casino. The casino is located on the west side of Maricopa Road immediately south of Farrell Road (phone 520/802-5080).

Annual celebrations on the reservation open to the public include the fourth of July fireworks and picnic in the Milton "Paul" Antone Memorial Park; the annual election barbecue held on the second Saturday in January; the Ak-Chin St. Francis Church Feast and Past Chairman's Recognition Day observed October 4 at the St. Francis church; and the Ak-Chin Him-Dak (the Ak-Chin "Way") Anniversary Celebration that takes place on the second Saturday of April at the Ak-Chin museum.

Group tours of the tribal farm can be arranged by calling 520/568-2227.

Tribal Museum: The reservation has the admission-free Ak-Chin Him-Dak community museum and culture center. It is located just north of Farrell Road in the Ak-Chin community 1.8 miles west of Maricopa Road.

The museum is described as an "EcoMuseum," a place distinct from a traditional museum "in that land and territory replace the building. Residents of the community are the curators and the audience. Each family is encouraged to create, maintain and enjoy exhibits of their self-development.

"Thus our EcoMuseum is a reflection of ourselves as we define values and identities and attempt to share our spirit with visitors."

The administrative headquarters house a large collection of prehistoric artifacts recovered during archaeological excavations of areas cleared for farming; O'odham baskets and family memorabilia; more than 7,000 photos; tribal, government, departmental, personal, and enrollment records; bibliographic resources; and technical and doctoral studies concerning the O'odham and Ak-Chin. It exists primarily for people in the community, but visitors are more than welcome. Those wanting further information can write to the Ak-Chin Him-Dak, P.O. Box 897, Maricopa, AZ 85239, or phone 520/568-9480 or Fax 520/568-9557.

Ak-Chin Indian Community
42507 W. Peters & Nall Road,
Maricopa, AZ 85239
Phone 520/568-2618; Fax 520/254-6133
Population: 500
Acreage: 21,840

*Mission San Xavier
del Bac, Arizona*

MAACK

TOHONO O'ODHAM NATION

When Father Eusebio Francisco Kino became the first European to establish his permanent residence in the northeastern reaches of the Sonoran Desert in 1687, he also became the first person to describe, in writing, native inhabitants whom he variously labelled "Pima," "Sobaipuri," and "Soba." They, and non-riverine peoples whom Kino's European contemporaries called "Papagos," spoke mutually intelligible dialects of a tongue later linguists would call "Piman," but whose speakers regarded themselves then, as now, as "O'odham" ("People"). Their northern boundary lay in lands immediately north of the Gila River and included today's Salt River, Gila River, and Ak Chin reservations, while the southern boundary lay equidistant south of the present U.S. and Mexico border along the Magdalena and Concepción rivers. The Northern O'odham's eastern range extended to the San Pedro river and headwaters of the Sonora and San Miguel rivers, while the western edge was marked by the Gulf of California and the Tinajas Altas and Gila mountains. It was a vast and arid territory, one halved into northern and southern segments when the Gadsden Purchase of 1854 divided the region—one called by Spaniards the Pimería Alta (northern Pima lands)—between the United States and Mexico.

By the end of the nineteenth century, most Mexican O'odham had either migrated to the United States or had become assimilated into the general Mexican population. At the same time, the O'odham in the United States had become conceptualized by non-Indians as "the Papago" and "the Pima," the latter living on the Gila and Salt rivers and the former living south of Tucson on the Santa Cruz River and scattered throughout the riverless desert country west of the Santa Cruz. The "Pimas" and "Papagos" were further defined—whether initially by themselves or by outsiders is unclear—as the "River People" ("Akimel O'othham," as Gila River Pimas now spell it) and the "Desert People" (Tohono O'odham). This definition ignores the fact that the aboriginal culture of "Papagos" who lived in the Santa Cruz River Valley, as evidenced by their ability to practice irrigation agriculture, also qualified them as "River People."

In 1874, an executive order signed by President Ulysses S. Grant created the Papago Indian Reservation surrounding the late eighteenth-century Spanish church of Mission San Xavier del Bac (Wa:k). It is situated on the Santa Cruz River about nine miles south of downtown Tucson, Arizona. Another executive order in 1882 set aside the Gila Bend Indian Reservation as additional lands for Papagos. Finally, in 1916, a third Papago Indian

Reservation was created by executive order with headquarters at Indian Oasis, today's Sells (named for Commissioner of Indian Affairs Cato Sells). There have been many adjustments in the initial boundaries of these reservations, but the modern result is three non-contiguous geographical units that in combination make the Papago Indian Reservation—the home of the Tohono O'odham Nation—the second largest Indian reservation in the United States. Only the Navajo Indian Reservation exceeds it in size. The three units of the reservation are commonly known as the San Xavier, Gila Bend, and Sells reservations.

There remains confusion over the reservation's name because in January, 1986, enrolled members voted to adopt a new tribal constitution and by-laws, a document which included a name change from the Papago Tribe of Arizona to the Tohono O'odham Nation. No one, however, has yet applied to the U.S. Board on Geographic Names, the federal agency responsible for the designation of official place names in the United States, to update the name of the reservation in conformity with the now official label for the group occupying it. The result

36

BURKHALTER

HEATH

Left, *The west transept of Mission San Xavier de Bac on the San Xavier district of the Tohono O'odham Nation*

Saint Augustin's Catholic Church, Chuichu, Tohono O'odham Nation, Arizona

is that one often sees the name Tohono O'odham Indian Reservation ("Desert People Indian Reservation") on maps when "Tohono O'odham Reservation" would be less redundant, and "Papago Indian Reservation" remains technically proper in the eyes of the federal government until the Board on Geographic Names takes action.

The Tohono O'odham Nation is divided into eleven political districts that share boundaries with cattle grazing districts. Nine of them are on the Sells portion of the reservation while the physically separated San Xavier and Gila Bend reservations are the remaining two districts. The Gila Bend Reservation district is called the San Lucy District after its only village. Federal, state, and tribal government (including schools) and cattle raising provide most of the employment for residents of the nine districts of the Sells reservation and of the Gila Bend Reservation, while government, off-reservation employment in contiguous Tucson, employment in the tribal gambling casino, and leasing of lands for copper mining are the chief sources of income for O'odham living at San Xavier.

Tohono O'odham also have a small tract of land adjacent to the community of Florence, and in 1997 the Bureau of Land Management turned over to a group of Hia Ced O'odham ("Sand Papago") a minuscule piece of their ancestral homeland south of Ajo that contains one of their historic burial grounds.

The reservation's population and administrative center is located in Sells sixty miles west of Tucson on Arizona State Highway 86. The other large center of population on the Sells reservation is at Santa Rosa on Reservation Route 15 approximately forty-five miles south of Casa Grande.

The San Xavier and Gila Bend Indian reservations are comprised essentially of single communities. The former, with its village of Wa:k (Bac), is located nine miles south of Tucson just to the west of Interstate 19 (exit 92), while San Lucy, the only settlement on the Gila Bend Indian Reservation, is two miles north of Gila Bend off Interstate 8 (exits 115, 116, and 119).

Recreational Opportunities

In spite of the fact that the Sells unit of the Tohono O'odham's reservation boasts vast expanses of what arguably are among the most spectacular vistas of Arizona Upland Sonoran Desert vegetation in the world, with miles of saguaro cacti stands unblemished by billboards, power poles, or other human obstructions, the Tohono O'odham Nation does not actively encourage tourism within its boundaries. People living in the reservation's widely scattered settlements, and there are more than sixty of them, expect outsiders to respect their privacy. And like cattle growers everywhere, they do not appreciate off-road travelers creating ruts that may lead to erosion, disturbing water holes, or damaging gates, fences, and corrals. Given problems with the movement of illegal aliens and drug traffic across the United States and Mexico boundary that marks the southern limit of the reservation, casual travel south of Arizona State Highway 86, especially, is not recommended at this time.

Visitors are decidedly welcome in the Nation's Desert Diamond Casino, a twenty-four-hour gambling operation that includes high stakes bingo, slot machines, and card games and that is located at 7350 S. Nogales Highway one mile south of Valencia Road on the eastern edge of the San Xavier Reservation.

On the north side of the San Xavier Reservation west of S. Mission Road is the Tohono O'odham Swap Meet, 5721 S. Westover (phone 520/578-9183). Hours are Friday from 8:00 a.m. to 4:00 p.m. and Saturday and Sunday from 5:00 a.m. until trading ends, usually late at night.

The central attraction on the San Xavier Reservation, and it is one that draws thousands of visitors annually from all over the world, is Mission San Xavier del Bac, 1950 W. San Xavier Road, Tucson, AZ 85746. This famous mission south of Tucson is reached via Interstate 19 (exit 92). Offering the best example of Spanish ultrabaroque architecture and religious art in the United States, the church at Mission San Xavier was completed in 1797 by Spanish artisans and O'odham laborers and masons in the employ of Franciscan missionaries. The building, with its highly decorated interior featuring polychrome wall paintings and religious statuary crafted in eighteenth-century guild workshops in Mexico has risen out of the Sonoran Desert like an Arabian Nights fantasy for two centuries. Still administered by Franciscans, it is the active parish church for the San Xavier District of the Tohono O'odham Nation. The mission, which includes a museum and gift shop, is open to the public at no charge seven days a week from 7:00 a.m. to 6:00 p.m. Weekday masses are at 8:30 a.m.; Saturday, at 5:00 p.m.; and Sunday, at 8:00 a.m., 9:30 a.m. (the parish mass), 10:00 a.m., and 12:30 p.m. Hours may vary in summer and winter. Phone 520/294-2624 for further information.

ANNERINO

Tohono O'odham stick game

▼▼▼▼▼▼▼▼▼▼▼▼▼▼▼▼▼▼▼▼▼▼▼▼▼

Other religious occasions at San Xavier that involve public processions are Corpus Christi (the Feast of the Holy Eucharist), a moveable feast held on a Thursday or Sunday in June or July; the Feast of St. Francis of Assisi, October 3 (vigil) and 4 (feast day); the celebration of the Holy Cross (Santa Cruz), May 3; and the Feast of Our Lady's Assumption, mid-August. Call the parish office at Mission San Xavier, 520/294-2624, for information.

San Xavier Plaza, 1959 West San Xavier Road, is located directly across from San Xavier Mission. Open daily from 8:00 a.m. to 5:00 p.m., the San Xavier Plaza includes an O'odham-operated snack shop, one that features Indian fry bread and other traditional O'odham foods as well as more familiar American fare. The remaining shops in the plaza have for sale authentic Southwest Indian jewelry, kachina dolls, pottery, baskets, and other arts and crafts as well as audio recordings of Indian music in different formats. The Tohono O'odham weave more baskets than all the other Southwest tribes combined. It is a coiled basketry. And there is a handful of Tohono O'odham painters, Mike Chiago and Leonard Chana among them, whose paintings are in considerable demand.

All shops on the plaza are Indian owned and operated. The management office is at 2018 W. San Xavier Road, Tucson, AZ 85746 (phone 520/294-5727).

On weekends, but sometimes during the week as well, individual O'odham families sell soft drinks and their traditional foods—fry bread, flour tortillas, chilis, and beans—beneath roofed shelters called ramadas in Spanish and regional English (vato in O'odham) that are set up just to the southwest as well as on the southeast side of the mission.

There are public religious fiestas that take place at Mission San Xavier during the year. Most of these are sponsored by one of five twelve-member feast committees who assume responsibility for one year's observances during a five-year rotating cycle. The most important of these events is the annual December 2-4 fiesta in honor of the community's patron saint, San Francisco Xavier. The patronal day is December 3, but the celebration begins the evening before, on the vigil, with a rosary begun in the church that continues as those participating leave the church and walk in procession counter-clockwise around the large parking area south of the church. The procession is led by altar boys carrying a cross and candles, followed by feast committee members carrying the upright statue of San Xavier that normally is in a niche on the altarpiece behind the high altar. They are followed by the parish choir singing Spanish hymns, and they in turn are followed by the clergy and general congregation and by any spectators who may care to join in. As the procession leaves the church, an O'odham band begins to play (drums, saxophone, guitar), the mission bells are rung, and fireworks are set off—all as recitation of the rosary continues unabated. When the procession re-enters the church, the statue of San Xavier is placed on the northwest corner of the crossing, the benediction of the Most Blessed Sacrament is given, and the service ends. Everyone then walks to the dance ramada southwest of the church where social dancing takes place, usually at least until midnight.

On December 3 there is a mass in the church in the morning, and in the evening the ceremonies—and social dance following—of the night before are repeated, but now with larger crowds and greater splendor. The observance is concluded on the morning of December 4 with a special mass and ceremony for the inauguration of the new feast committee.

The San Xavier community hosts an annual powwow, usually early in March of each year. Indians from as many as forty tribes from the United States and Canada take part in a two-day competition among costumed dancers for prizes offered for the best performances. Many booths are also set up offering traditional foods for sale. The Wa:k Powwow—for which there is a nominal admission charge—takes place in the playing field behind the mission. Still photographs, but not movies or video, are allowed. For further information, call 520/294-5727.

The Tohono O'odham Nation sponsors an annual rodeo the first weekend of each February at the tribal rodeo grounds on the far northwest side of Sells on the south side of State Highway 86. For further information, call 520/383-2221 ext. 228.

A favorite destination for hikers and rock climbers is the summit of 7,734-foot high Baboquivari Peak. The crest of the Baboquivari Mountain Range forms the eastern boundary of the Sells unit of the reservation south of Highway 86, meaning the eastern half of the peak is off the reservation while the western half is on it. The summit can be approached from either direction. The trailhead from the western, reservation side is in Baboquivari Park, a picnic area and overnight campground operated by the Baboquivari District. The park can be reached by taking Indian Highway 19 south of

Sells 12.2 miles to Topawa. At Topawa, a sign directs visitors to the east on a graded road, Indian Highway 10, approximately another 12 miles to the park.

A full-time manager resides in a house at the park every day of the week except Wednesday and Thursday, and a hiking and use permit can be obtained from him there. Should he not be available, one can get the necessary permit at the Baboquivari District office in Topawa (phone 520/383-2366).

Drive on State Highway 386, a paved road, to the 6,875-foot summit of Kitt Peak, site of the Kitt Peak National Observatory, for a spectacular view of the Sells portion of the reservation. This world-famous observatory is located on land leased from the Tohono O'odham Nation, and is open daily, at no charge, from 9:00 a.m. to 4:00 p.m. (phone 520/318-8600). There is an excellent visitors center on top of the mountain, with displays and programs related to astronomy as well as a gift shop whose wares include Tohono O'odham baskets, pottery, and other crafts. One can also visit the McMath solarscope and two of the twenty-three telescopes on the mountain. Below the observatory is a developed picnic area where water and toilet facilities are available.

The vistas from Kitt Peak and the highway ascending it are truly breathtaking and provide visitors with a bird's eye view of the Arizona Upland portion of the Sonoran Desert. The vegetation at the summit includes pines and juniper, plants that do not survive at lower elevations in the desert.

O'odham handmade goods are available at Margaret's Indian Arts & Crafts Shop in Sells (520/383-2800) as well as in reservation trading posts at Santa Rosa (520/361-2449), in Pisinemo (520/362-2358), and at Quijotoa at the junction of State Highway 86 and Indian Highway 15 (Gu-Achi Trading Post; 520/361-2613).

Tohono O'odham Nation
P.O. Box 837, Sells, AZ 85634
Phone 520/383-2221; Fax 520/383-3379

PASCUA YAQUI TRIBE

The homeland of the Yaqui Indians is not in the United States, but in Mexico in the southern reaches of the State of Sonora. In the late eighteenth century, Spaniards and others began to invade Yaqui homelands and a period of armed conflict ensued between Yaquis and outsiders that lasted into the 1930s. Yaquis in large numbers began entering the United States, particularly Arizona, immediately preceding and following the Mexican Revolution of 1910.

The results of the Yaqui diaspora in Mexico proved to be permanent for many Yaquis, and since 1910 lasting Yaqui communities have been established in Arizona near Phoenix, Marana, and Tucson. You can reach the Tucson reservation by taking the Valencia Road exit west off Interstate 19 (exit 95), following it five miles west to Camino de Oeste, and turning south on Camino de Oeste about a half mile.

Federal recognition of the Yaqui Tribe was slow in coming. In 1964, an Act of Congress transferred 202 acres of land southwest of Tucson to the Pascua Yaqui Association to create a community that was named New Pascua. These were not, however, regarded as lands held in federal trust for the Yaquis, and it was not until 1978 that the Yaquis received federal recognition as "American Indians." An Act of Congress approved in 1994 granted historical status to the tribe, allowing it to enroll Yaqui individuals deemed by it to be members of the tribe. Tribal rolls, except for new births, closed October 31, 1997. In the meantime, 690 acres had been added to the Pascua Yaqui Reservation.

The majority of enrolled Yaquis do not live on the reservation, but live in other Yaqui communities—two others in Tucson, one at Marana, and one south of Phoenix—or are scattered elsewhere throughout the United States.

Yaquis refer to themselves as the "Yoeme," and survival of the Yoeme language among the children is one of the priorities of tribal leaders. Classes in Yoeme are taught on the reservation as well as in elementary schools where Yaqui children are enrolled in large numbers. Many Yaquis are also comfortably bilingual in Spanish and English.

Recreational Opportunities:
The Yaquis operate a gambling casino, the Casino of the Sun (phone 520/883-1700), twenty-four hours a day at 7406 S. Camino de Oeste on the Pascua Yaqui Reservation.

The Yaquis celebrate Lent and Holy Week with costumed religious dramas, Yaqui versions of dramas taught them by Jesuit missionaries as early as the seventeenth century.

The observances starting on Ash Wednesday continue for seven weeks on each Friday at about 6:00 or 7:00 p.m. The Saturday before Palm Sunday there is a fiesta all day and night into Palm Sunday. During Holy Week, the week preceding Easter Sunday, ceremonies begin and last all night on Wednesday and all day and all night Thursday, Friday, and Saturday. The grand culmination, when the forces of good triumph with the burning of a straw figure representing Judas of Iscariot, usually takes place before noon on Holy Saturday. This defeat of evil is followed by a celebration lasting the rest of the day and all night. Church services are held on Easter Sunday followed by a small ceremony that ends midday.

Although visitors are invited to witness the Yaquis' Lenten and Easter observances, photography, sketching, note-taking, and audio or video tape recording—like alcoholic beverages—are strictly prohibited. One can bring soft drinks and food, but there are many food booths set up to respond to the hunger and thirst of spectators. For more information phone 520/883-5001.

For several years the Yaquis who live in Old Pascua and who are members of the Roman Catholic Parish of Blessed Kateri Tekawitha have held a fund-raising festival at the Old Pascua Neighborhood Center, 785 W. Sahuaro Drive, Tucson. For information on each year's festival, phone 520/791-7774.

Yaqui arts and crafts are available for sale on the reservation at the Victor Flores Gymnasium, 7474 S. Camino de Oeste (phone 520/883-5159).

Tribal Museum: There is no tribal museum, but there are excellent outdoor murals painted by Yaqui artists on tribal buildings in New Pascua as well as at the neighborhood center in Old Pascua.

Pascua Yaqui Tribe
7474 S. Camino de Oeste, Tucson, AZ 85746
Phone 520/883-5000; Fax 520/883-5014
Population: 12,000
Acreage: 892

The Vermilion Cliffs-Paria Canyon Wilderness Area, Arizona, between the Navajo and Kaibab Paiute reservations

PLATEAU COUNTRY

HUEY

The Colorado Plateau stretches from east to west across the northern third of Arizona, across a large area of southern Utah, and into northwestern New Mexico and southwestern Colorado. The region is in reality a gathering of many smaller plateaus, mesas (table-like formations rising out of plateaus), and cliffs, places with colorful names like Shivwits Plateau, Hurricane Cliffs, Kanab Plateau, Black Mesa, Kaibab Plateau, Kaibito Plateau, Moenkopi Plateau, Echo Cliffs, Grey Mesa, Shonto Plateau, and Skeleton Mesa. Coconino and Hualapai plateaus and Aubrey Cliffs, also part of the Colorado Plateau, lie south of the Grand Canyon, and Indian reservations there are separately considered in this guide.

The Colorado Plateau is famed for its horizontal vistas and its exposed and colorful rock formations. Names like Painted Desert, and Vermilion Cliffs, Pink Cliffs, Red Hill, Rainbow Plateau, and Sunset Crater tell part of the story. Most dramatic, however, is the view of colored rock layers exposed in the sheer walls of the Grand Canyon. Here the Colorado River has knifed its way through the plateau to depths at times a mile beneath the surface. The river's cutting has afforded visitors one of the most breathtaking and awe-inspiring views in the world.

The Indians who continue to make their homes in the Arizona and Utah portions of the northern Colorado Plateau are two groups of Southern Paiute, the Hopi, and the Navajo.

KAIBAB PAIUTE TRIBE

The Kaibab-Paiute Indian Reservation in northwestern Arizona is one of the more remote reservations in the Southwest. The people who live here are spread among five small settlements: Kaibab, Steamboat, Juniper Estates, Six-Mile, and Redhills. The reservation is reached by taking U.S. Highway 89A between Jacob Lake, Arizona, and Kanab, Utah, to Fredonia, Arizona, where Arizona State Highway 389 carries the traveler west to the Kaibab-Paiute headquarters just south of Pipe Spring National Monument.

Kaibabs prefer privacy to tourism. I recall in 1965 driving into the yard of a Kaibab home only to be confronted by a neatly lettered sign that read: "Don't go away mad. Just go away." So I did.

The Kaibab people are one of what historically were sixteen identifiable groups of Southern Paiute, people whose native speech is a part of the Southern Numic branch of the Uto-Aztecan language family. They call themselves kaivavitun-ingwi—Mountain Lying Down People—in their own language, and their aboriginal territory, bounded on the south by the Grand Canyon, once extended as far north into southern Utah as it did south into northern

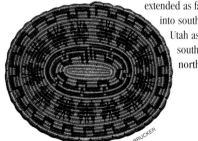

Paiute Butterfly basket

BRUCKER

Arizona. Although at one time primarily dependent on hunting and gathering for their subsistence, the Kaibab people seem to have borrowed horticulture—raising corn, squash, and beans—from neighboring farming peoples to the west and east at an early period. In modern times they have managed to make a living through a combination of income derived from wage labor, livestock raising, social security benefits, and, until 1996, from tribal income from a casino, the Pipe Springs Resort. The casino, however, is now defunct and prospects for its future—partly because of the region's remoteness from sufficient numbers of potential gamblers—are not good.

The Kaibab, like other Southern Paiutes, began to be affected by the passage of Spaniards through their region in the eighteenth century. It was not, however, until after the mid-nineteenth century when Mormon settlers began to move onto their lands that sustained dealings with non-Indians began.

Between 1870 and 1900, many Kaibab people moved to be near the Mormon settlement at Kanab, Utah, where jobs as wage laborers were available. Several families also settled to the south in Arizona near Moccasin Spring, and in 1900 the Mormon church at Kanab obtained for the Kaibab who had moved there a third of the flow from the spring, thereby enabling the Indians to start a small farm. The Kaibab-Paiute Reservation was established by executive order in 1907 and expanded in 1913 and again in 1917 to its present size. The entire reservation lies in Arizona, its northern boundary being the southern Utah border.

Winsor Castle at Pipe Springs National Historic Site, Arizona, just south of the Kaibab Paiute Reservation

Paiute Baskets

Recreational Opportunities

The Kaibab-Paiute Reservation is in a scenic setting, one backed by the Vermilion Cliffs. Visitors who merely drive across the reservation or who drive on its other developed roads will be rewarded by the views. Now that the tribe's casino is no longer operating, however, the principal attraction once again has become Pipe Spring National Monument (phone 520/643-7105). Sitting on forty acres of land surrounded by the reservation, Pipe Spring, established as a National Monument in 1923, features well-preserved and furnished late nineteenth-century ranch buildings—including a fortified stone house known as Winsor Castle—built by Mormon pioneers. A cafeteria here serves authentic cowboy fare on the site until 4:00 p.m. each day. There are both guided and self-guided tours and there is a small gift shop where traditional Paiute crafts, including leather beadwork and the shallow coiled baskets known as wedding baskets, are for sale. Paiute women are occasionally at the monument doing beadwork. The National Park Service charges a small entrance fee to visit the monument.

Visitors are encouraged to visit the reservation on the second Saturday of each October when the tribe holds its annual Heritage Day Celebration in Kaibab at the reservation's multi-purpose building (phone 520/643-7289). The Kaibab Classic Basketball Tournament is held in the multi-purpose building the last weekend of each April (520/643-7289).

Tribal Museum: The tribe has no museum, but there are informative displays at Pipe Spring National Monument.

Kaibab Paiute Tribe
HC 65 Box 2, Fredonia, AZ 86022
Phone 520/643-7245; Fax 520/643-7260

SAN JUAN SOUTHERN PAIUTE TRIBE

Like the Chemehuevi and Kaibab peoples, the San Juan Paiutes were one of sixteen aboriginal groups of Southern Paiute. Their pre-European homeland was bounded on the north by the San Juan River, on the south by the Little Colorado River, on the west by the Colorado River, and on the east by lands that were the domain of Hopi and Navajo Indians. Today, these aboriginal homelands are a part of the Navajo Indian Reservation, and the San Juan Paiutes have no reservation of their own. Even so, these Southern Paiutes continue to live in areas north and west of Navajo Mountain in southeastern Utah as well as in traditional sites north and west of Tuba City, particularly at Willow Springs and Hidden Springs on U.S. Highway 89 south of Page and north of Flagstaff. The vast majority of travelers driving along this highway doubtless assume all the Indians they are seeing here are Navajo when, in fact, many are surviving San Juan Paiutes who are struggling to maintain their separate cultural identity and to acquire lands they can claim as their own. Although they lack their own reservation, since 1990 they have been recognized by the federal government as an independent tribe and they elect their own council and hire their own managers and directors. The tribal headquarters is about a mile south of Hidden Springs Mission on U.S. 89.

Recreational Opportunities

The San Juan Paiutes hold a powwow each year during the second week of June (call 520/283-5537 for details). It takes place in Arizona outdoors at Hidden Springs near a running spring. Admission is free and there are food stands where spectators can buy food. There is no seating, so visitors should bring their own chairs.

Tribal Museum: Although there is no tribal museum, traditional Southern Paiute baskets are sold through the San Juan Southern Paiute Ying-Up Weavers Association, P.O. Box 1989, Tuba City, AZ 86045 (phone 520/283-5541). The best known Paiute craft product is the so-called "Navajo wedding basket," ying-up in Paiute. These are a Paiute adaptation of what until the end of the nineteenth century had been a Navajo form of coiled basket. These baskets, banded in stepped designs in red and black against a light background, are essential elements in many Navajo ceremonies, and Navajos have become heavily dependent on Paiute weavers for these beautiful objects. The baskets have become popular among non-Indians as well.

San Juan Southern Paiute Tribe
P.O. Box 1989, Tuba City, AZ 86045
Phone 520/283-4589 or 4587;
Fax 520/283-5761
Population: 225
Acreage: 0

Hopi dancers

Right, Hopi quilter Marling Sekaquaptewa and one of her quilts

COHEN

HEATH

▼▼▼

THE HOPI TRIBE

The Hopi Indians and the Tewa-speaking peoples who since 1680 have lived next to Hopis in the village of Hano on First Mesa are the only Pueblo Indians in Arizona. Tewas were invited by Hopis to come live among them in the wake of the 1680 revolt against Spaniards by the Pueblo Indians of New Mexico. The Hopis, for their part, had lived in northeastern Arizona for many hundreds, if not thousands, of years. Their village of Old Oraibi was begun in its present location over eight hundred years ago, perhaps qualifying it as the community in the United States with the longest unbroken habitation by people of one ethnic group. The Hopi village of Shungopavi was founded earlier, but in a location different than the present one on Second Mesa that post-dates the Pueblo Revolt of 1680.

Hopis were able to develop real towns, something like small urban centers, in a harsh and dry environment because of their genius as agriculturists. They and other Pueblo Indians in the Southwest became adept at developing and growing drought-resistant varieties of corn and beans. It was this ability, and lessened dependence on far spread hunting and gathering, that made it possible for large numbers of people to live concentrated in one place. Visitors from Iowa, Nebraska, and Illinois are bemused when they see sparse, wind-blown corn stalks struggling to stay alive in fields of shifting sand. What they do not know, however, is that the yields from these desert-adapted Hopi varieties of corn are phenomenal.

The Hopis' dispute with Navajos over land led to a federal court decree in 1962 that said Hopis and Navajos should work out ways between them for the joint use of 1.8 million acres of land beyond the confines of Hopi grazing District Six, an area of approximately 632,000 acres immediately surrounding the Hopi villages. Not surprisingly, this arrangement did not work, and in 1974 Congress partitioned the joint-use area into halves, saying Hopis, about a hundred of them, who lived on the Navajos' half should leave, and they did. More than eight thousand Navajos who lived on the Hopis' half were also told they would have to leave, but many have refused to do so. The dispute is one likely to simmer into the foreseeable future. Hopis and Navajos have serious disagreements on a great many issues involving land, water, and mineral resources.

Today's eleven principal Hopi villages are situated either on top of or near the base of one of three

Hopi basket dancers Mary, Juanita, and Wilhelmina Saufkie

TEIWES

mesas that finger south from the much larger Black Mesa. First Mesa, on the east, includes Walpi, Sichomovi, and Hano (Tewa Village) on its flat summit with Polacca, a community dating from 1890 and which has neither its own plaza nor ceremonial life, down below. The top of Second Mesa has three villages: Shongopavi, Mishongnovi, and Sipaulovi. Third Mesa's surface is where Oraibi is located, while Kykotsmovi ("New Oraibi") is at its base. Although somewhat geographically removed, Hotevilla and Bacabi are a part of the Third Mesa group of villages.

Detached from the Hopi Reservation to the west are two additional Hopi communities, Upper Moenkopi and Lower Moenkopi. Another "Hopi community" is a government town, Keams Canyon, where the Phoenix Area Indian Health Service operates a hospital and where the Bureau of Indian Affairs maintains its Hopi Agency headquarters. Homes, a store, and arts and crafts shops have also grown up near the junction of Arizona State Highways 87 and 264 at the foot of Second Mesa where they have a "Second Mesa" address.

Hopi tribal headquarters are in the community formerly known as "New Oraibi," but which is now officially Kykotsmovi. Most Hopis call it "K-Town."

Visitors have several choices about how best to reach the Hopi Reservation. The reservation is bisected by State Highway 264 between U.S. Highways 160 on the west and 191 on the east. State Highway 87 leads northward onto the reservation from Interstate 40 near Winslow (exit 257), while a somewhat more picturesque route is Reservation Highway 2 going north from Leupp to Kykotsmovi. Leupp, in turn, is most readily reached by taking State Highway 99 north from Interstate

Hopi Kachina dolls

HUCKO

One popular public perception is that all Hopi religious ceremonies involve kachina dances. In fact, the masked kachinas do not arrive in the villages until January or February and their appearances end in July. Religious observances the other half of the year include the snake-antelope ceremony or flute ceremony in alternating years in each village; the butterfly dance; the buffalo dance; the wuwuchim ceremony; and the ceremonies of three women's societies: Maraw, Lakon, and Owaqol. All are extremely colorful and, to outsiders, wonderfully picturesque and exotic. To Hopis, however, as well as to other Indians who have public religious rituals, these ceremonies are charged with deep religious significance. All of them are meant as blessings, and depending on the particular ceremony, they are intended to bring rain, promote the growth of crops, insure an abundance of game, promote fertility, insure good harvests, bring success in war, and to bring about general well being and harmony, not only among Hopis, but among all the world's people.

Because these ceremonies, like those in other Southwest Pueblo communities, have become so popular to outsiders, many of them are no longer open to the general public. Decisions concerning public access to these religious observances are in the hands of the local villages where they occur. To learn what the situation is from year to year call the village community development offices, at area code 520: Bacabi Village (734-9360); First Mesa Consolidated Villages (737-2670); Hotevilla Village (734-2420); Kykotsmovi Village (734-2474); Mishongnovi Village (743-2520); Shongopavi Village (737-2570); Sipaulovi Village (734-2353); Moenkopi Village (283-8051); and the Hopi Civic Center (743-6686).

Although there is a Hopi tribal government with a democratically elected Council, Hopi villages have a great deal of autonomy in the management of their own affairs. Indeed, there are villagers, so-called "conservatives," who prefer not to recognize the council's authority. That is why it is important to make inquiries at individual villages if planning more than a brief visit.

The greatest pleasure in visiting Hopi country comes from the opportunities one has to sample a hint of Hopi life and hospitality. Shopping in stores where Hopis shop and eating in restaurants or cafes where Hopis eat gives one a chance to listen, observe, and to feel something of the tenor of Hopi life. In many places, both in villages and alongside

40 at Leupp Corner (exit 245). Regardless of the route, travelers cross large expanses of the Navajo Indian Reservation before arriving on the Hopi Reservation. The latter is totally encircled by the former.

Recreational Opportunities

Visitors go to the Hopi Reservation primarily to see compact villages built in an ancient manner of stone masonry on high mesas, among the oldest settlements in the United States. Traditional villages are made up of contiguous multi-storied units constructed around plazas and which have one or more kivas, subterranean chambers constructed primarily for religious purposes. Visitors also go to Hopiland to buy high quality locally made jewelry, pottery, basketry, carved kachina dolls, and visual art; and, if they are fortunate, to witness public portions of Hopi religious dramas performed by masked kachinas, other costumed performers, and ritual clowns.

Kachinas are the living essence of plants, animals, and such inanimate objects as the moon. They spend half the year living underground, but for six months, between the winter and summer solstices, they assume material shape through the bodies of

male impersonators. When wearing their masks, impersonators are the kachinas. Hopi children are instructed in the identification of some three hundred kinds of kachinas with dolls carved in their likenesses. These wood carved and decorated dolls have also become a favored item of Hopi sculptural art among non-Hopis.

Persons allowed to be present at Hopi religious ceremonies should accord the ceremonies the same respect due ceremonies in a church, mosque, or synagogue, and one's behavior should be the same. Just as at a Christian, Muslim, or Jewish service, men should wear long pants and shirts. Women should dress modestly. Questions should no more be asked of participants or of others than they would in an indoor non-Indian religious ceremony. One should choose a place from which to listen and observe and should remain stationary in that place. And although the sacred space is outdoors rather than indoors, as is the case with rituals of most so-called "major religions," wearing hats or holding umbrellas—which might block the view for others—is not recommended. Never follow participants in the ceremony when they leave the plaza. Photography, video and audio recording, sketching, and note-taking are prohibited as, indeed, is the case in Hopi villages under any circumstances.

Stagecoach and Rabbit Ears, Monument Valley, Navajo Reservation, Arizona

HEATH

roads leading to them, there are signs indicating that the owners of individual homes are selling pottery, jewelry, kachina dolls, or baskets, and potential buyers are often invited into homes. Individual entrepreneurs among the Hopi also sell piki bread, thereby affording visitors another reason to enter a home.

Hopi pottery is traditionally made on First Mesa, especially by the Tewas of Hano Village. Second Mesa is known for its coiled baskets and Third Mesa for its wicker baskets. Kachina doll carvers, silversmiths and other jewelers, textile weavers (who are men among the Hopi), and painters and sculptors are in communities throughout the reservation. Hopi silversmiths are especially well known for their silver overlay work.

There are a great many places visitors can shop for Hopi arts and crafts on the reservation, with old ones closing and new ones opening frequently. Visitors driving along reservation highways will see signs in the yards of some homes on all three mesas inviting them to shop for Hopi arts and crafts. Among some of the better known reservation outlets in operation in 1997 were Bear Strap, Hopi Cultural Center #2, P.O. Box 683, Second Mesa, AZ 86043 (phone 520/734-2406); Honani Crafts Gallery, specializing in fine Hopi silver and gold overlay jewelry, P.O. Box 221, Second Mesa, AZ 86043 (520/737-2463); Hopi Arts & Crafts-Silver Crafts Cooperative Guild, P.O. Box 37, Second Mesa, AZ 86043 (520/734-4263); Alph Secakuku,

kachina dolls, silver jewelry, and pottery, Box 431, Second Mesa, AZ 86043 (520/737-2256); Phil Poseyesva, silversmith, P.O. Box 421, Second Mesa, AZ 86043 (520/737-9306); Hopi Gallery, P.O. Box 316, Second Mesa, AZ 86043 (520/737-2211); and Is-ka-sok-pu, P.O. Box 329, Second Mesa, AZ 86043 (520/734-2278).

Also: Shalako Arts & Crafts, P.O. Box 146, Second Mesa, AZ 86043 (520/734-2384); Monongya Gallery, P.O. Box 287, Old Oraibi, AZ 86039 (520/734-2344); Sockyma's Arts & Crafts, P.O. Box 96, Kykotsmovi, AZ 86039 (520/734-6667); and McGees Indian Art Gallery, P.O. Box 607, Highway 264, Keams Canyon, AZ 86034 (520/738-2295).

Situated one and a half miles east of the Hopi Cultural Center on Highway 264 at Second Mesa is the Tsu-kurs-ovi (Tsakurshovi) store operated by Janice and Joseph Day to supply Hopis with traditional items used in Hopi ceremonies (P.O. Box 234, Second Mesa, AZ 86043; phone 520/734-2478). Here one can see close at hand samples of ceremonial paraphernalia, including items of dress, traditional musical rattles, and herbs and sweet grass needed by Hopis for religious observances.

The paved road leading from Polacca to the top of First Mesa cannot be negotiated all the way by RVs, buses, or vehicles pulling trailers. Visitors in such conveyances will have to walk part of the way to the mesa top. Others will drive through Hano and Sichomovi to the end of the paved road in front of the Punsi Center operated by First Mesa Consolidated Villages. Visitors are not allowed to stroll unattended through Walpi and most of Sichomovi but must be accompanied by a guide. Guides, whose services are offered between 9:30 a.m. and 4:30 p.m. during the summer months and between 9:30 a.m. and 4:15 p.m. the rest of the year, are free of charge, although contributions can

be left at the Center. There is the usual prohibition against photography, sketching, and tape-recording.

Weekends during the summer are when ceremonies regularly occur at Walpi, and outsiders can visit Walpi on those occasions only at the invitation of a Walpi resident. The village otherwise is closed to outsiders when religious observances are taking place.

Polacca is headquarters for the Hopi Polewyma Travel and Tours company, P.O. Box 210, Polacca, AZ 86042 (520/525-9490). The company provides Hopi guides for tours of the Hopi villages and visits with Hopi artists and craftspeople. Tribal Museum: The Hopi Cultural Center Museum, P.O. Box 7, Second Mesa, AZ 86043 (520/734-6650) is on state highway 264 northwest of its junction with state highway 87. There is a nominal charge to visit the museum, one with excellent photographic and other exhibits that was established in 1970.

The museum includes displays of Hopi silver and other jewelry, basketry, kachina dolls, and weaving. The museum also maintains a photographic archive and research library that are available to scholars and others with legitimate interests.

The Hopi Tribe
P.O. Box 123, Kykotsmovi, AZ 86039
Phone 520/734-2441; Fax 520/734-2435
Population: 9,000
Acreage: 1,561,213
(of which 911,000 are Hopi partitioned lands)

Shawl dancers

ANNERINO

NAVAJO NATION

Navajos, who call themselves the Diné ("People"), speak a language belonging to the Athapaskan family. Indeed, linguists classify Navajo as an Apachean language, a tongue largely mutually intelligible with the language spoken by Western Apaches and, to some extent, with the languages of Chiricahuas, Jicarillas, and Mescaleros.

Most archaeologists believe Navajos and other Athapaskans entered the Southwest in the sixteenth century about the time the first Europeans began making explorations into the area. Primarily hunters and gatherers, they soon learned agricultural techniques from more sedentary neighbors and became adept at growing corn. After Spaniards introduced sheep, goats, and horses in large numbers beginning in the seventeenth and eighteenth centuries, Navajos became pastoralists as well as raiders.

The Navajos were militarily defeated by the United States in 1864. Most of them were removed from their homelands in Arizona and western New Mexico in a tragic event in Navajo history recalled by them as "The Long Walk." They were forced to move on foot in the dead of winter some 350 miles to Bosque Redondo on the Pecos River in eastern New Mexico. Survivors of the march remained exiled there until 1868 before being allowed to return to a portion of their former territory. By the end of the nineteenth and early twentieth centuries, Navajos had become almost totally dependent on sheep as their source of livelihood.

To write about Navajos among contemporary Indians of the United States requires the use of

superlatives. With more than 210,000 members, the Navajo tribe is by far the largest in the United States. With more than 16 million acres (26,000 square miles) of land, the Navajo Nation's real estate holdings dwarf those of all other tribes. The vast reservation covers much of northeastern Arizona and sprawls into large areas of adjoining southeastern Utah and northwestern New Mexico. It completely surrounds the Hopi Indian Reservation; embodies the San Juan Paiute Tribe; and has within its boundaries Canyon de Chelly National Monument, Navajo National Monument, Hubbell Trading Post National Historic Site, and Rainbow Bridge National Monument. It shares portions of exterior boundaries with Wupatki National Monument, Petrified Forest National Park, Grand Canyon National Park, Glen Canyon National Recreation Area, Chaco Culture National Historical Park, and Grand Staircase/Escalante National Monument.

RUNNING

Redwing Nez, Navajo

Partially to express their independence from state government, Navajos have refused to follow Arizona's lead in ignoring daylight savings time. When daylight savings time goes into effect the first week in April and remains in effect until the last week of October throughout forty-seven of the forty-eight contiguous states, so is it in effect on the Navajo (but not on the Hopi) Reservation. This is notwithstanding the fact that most of the reservation lies within Arizona.

The Navajo Nation's administrative headquarters are in Window Rock, Arizona, on State Highway 264 not far from the New Mexico State line just

northwest of Gallup, New Mexico. Window Rock and adjacent St. Michaels comprise the reservation's largest urban area, but there is a large community at Tuba City, Arizona, as well. Other communities of significant size are those at Ganado, Fort Defiance, Lukachukai, Many Farms, Chinle, and Kayenta in Arizona and at Shiprock in New Mexico. Beyond these larger settlements, the reservation is a rural land of thin population density. Visitors can travel for miles and see only an occasional hogan or other house or a family cluster of houses. The region remains one of wide open spaces.

Recreational Opportunities

The Navajo Reservation is a land of plateaus, mountains, and mesas, of scenic panoramas that are among the best in the world. And the Navajo Nation, anxious to bolster its economic base and to improve its share of tourism dollars spent in Arizona and New Mexico, has created a Navajoland Tourism Office (P.O. Box 663, Window Rock, AZ 86515; phone 520/871-6436) that makes every effort to see that the welcome mat on the reservation is spread out for visitors who are respectful of tribal traditions and law and of the privacy of individuals. So do countless individual Navajo entrepreneurs take advantage of an influx of tourists, especially during the weeks of late spring, summer, and early autumn when roadside booths where jewelry and rugs are sold by knowledgeable Navajo salespeople.

Much of the reservation is very cold between November and February, and there is considerable snow in some areas. However, winter sport facilities, such as those for skiing, have not been developed. Sightseeing; photography; camping; hiking on established trails; fishing; hunting; taking in tribal fairs or other public events; and shopping for

HUEY

HOUSER

Camel Butte, Monument Valley,
Navajo Reservation, Arizona

Navajo weaver Susie Black

Navajo rugs, jewelry, pottery, and other crafts are more than enough reasons for visitors to spend time in Navajoland.

Sightseeing and Arts and Crafts: Rock climbing and off-trail hiking are prohibited on the reservation. Similarly prohibited is off road travel by four-wheel vehicles, dune buggies, jeeps, and motorcycles. Permits are required for back country use, including hiking. These can be obtained through the Navajo Parks and Recreation Department, P.O. Box 9000, Window Rock, AZ 86515 (phone 520/871-6647 or 7307; fax 520/871-6637 or 7040).

There are many different ways one might choose to tour the Navajo Indian Reservation. The Navajoland Tourism Department has published a suggested itinerary with Window Rock, the Navajo Nation's capital, as the starting point. That itinerary, with minor changes, is followed here.

Window Rock is readily reached from Gallup, New Mexico, via State Highway 264 or, if one is approaching from the west, via Indian Route 12, which heads north from Interstate 40 at exit 357 at Lupton, Arizona.

The Navajo Nation Council Chambers in Window Rock is a beautiful structure erected in a shape to emulate that of a Navajo dwelling (hogan). As traditional, its entrance faces east to allow easy access for the Holy People so important in Navajo religion. Murals depicting Navajo history painted by Navajo artist Gerald Nailor adorn the interior walls of the council chamber. Visitors are welcome.

The Navajo Arts and Crafts Enterprise (NACE, P.O. Box 160, Window Rock, AZ 86515; phone 520/871-4090 or 4095), which shares a building on Highway 264 with the Navajo Tribal Museum, also has outlets on the reservation at Cameron and Chinle. Wholly owned and operated by the Navajo Nation as a non-profit enterprise, income derived by NACE from sales of Navajo and other authentic Indian arts and crafts is reinvested in the business in support of native craftspeople. Traditional Navajo jewelry is world renowned, and silversmiths can be seen here crafting earrings, belt buckles, concho belts, bracelets, brooches, bola ties, and necklaces out of sterling silver and high quality semi-precious stones, especially turquoise. Also for sale here are baskets, Navajo pottery, dolls, rugs, kachina dolls, and NACE's own line of Christmas cards and T-shirts. The store is open Monday through Friday from 8:00 a.m. to 5:00 p.m. during the winter and Monday through Saturday from 8:00 a.m. to 6:00 p.m. in the summer.

The window rock from which the community takes its name is located in the Window Rock Tribal Park two miles north of Highway 264 and is well worth a visit. Water and wind have abraded a large hole in a local sandstone formation creating one of the region's better known landmarks. There is no admission fee to visit the park, where picnicking (but no camping) facilities are available. Neither is there a fee to visit the Navajo Nation Zoological and Botanical Park located next to the Navajo Nation Inn at the junction of Arizona State Highway 264 and Indian Route 12. The park has an exhibition center, trails, examples of traditional Navajo dwellings, and animals native to the reservation, including examples of domestic livestock—most notably different varieties of sheep and goats—culturally important to Navajo people. The park is open from 8:00 a.m. to 5:00 p.m. daily except on Christmas and New Year's Day (phone 520/871-6573 for further information).

Stanley Perry, operator of Step on Tour Guide (P.O. Box 2381, Window Rock, AZ 86515; phone after 5:00 p.m., 520/871-2484) arranges private visits to artisans in the Window Rock vicinity and elsewhere on the reservation. Arrangements can be made at the Navajo Nation Inn (P.O. Box 2340, Window Rock, AZ 86515; phone 800/662-6189 or 520/871-4108) for vehicle tours of Window Rock, Navajo, Wheatfields, Tsaile, Chinle, Ganado, and St. Michaels.

Some visitors on leaving Window Rock will enjoy driving north on Indian Route 12 about three miles to a turnoff west to Fort Defiance. The U.S. Army erected a fort here in 1851, and in 1868, when the first Navajo reservation was created, Fort Defiance became headquarters for the Navajo Indian Agency

HUEY

RUNNING

Western Painted Desert,
Navajo Reservation, Arizona

Navajo woman with Indian corn

of the Department of the Interior. Two places worthy of a visit in Fort Defiance are Our Lady of the Blessed Sacrament Catholic Church, built in 1915 by Franciscan friars out of native sandstone, and the Good Shepherd Mission begun by Episcopalians after their arrival here in 1892. The Chapel of the Good Shepherd, the first building on the left inside the mission's entry gate, was built in 1954 and was designed by famed Southwest architect John Gaw Meem.

From Fort Defiance one can drive back to State Highway 264 via Indian Route 112 to St. Michaels. St. Michaels, about three miles west of Window Rock, dates from 1896 when Franciscan missionaries began a mission here on what was then—and has remained—440 acres of private (non-tribal) land. In addition to a handsome stone church on the mission's grounds, the friars operate the modest but tastefully arranged St. Michaels Historical Museum during the summer months between Memorial Day and Labor Day. The museum is intended to give an overview of the early influence of Franciscan friars among the Navajo. There is no admission charge, but donations are welcome (phone 520/871-4171).

The highway west from St. Michaels takes the traveler twenty-five miles to its junction with U.S. Highway 191 between Chambers and Chinle. Located here is the community of Ganado and the Hubbell Trading Post National Historic Site (P.O. Box 150, Ganado, AZ 86505; phone 520/755-3475). The Hubbell Trading Post—typical of dozens of trading posts scattered throughout the Navajo Reservation—was begun by trader John Lorenzo Hubbell in 1878. The rug room and office for the trading post, which remains in use today

and is operated for the National Park Service by the Southwest Parks and Monuments Association, is in a handsome stone building erected in 1883. Next door is the Hubbell home that since 1967, when the National Park Service acquired the Hubbell property from the family, has been maintained much as it had been in use for many decades. Free tours of the home are offered daily.

Detached from the house, store, and adjacent wool barn, between them and the road connecting with Highway 264, is a National Park Service visitor center where, most of the time, there are, in addition to exhibits, a Navajo woman demonstrating rug weaving and a Navajo man demonstrating silversmithing. Books related to the region and to Navajo culture are also on sale in the visitor center.

The Hubbell Trading Post National Monument—which offers for sale some of the highest quality Navajo rugs and jewelry—is open seven days a week except on Thanksgiving, Christmas, and New Year's Day. Its summer hours are from 8:00 a.m. to 6:00 p.m. and its winter hours from 8:00 a.m. to 5:00 p.m.

About a mile before reaching the Hubbell Trading Post, on the north side of Highway 264 is the turnoff to the Ganado Mission and Sage Memorial Hospital. Started as a Presbyterian mission to the Navajos in 1903, a hospital was added to the complex in 1911. Since 1974, the hospital and various community outreach programs here have been run by the Navajo National Health Foundation, a group with an all Navajo board of directors.

From five miles west of Ganado, U.S. Highway 191 goes north thirty-seven miles to a turnoff at Indian Route 7 to Chinle. Of interest in Chinle, behind the modern hogan-shaped Catholic church, is the church built by Franciscans here in 1912.

The entrance to Canyon de Chelly National Monument (P.O. Box 588, Chinle, AZ 86503; phone 520/674-5500 or 5501) is three miles east of Chinle. Canyon de Chelly is unusual among national monuments in that it is on 130 square miles of land owned by the Navajo Nation. Although famous primarily for its spectacular scenery and prehistoric pueblo ruins, Canyon de Chelly today is also homeland for many Navajo families who raise sheep, grow corn, and, more recently, act as tour guides.

Anyone wanting to enter the Canyon and visit at floor level any of its four principal branches—Canyon de Chelly, Monument Canyon, Black Rock Canyon, or Canyon del Muerto—must be accompanied by a park ranger or by an authorized guide. The exception is White House Ruins which can be visited without a guide by hiking a trail from White House Trail Overlook reached via a short road that heads north from Indian Route 7 about five miles from monument headquarters. Route 7 runs along the south boundary of the monument.

Authorized guides can be hired by making arrangements at the monument's visitor center with the Tsegi Guide Association (520/674-5500) or by contacting DeChelly Tours (520/674-3772 or 5433); Canyon Hiking Services (P.O. Box 362, Chinle, AZ 86503); Justin Tso Horse Rental (520/674-5678); or Twin Trail Horseback Tours (520/674-8425). Tours on foot, on horseback, or in rented or in one's own four-wheel drive vehicle can last from three hours to overnight stays. Visitors satisfied with viewing the canyons from above can drive along Indian Route 7 on the south or along Indian Route 64 on the north. White House Ruins, Mummy Cave,

*Historic commercial
wagon outside
Hubbell Trading Post
National Historic
Site, Arizona*

Massacre Cave, and Spider Rock are among famous sites viewed easily from the canyons' rims.

Leaving Canyon de Chelly, Indian Route 64 takes the traveler east twenty-eight miles to Tsaile, Arizona. Here near the scenic Lukachukai and Chuska Mountains is Navajo Community College. Founded in 1968, this first Indian-controlled community college in the United States features a six-storied, hogan-shaped cultural center. The Ned Hatathli Museum & Gallery, housed in the cultural center on the campus, offers for sale authentic Navajo rugs, silverwork, baskets, purses, pillows, and pottery. There is also a good selection of books. Hours are from 8:00 a.m. to noon and from 1:00 p.m. to 5:00 p.m. weekdays.

Indian Route 12 north from Tsaile heads to the community of Lukachukai. Near Lukachukai is

an unusual business operated by Annie Tsosie Kahn, Nizhoni Five Fingers, Inc. (P.O. Box 1347, Lukachukai, AZ 86507). Nizhoni Five Fingers operates workshops for Navajos and non-Navajos wanting to learn more about traditional Navajo beliefs and lifestyle. Women have the use of a traditional sweat lodge and both men and women can deepen their understanding of Navajo life surrounded by the natural beauty of the Lukachukai region.

Continuing south of Indian Route 12 brings one to its junction with New Mexico State Highway 134 (Indian Route 32). State Highway 134 goes east to Crystal, New Mexico, where there is a trading post. A few miles farther east the highway crosses 8,150-foot Narbona Pass through the Chuska Mountains. Two-and-a-half miles east of the pass is the Owl Springs Picnic Area.

State Highway 134 intersects U.S. Highway 666 at Sheep Springs where there is another trading post. Highway 666 north goes through Newcomb and Littlewater where there are also trading posts. Between Newcomb and Littlewater there is a scenic pullout where one can get a splendid view of the famed volcanic plug known as Shiprock but which Navajos know as Winged Rock. A favorite subject for photographers, Shiprock rises above the surrounding valley floor some 1,700 feet.

From Shiprock, U.S. Highway 64 goes west to Teec Nos Pos, Arizona, and its junction with U.S. Highway 160. There is a fine selection of Indian arts and crafts in the Teec Nos Pos Trading Post.

North of Teec Nos Pos on U.S. Highway 160 is the Four Corners Monument Navajo Tribal Park at the only point in the United States where four states come together. At this juncture, the Navajo Reservation in Utah, Arizona, and New Mexico adjoins the Ute Mountain Indian Reservation in Colorado. Located a half mile west of the main highway, the park includes a tribally operated visitor center, a demonstration center, Navajo arts and crafts booths, picnic tables, and portable restrooms. The park is open from 8:00 a.m. to 7:00 p.m. during the summer and from 8:00 a.m. to 5:00 p.m. the rest of the year (phone 520/871-6647 or 7307 for further information).

From Four Corners, travelers choosing not to drive into Colorado can double back to Teec Nos Pos and continue west on U.S. Highway 160 to Kayenta. This scenic route goes past Red Mesa, Baby Rocks Mesa, Comb Ridge, and Church Rock before arriving at Kayenta, the gateway to Monument Valley and home for many workers in the nearby Peabody Coal Mine on Black Mesa.

In Kayenta a Burger King on U.S. Highway 160 west of its junction with U.S. Highway 163 boasts a fine photographic exhibit related to the Navajo Code Talkers, Navajos who during World War II used their native language as a code neither the Germans nor Japanese were able to decipher.

Just east of the Burger King on the north side of the highway is the Kayenta Visitors Center, a tribally operated store in the shape of a hogan enclosing forty booths where Navajo vendors sell their wares. The center also has an information booth, museum, outdoor amphitheater, and a food court where Navajo dishes are the specialty.

Most visitors to Kayenta will want to take the drive north on U.S. Highway 163 to Monument Valley, a high, red plateau from which dark igneous spires rise like desert sentinels, a panorama made famous through many western movies that have been filmed here. Dramatic geologic features with wonderful names like Half Dome, Boot Mesa, Chaistla Butte, Agathla Peak, Owl Rock, West Mitten, East Mitten, Gray Whiskers, Totem Pole, Rain God Mesa, and, in Utah, Bears Ears, Sentinel Mesa, Big Indian, Brigham's Tomb, King on His Throne, Stagecoach, Castle Butte, and Bear and Rabbit reveal their dramatic splendor within easy view of surfaces that for the most part are paved.

Rock glow in corkscrew, Antelope Canyon, Navajo Reservation, Arizona

HOPKINS

Candice John demonstrates grinding corn

ANNERINO

Mountains, and in the areas of Chinle and Rough Rock. Indian Country Tours, 611 West Hopi Drive, P.O. Box 388, Holbrook, AZ 86025 (800/524-4350 or 520/524-2979) takes groups of twenty-five or more visitors in motorcoaches on one to three-day trips to the Hopi villages, Canyon de Chelly and Hubbell Trading Post, Monument Valley, Window Rock and Ft. Defiance.

Leaving Monument Valley Navajo Tribal Park, the visitor takes Indian Route 42 back to its junction with U.S. Highway 163. Here one is encouraged to continue northwest on Indian Route 42 to Goulding's Trading Post Museum and Lodge. Resting on 640 acres of privately owned, patented land surrounded by Navajo lands, Goulding's dates from the 1920s when Harry Goulding opened a trading post here on land that had formerly belonged to Paiute Indians. The museum at Goulding's is open from late March through early October from 7:00 a.m. to 9:00 p.m., and although there is no admission fee, donations are accepted. Guided tours of the region can be arranged at Goulding's Lodge, Box 360001, Monument Valley, UT 84536 (801/727-3231). The lodge also features a three-times-nightly slide show, "A Celebration of Monument Valley."

Returning to Kayenta and U.S. Highway 160, the route continues southwest through Tsegi and through Black Mesa to the junction with State Highway 564 leading ten miles northwest to Navajo National Monument and its prehistoric pueblo ruins of Keet Seel and Betatakin. A third pueblo ruin, Inscription House, is closed to the public because of its fragile condition and because there is no legal access to the site through surrounding Navajo lands. The Monument's address is HC-71, Box 3, Tonalea, AZ 86044-9704 (phone 520/672-2366 or 2367).

Just after crossing into southern Utah, Indian Route 42 takes the traveler southwest three miles back into Arizona and headquarters for Monument Valley Navajo Tribal Park. From May through September 7, hours are 7:00 a.m. to 7:00 p.m. For the rest of the year they are from 8:00 a.m. to 5:00 p.m. The park is closed Christmas, New Year's Day, and Thanksgiving Day. During the summer there are Indian dances on the patio at the park visitor center from 8:00 p.m. to 9:30 p.m. There is a campground inside the park. Further information can be obtained by writing the Monument Valley Navajo Tribal Park, P.O. Box 93, Monument Valley, UT 84536-0289 (phone 801/727-3353 or 3287).

The seventeen miles of roads inside the park are unpaved and surface conditions change after each storm, a situation that can cause problems for low clearance vehicles. Persons taking the self-guided tour should buy a map at the visitor center. Tour guides can be hired at the visitor center to take tourists through the park.

There are several tour operators who specialize in guiding visitors through Monument Valley. Among these, listed here in alphabetical order, are Bennett Tours, P.O. Box 360285, Monument Valley, UT 84536 (800/438-1544 or 801/727-3283); Bigman's Horse Tours, P.O. Box 360426, Monument Valley, UT 84536 (800/438-1544); Black's Van and Hiking Tours, P.O. Box 310393, Mexican Hat, UT 84531 (801/739-4285); Crawley's

Tour, P.O. Box 187, Kayenta, AZ 86033 (520/697-3463 or 3724); Ed Black's Monument Valley Horseback Trailriders, P.O. Box 4226, Mexican Hat, UT 85431 (800/551-4039 or 801/739-4285); Fred's Adventure Tours, P.O. Box 310308, Mexican Hat, UT 84531 (800/739-4294); Golden Sands, P.O. Box 458, Kayenta, AZ 86033 (520/697-3684); and Homeland Tours, P.O. Box 662, Kayenta, AZ 86033 (520/697-3667).

Also, Jackson Tours, P.O. Box 360375, Monument Valley, UT 84536 (801/727-3353); Navajo Guide Tour Service, P.O. Box 360456, Monument Valley, UT 84536; Roland's Navajoland Tours, P.O. Box 1542, Kayenta, AZ 86033 (800/368-3524 or 520/697-3524); Totem Pole Guided Tours, P.O. Box 360306, Monument Valley, UT 84536 (800/345-8687 or 801/727-3313); Tours of the Big Country, P.O. Box 309, Bluff, UT 84512 (801/672-2281); Triple Heart Ranch Tours, Mexican Springs Trading Post, Mexican Springs, NM 87320 (505/733-2377 or 303/882-4155); and Tsebiinizghai Tours, P.O. Box 360001, Monument Valley, UT 84536-0001 (800/874-0902 or 801/727-3225).

Some of these tour operators guide patrons to other parts of the reservation as well. Justin Tso's Horseback Tours are offered reservation wide and Triple Heart Ranch Tours, which are also horseback outings, can additionally be taken in the vicinity of Mexican Springs, New Mexico, in the Chuska

*Rainbow Bridge,
Rainbow Bridge National
Monument, Navajo
Reservation, Arizona*

HUEY

From May through early September, the park is open from 8:00 a.m. to 6:00 p.m. daily; from early September to mid-December and from March into May, the park closes at 5:30 p.m., and from mid-December to March, it closes at 4:30 p.m. Tsegi Canyon, on whose branches the ruins are located, lies in a region whose mesas are over 6,000 feet above sea level. Piñon pine, quaking aspen, ponderosa pine, and great sandstone cliffs provide a beautiful setting for the region.

A one mile round trip takes hikers over Sandal Trail from the visitor center to an overlook providing a fine view of Betatakin Ruin. Those hiking the full five-mile round trip to the ruins must be accompanied by a ranger, and no more than twenty-five people are allowed in a group. A permit is required to use the twelve-mile round trip trail to Keet Seel Ruin, and visitors are limited to twenty per day. Horseback tours with a Navajo guide can also be arranged at the visitor center. Tickets for tours are offered on a first-come first-served basis; no reservations are taken.

There is a campground near the monument's visitor center for people staying overnight and there is a primitive campground on Navajo lands near Keet Seel Ruins.

Once back on U.S. Highway 160 at Black Mesa, the road continues southwest beyond its junction with Arizona State Highway 98 (which goes to Page) past giant sandstone formations called Elephant Feet because of the shape into which wind and water have eroded them. Just beyond Elephant Feet is Red Lake (Tonalea), the last trading post before reaching Tuba City and the junction with U.S. Highway 89.

Tuba City was laid out in 1878 as a Mormon settlement. Most of it was later added to the Navajo Reservation and the non-Indian Mormons sold out and left in 1904. Since then it has been a place where Navajo and Hopi communities have existed side by side and where people of these two cultures have closely intermingled. Tuba City is a large community, one, like Window Rock, with traffic control signals. Tuba City has several conveniences plus a flea market that operates every Friday from about 9:00 a.m. to 3:00 p.m. and where one can often get homemade mutton stew, Navajo fry bread, and good prices on Navajo and other Indian arts and crafts. The flea market is located behind the community center along the four-lane section of Main Street.

There are several establishments of historic interest in Tuba City. Heading the list is the Tuba Trading Post first opened in 1870. It sells products of native artists, T-shirts, and a wide selection of books about the Southwest. Open Monday through Saturday from 7:30 a.m. to 7:00 p.m., like the rest of Arizona it remains on Mountain Standard Time regardless of its location on the Navajo Reservation. The trading post's phone number is 800/644-8383 or 520/283-5441.

Buildings of interest in Tuba City, in addition to the trading post, are the Old Mormon Laundry Building on the east side of Main Street, constructed with limestone block walls early in the twentieth century;

the First Presbyterian Church, a limestone block structure that was the first church built by Presbyterians on the Navajo Reservation; and the Bureau of Indian Affairs Boarding School Compound, a large facility closed for many years. The buildings in the compound include three very large, two-story structures crafted by Hopi and Navajo stonemasons out of red sandstone—the largest natural red sandstone structures ever erected on the reservation. These were the school's original student dormitories. Tuba City residents are now hoping to restore the school's buildings and adapt them for modern uses.

Continuing the tour of the Navajo Reservation, U.S. Highway 160 takes the traveler west to U.S. Highway 89. En route, the road passes within a hundred feet of dinosaur tracks left in mud flats of what some two hundred million years ago was the edge of a tropical sea. The tracks can be seen within a hundred feet of the unpaved road to Moenkopi, and are located five miles east of U.S. Highway 89 and a quarter mile north of U.S. Highway 160. Signs lead the way to roadside stands by the tracks, and for a small gratuity, a Navajo entrepreneur will point out the tracks.

Six miles north of the southern boundary of the Navajo Nation near the junction with Arizona State Highway 64 heading west to the east entrance to the Grand Canyon are the Navajo Arts and Crafts

Prehistoric roof timbers at Navajo National Monument, Arizona

Enterprise and the Navajo Tribal Tourist Office. They are in a hogan-shaped building on the west side of the highway. The former sells authentic Navajo rugs, jewelry, and pottery, and the latter, in addition to dispensing information, has available the camping and hiking permits required for either activity on the reservation.

Arizona State Highway 64 to the Grand Canyon goes past a turnout leading to an overlook of the Little Colorado River Gorge. The overlook is inside of what is called the Little Colorado River Gorge Navajo Tribal Park.

About a mile north of the junction with Arizona State Highway 64 on U.S. Highway 89 is the Cameron Trading Post, P.O. Box 339, Cameron, AZ 86020 (phone 1/800/338-7385 or 520/679-2231). Located immediately south of the highway's crossing of the Little Colorado River on the west side of the highway, the Cameron Trading Post has a gallery, gift shop, market, motel, restaurant, and service station. Each October it hosts a Collector's Auction at which quality Indian-made items, especially heirloom Navajo rugs, are sold. Auction participants are also treated to a contest among Navajo employees for the best traditional outfits and to traditional Indian dances.

Heading north on U.S. Highway 89 past its junction with U.S. Highway 160, one drives past Willow Springs to Hidden Springs and the tribal headquarters of the San Juan Southern Paiute Tribe. The highway continues north through a break in Echo Cliffs at The Gap. Continuing on U.S. 89, the highway goes through Cedar Ridge to Bitter Springs and the junction of U.S. 89 and U.S. 89A. The scenery along the way is enlivened by the presence of the colorful layers of Echo Cliffs on the east.

At Cedar Ridge, Indian Route 6110, an unpaved road, goes west to an overlook of the Colorado River at the site of the once-proposed Marble Canyon Dam. Although marked on some maps as the Marble Canyon Navajo Tribal Park, there are no facilities here and local Navajos who depend on raising sheep for their livelihood may object to tourists crossing their lands.

U.S. 89 goes to Page, Arizona, on the south edge of Lake Powell and Glen Canyon National Recreation Area. Page sprang into existence in 1957 as the staging site for construction of Glen Canyon Dam. Navajos traded the land for Page to the U.S. government for lands in southern Utah. Lake Powell, with its opportunities for fishing and for all kinds of recreational boating and water sports, attracts a great many tourists during the summer. Glen Canyon Dam and Glen Canyon Bridge are themselves tourist attractions along with the Powell Museum which features exhibits concerning the region's Indians; the founding of Page; and the two trips down the Colorado River made by John Wesley Powell in the nineteenth century. One can make arrangements at the museum for river rafting trips, jeep tours, or boat tours of the lake (phone 520/645-9496).

It is by boat on Lake Powell that visitors can most easily reach Rainbow Bridge National Monument in the Utah portion of the Navajo Reservation. Rainbow Bridge, with its 275-foot span making it the largest natural bridge in the world, is regarded as sacred by Navajo Indians.

Reaching the 160-acre monument is alternatively possible via hiking trails from Navajo Mountain Trading Post or from the ruins of Rainbow Lodge after receiving permission from the Navajo Nation, Parks and Recreation Department, Box 9000, Window Rock, AZ 86515 (520/871-6647 or 7307).

For persons not interested in a strenuous, if scenic, 28-mile round trip hike and who wish simply to view the spectacular bridge, it is a simple matter to reach the site by boat. Dangling Rope Marina lies close by, and there is a courtesy dock at the monument.

To make reservations to visit Rainbow Bridge by boat, contact Lake Powell Resorts and Marinas, 2916 N. 35th Avenue, Suite 8, Phoenix, AZ 85017-5261 (800/528-6154).

From Page it is also possible to visit slot canyons, including Antelope-Corkscrew Canyon. These narrow canyons are cut through varicolored walls of sandstone, and with light filtering through the cracks from above, they are often the subjects of prize-winning photographs. Recommended only for avid hikers in good physical condition, tours can be arranged through the LeChee Chapter, P.O. Box 1257, Page, AZ 86040 (520/698-3272); Overland Adventures, P.O. Box 1144, Page, AZ 86040 (520/645-5501); or Duck Tours, P.O. Box 2253, Page, AZ 86040 (520/645-2955).

On the far east side of the Navajo Reservation, in the so-called checkerboard area, the regional center is Crownpoint, New Mexico. Located north of Thoreau, New Mexico, on State Highway 371, the great attraction here for visitors is the monthly rug auction held in the gymnasium of the Crownpoint Elementary School. Weavings sold at this auction come from throughout the reservation and can usually be purchased from the weavers themselves at prices well below retail. For further information, contact the Crownpoint Rug Weavers Association, P.O. Box 1630, Crownpoint, NM 87313 (phone 505/786-5302).

Canyon de Chelly National Monument, Navajo Reservation, Arizona

HEATH

Another organized group of traditional weavers is made up of more than forty women who live on the Ramah Navajo Reservation. They have formed the Ramah Navajo Weavers Association and can be contacted at P.O. Box 153, Pine Hill, NM 87357 (phone 505/775-3253).

Crownpoint is the southern gateway to Chaco Culture National Historical Park (Star Route 4, Box 6500, Bloomfield, NM 87413; phone 505/786-7014). To reach the park from Crownpoint, take State Highway 371 north to its junction with State Highway 57 and follow Highway 57 to where it becomes a graded dirt road leading north directly into the park. The park can be reached from the north by heading south from State Highway 44 either from Blanco or Nageezi. There are no visitor services in the park, including public telephones, fuel wood, or gasoline, so visitors need to arrive prepared.

Chaco Culture National Historical Park is the location of several well-preserved prehistoric pueblo ruins, including Pueblo Bonito, Chetro Ketl, Pueblo Arroyo, and Kin Kletso.

Fishing, Hunting, Boating: A reservation license is required for fishing, hunting, or boating. These licenses are obtainable through Navajo Fish and Wildlife, P.O. Box 1480, Window Rock, AZ 86515 (phone 520/871-6451 or 6452; fax 520/871-7040).

A variety of big game (chiefly deer and turkey) hunts are offered beginning in mid-September and continue into December. Most small game is in season year around (call Navajo Fish and Wildlife for particulars).

There are sixteen lakes on the reservation where fishing, especially for rainbow trout, is good to

excellent. The most popular of these are Wheatfields and Tsaile in Arizona and Whiskey Lake in New Mexico. Fishing can be either from the shore or by boat, with motor restrictions applying on all but two of the lakes.

Tsaile Lake (260 acres) is just south of the campus of Navajo Community College. Tribal fishing licenses are available at the service station at the junction of Indian Routes 12 and 64.

Wheatfields Lake (270 acres), is noted for the best rainbow and brook trout fishing on the Navajo Reservation. It is about ten miles south of Tsaile on Indian Route 12. The necessary tribal fishing license can be purchased at the Wheatfields store or in the nearby communities of Tsaile and Navajo.

HUCKO

Pioneer Days celebration at Navajo Mountain, Navajo Reservation, Arizona

Whiskey Lake (250 acres) is about thirty miles north of Gallup, New Mexico, and is reached from Gallup via U.S. Highway 666 to Tohatchi, Indian Route 31 west to its junction with Indian Route 33, and north on Route 33 to the lake.

Morgan Lake (1,200 acres) in New Mexico is south and east of Shiprock. Anglers here catch largemouth bass, bluegill, and channel catfish. There are

no motor restrictions on boats on Morgan Lake. Other New Mexico reservation lakes are Blue Canyon Lake, just off Indian Route 12 north of Fort Defiance; Chuska Lake (25 acres), twenty-five miles north of Gallup just off of U.S. Highway 666; Assiyi Lake (Pond; 36 acres), eleven miles northeast of Navajo on unpaved Indian Route 31 and 231; Todacheene Lake (Pond; 1 acre), north of New Mexico State Highway 134 and the community of Crystal; Berland Lake, north of Aspen Lake on Indian Route 30; Toadlena Lake (35 acres), about five miles north of Berland Lake; and Red Lake (600 acres), to the north of the community of Navajo and west of Reservation Route 12.

Other reservation fishing lakes in Arizona are Antelope Lake (3 acres), a few miles south of Arizona State Highway 264, with the turnoff west of Window Rock; Ganado Lake (300 acres), about three miles north of Ganado on Indian Route 27, and where channel catfish and occasional largemouth bass are caught; Trout Lake (26 acres), south of Indian Route 7 between Chinle and Sawmill; Many Farms Lake (1,000 acres), with largemouth bass and catfish and where no motor restrictions apply, just outside of the community of Many Farms, north of Chinle on U.S. Highway 191; and Round Rock Lake (50 acres) on Indian Route 12 north of Wheatfields and Tsaile south of the community of Round Rock.

Roads into some of these lakes may restrict the ability of one to pull a boat trailer, so call ahead: 520/871-6647.

Fishing, hunting, and hiking—with the proper permits—are also available on the Alamo (Puertocito) Navajo Reservation (phone 505/854-2686); on the Cañoncito Navajo Reservation (phone 505/831-4221); and on the Ramah Navajo Reservation (per-

Liana Lynn Cleveland dressed for traditional song and dance

ANNERINO

▼▼

mits are available at local stores, including the service station on Pine Hill Road; phone 505/775-3310 or 3389).

Public Events: Special tribal events open to the public, in addition to the monthly rug auctions at Crownpoint, include a series of regional fairs and rodeos as well as the Navajo Nation Fair held in Window Rock each September (for details concerning the latter, call 520/871-6478). The Navajo Nation Fair, which properly bills itself as the "world's largest American Indian fair," annually attracts more than a hundred thousand visitors for the five-day event. The all Indian rodeo held in conjunction with the fair attracts some nine hundred contestants from eight different rodeo associations throughout the United States and Canada. Other events include horse racing, an inter-tribal powwow, arts and crafts exhibits, Miss Navajo Nation competition, an Indian fry bread contest, a baby contest, concerts, agricultural and livestock exhibits, food concessions, a carnival, and the Navajo Nation parade through the Window Rock area. There is a Saturday night performance that showcases such traditional dances as those of the Zuni Olla Maidens, Apache Crown Dancers, and traditional dance groups from the Hopi, Ute, and Navajo tribes.

The annual Eastern Navajo Fair takes place in Crownpoint, New Mexico, in August (phone 505/786-5841 or 5244 for details), as does the Central Navajo Fair in Chinle, Arizona (520/647-3614, 3611, or 2052).

The Northern Navajo Fair is held every October in Shiprock, New Mexico (505/368-5312). Touted as "The oldest and most traditional Navajo fair," there are a rodeo, a carnival, traditional Navajo

singing and dancing (including masked Yei-bi-chei dancers), Navajo food, a country & western concert, a parade, agricultural and arts and crafts exhibits, Miss Northern Navajo Pageant, and a baby contest.

Rock Point, Arizona, north of Chinle and south of Mexican Hat on U.S. Highway 191, holds the Northeast Fair and Rodeo in June. It includes a powwow, singing and dancing performances, and a carnival (520/659-4224).

The Western Navajo Fair in Tuba City, Arizona, also takes place in October (520/283-5782), while September is the month for the Southwest Navajo Fair held in Dilcon, Arizona (520/657-9244 or 3376). Dilcon is six miles east of State Highway 87 on Indian Route 15 at its junction with Indian Route 60. It is most easily reached by taking Highway 87 north from Interstate 40 at exit 257 east of Winslow, Arizona. Both a trading post and chapter house are located here.

Each December the Navajo Nation Library sponsors the Christmas Arts and Crafts Fair in the Window Rock Civic Center (phone 520/871-6376 or 7303 or 6517). Also in December, Navajo Community College hosts an arts and crafts bazaar (520/724-3311).

Typical of other events are the Navajo Song and Dance Festival held in February in the Rock Point Community School at Rock Point, Arizona (520/659-4221 or 4224); February's annual Shiprock Balloon Festival and Dance in Shiprock, New Mexico (505/598-0887); the annual March "Stars in the Desert" celebration in Tuba City that includes a junior rodeo and a children's walk/parade (520/283-4239); and the yearly Navajo Nation Diné Drama and Video Festival held in March at the Greyhill Academy High School in Tuba City (520/283-6271). The annual Damon-Bahe Boxing Tournament, with boxers from Arizona, New Mexico, Colorado, and Utah, takes place in Chinle in April (520/674-3607), and that same month or early in May at the Chinle High School there is a fine arts and academic showcase featuring high school artwork, crafts, jewelry, and food—all of which is for sale (520/674-9761).

Every May in Naschitti, New Mexico, which is north of Gallup on U.S. Highway 666, there is the Ilhozo Ji. This is a cultural event intended to bring students (kindergarten through the sixth grade), grandparents, parents, and clanspeople together for one day in a program that includes songs and dances, a pageant, and special guests (505/732-4204). Also in May, a bazaar featuring a fun run, cake walk, arts and crafts show, bingo, food, and children's games is held at the St. Michaels School in St. Michaels, Arizona (520/871-4636).

There is always a big Fourth of July celebration in Window Rock. It includes a rodeo, carnival, traditional Navajo singing and dancing, a video dance and midway, arts and crafts sales, and fireworks (520/786-5302). There is a similar Fourth of July celebration held in Kayenta (520/697-5520 or 5521).

Navajos at Ramah, New Mexico, have a community fair in September, one complete with a parade, powwow, traditional singing and dancing, Indian market, and a rodeo (505/775-3256, 3257, or 3258). In October, Alamo Community Day is celebrated on the Alamo Navajo Reservation with a parade, Indian market, powwow, and sales of traditional Navajo food (505/854-2686).

There are literally hundreds of rodeos in Navajoland every year, proving that Indians are the cowboys (and cowgirls). The Navajo Nation is said to host more Indian rodeos than the rest of the tribes in the United States or Canada combined. While most rodeos take place in the summer, during the winter there are team roping and bull riding competitions. To learn about locations and times of some of these events, contact Navajoland Tourism, P.O. Box 663, Window Rock, AZ 86515 (520/871-6659 or 6436).

Another excellent source of information about current public events in Navajoland is the Navajo Nation radio station, KTNN in Window Rock, Arizona (phone 520/871-2582 or 4487 or 2666). KTNN, which broadcasts on AM 660, while specializing in country and western songs, covers many reservation fairs and other public events live from the scene. Some of its interviews and advertising are conducted in the Navajo language. The Navajos on the Ramah Reservation also operate their own station, KTDB-FM at 89.7. The station is located on the reservation in the community of Pine Hill.

Tribal Museums: The principal Navajo Tribal Museum shares a building with the Navajo Arts & Crafts Enterprise (NACE) in Window Rock, Arizona, on the north side of U.S. Highway 264 just east of its junction with Indian Route 12. There are presently a few modest displays in the museum. Call 520/871-6675 for hours. There is also a small tribally owned museum in the Kayenta Visitors Center.

Navajo Nation
P.O. Box 9000, Window Rock, AZ 86515
Phone 520/871-6352; Fax 520/871-4025
Population: 219,000
Acreage: 17,500,815 acres
(includes Arizona, New Mexico, and Utah)

*Zuni parrot dancers,
Gallup, New Mexico*

ANNERINO

NEW MEXICO'S WESTERN PUEBLOS

When anthropologists write about the Western Pueblos they are referring to Zuni and Hopi. The Eastern Pueblos, in their terminology, are the remainder of Puebloan peoples in New Mexico as well the Ysletan peoples of El Paso, Texas, and the Tewa who live among the Hopis at Hano on First Mesa.

Today's All Indian Pueblo Council of New Mexico divides its members into the eight Northern Pueblos and the twelve Southern Pueblos, with Zuni, Ácoma, and Laguna among the latter.

Although it does not fit well with linguistic, other cultural, and historical conceptions, and it is not in keeping with modern political arrangements, it makes geographic sense to write about the people of Ácoma, Laguna, and Zuni, who live in the mesa and mountain country west of the Rio Grande, as New Mexico's western Pueblos.

The Zuni, followed in short order by the people of Ácoma and Laguna, were among the first still-extant peoples in the Southwest to be contacted by Europeans. Motivated by God, glory, and gold, in 1539 Mexico's viceroy sent the Franciscan friar Marcos de Niza north in search of the fabled Seven Cities of Cíbola. At least one of his party, a Moroccan slave named Esteban, got as far as the Zuni villages in today's western New Mexico where the Zunis killed him. Friar Marcos drew within sight of at least one of the Zuni villages before returning to Mexico with the story that there were indeed golden cities in the north. It was this assurance that in 1540 brought the ill-fated expedition of Francisco Vásquez de Coronado to the Southwest. The Zuni pueblos were the first the expedition encountered in the region. From Zuni, Coronado moved eastward through lands of the Ácomas and Lagunas before descending to the Rio Grande.

The probable path taken by the Coronado expedition follows closely a major east and west route used today by travelers between Zuni and Albuquerque, the largest city in New Mexico. New Mexico State Highway 53 runs the length of the Zuni Indian Reservation and continues eastward to connect with Interstate 40 at Grants. Interstate 40 skirts the northern end of the Ácoma Indian Reservation and bisects the Laguna Indian Reservation before it begins to make a long and gradual descent into the Rio Grande Valley. Were Coronado to return, he would not recognize the modern paved highways and towns and cities that have grown up along them, but the red sandstone cliffs and mesas, green forests, and large expanses of black lava would be totally familiar to him. And at the communities of Zuni, Ácoma, and Laguna, he might recognize at least some semblance of the puebloan architecture he encountered in 1540.

PUEBLO OF ZUNI

Whatever remained of Zuni subsistence economy disappeared by the end of World War II, and Zunis, like all other Indians in the Southwest, are now totally dependent on cash economy. Most of the reservation is used for livestock grazing, chiefly sheep but including cattle, and some five thousand acres are croplands irrigated by the federally constructed dam at Black Rock, three miles east of Zuni Pueblo. Zuni income derives from livestock; agriculture; wage labor, including employment by the tribe, federal government, and off-reservation businesses in nearby Gallup, New Mexico; and, above all, from the sale of incredibly beautiful items of silver jewelry with stone and shell inlay, crafted by Zuni silversmiths, as well as Zuni-made stone, shell, and antler fetishes. To a much lesser extent, Zuni earthenware pottery, which underwent a revival in the 1970s, provides a source of income.

Zuni Pueblo, tribal headquarters and, with nearby Black Rock, the only "urban" settlement on the reservation, is located on New Mexico State Highway 53 seventy-one miles west of Grants. It is thirty-five miles south of Gallup. Travelers take New Mexico State Highway 602 to its junction with State Highway 53 and continue west to the pueblo.

Recreational Opportunities
Zuni Pueblo is in a beautiful setting. The Zuni sacred mesa, Dowa Yalanne (Corn Mountain), provides a spectacular backdrop southeast of

Traditional Zuni white buffalo costume

Zuni turkey dance

BUTCHOFSKY

PLACE

the community. It was to this 1000-foot high mesa that Zunis retreated at intervals during the Spanish period seeking refuge from either real or threatened Spanish punitive expeditions. It is also the location of Zuni sacred shrines and is off limits to non-Zunis, but tourists can nonetheless appreciate, and photograph, its majesty from a distance.

Visitors to Zuni are encouraged first to visit the tribal office where information and various permits, including those for photography, are available.

There are several outlets in Zuni Pueblo for silver jewelry and Zuni-crafted stone animal fetishes. Nearly every Zuni household is involved in making jewelry. As a rule, men design the shapes and cut the silver while the women cut and mount the stones. Zunis are best known for their channel inlay and "needlepoint" jewelry, the latter a distinctive Zuni style in which tiny bits of turquoise are mounted in a wide variety of settings. Objects include buckles, bracelets, bolo ties, pins, brooches, necklaces, earrings, cuff links, and watch bands. Turquoise is the most popular inlay stone, but pins, buckles, and bolo ties may also

Zuni fetish

feature jet, mother of pearl, agate, and coral. Zunis also make necklaces of drilled and polished stone with carvings of animals, especially birds.

Zunis are justly famous for their carvings of fetishes in shapes of such animals as bears, mountain lions, eagles, moles, owls and other birds, frogs and turtles, corn maiden and maidens, and even horses, sheep, goats, and cows. Carvers have even been known to fashion such unlikely creatures, for Zuni, as whales, seals, alligators, manta rays, jackalopes (the horned rabbits of western folklore), dinosaurs, sea horses, and hippopotamuses. The fetishes are crafted from such stones as alabaster, serpentine, marble, dolomite, pipestone, jasper, onyx, jet, malachite, azurite, and turquoise. Carvers also work in mother of pearl, coral, abalone shell, and antler. Many fetishes feature intricate inlay, including inlaid eyes, typically of turquoise.

Minor Zuni crafts include beaded dolls and beaded rabbits' feet, pottery, and paintings by Zuni artists.

Zuni arts and crafts are on display and available for sale in Zuni Pueblo in several places on New Mexico State Highway 53, including the tribally owned Pueblo of Zuni Arts and Crafts, Zuni, NM 87327 (phone 505/782-5531 or 4481); Turquoise Village, P.O. Box 429, Zuni, NM 87327 (800/748-2405 or 505/782-5521); Running Bear of Zuni, P.O. Box 489, Zuni, NM 87327 (505/782-4907); and Old Pueblo Trading Post, P.O. Box 1115, Zuni, NM 87327 (505/782-2296). The only store owned and operated by Zuni craftspeople themselves is the Zuni Craftsmen Cooperative Association, P.O. Box 426, Zuni, NM 87327 (505/782-4521 or 4425). A mail order brochure is available from the Association; call for details.

PLACE

The Roman Catholic mission in Zuni Pueblo was founded in 1629. The old mission church is about two blocks south of Highway 53 on Old Mission Way in the pueblo proper. It was built about 1699, dedicated to Our Lady of Guadalupe, and has undergone restoration that began in 1966. After the church was restored, and at the invitation of the Franciscan priest in charge of the Catholic church in Zuni, artist Alex Seowtewa began in 1970 to paint panels of life-size Zuni katsinas (i.e., kachinas) on the walls. He had the help of three of his sons in creating these remarkable paintings, decorations that would not have been allowed in the mission's Spanish period. The church is generally open weekdays from 9:00 a.m. to 4:00 p.m.; and mass is celebrated there on Sundays at 10:00 a.m. Persons wanting to visit it on Saturday should call 505/782-4477 to make the necessary arrangements. No photography is allowed inside the church.

To walk around the old village is to journey into the past. The surviving old stone buildings, unpaved streets, the ceremonial plaza, the church and walled cemetery, and clusters of hornos, the huge beehive-shaped baking ovens introduced by Spaniards, give one at least a hint of a bygone era.

*Members of the
Cellicion Traditional
Zuni Dancers,
New Mexico*

HOUSER

Anglers can get a license from the Zuni Fish and Wildlife Department (phone 505/782-5851 or 5852) as well as from selected reservation stores. Ojo Caliente and Nutria Lakes as well as Eustace Lake, Galestino Ponds, Ojo Caliente Lake, Pescado Lake, and Tekapo Reservoir are stocked with northern pike, trout, channel catfish, and large-mouth bass. There are restrooms at Ojo Caliente Lake, and Nutria Lakes have fresh drinking water available. Hunting licenses, along with tribal hunting regulations, are also available through the Fish and Wildlife Department.

One of the more unusual annual public attractions for a reservation is the Zuni soap box derby held each spring in Black Rock. For information, call the Zuni newspaper, the Shiwi Messenger, at 505/782-2236.

Persons wanting to visit prehistoric sites, including the excavated ruins of Hawikuh, should ask about guide service at the tribal office.

Formerly, Zuni religious ceremonies that include ritual dramas by masked performers, many of them katsinas, were a great attraction for non-Zuni visitors. Unfortunately for non-Zunis, by the summer of 1995 the Zuni tribal government issued an executive order banning non-Indians from the middle plaza area "during the times of ceremonial/religious activity."

The ban extends to the Zunis' summer solstice pilgrimage and summer rain dances, the mud head kachina tribute ceremonials, and the tremendously popular Sha'lak'o ceremony held late each November or early each December as one of the

pueblo's winter solstice observances. The Sha'lak'o ceremony involves appearances by men masked as mudhead katsinas, Long Horn katsinas, and the Sha'lak'o themselves, ten-foot high masked couriers. Banning outside observers at these ceremonies has caused many Zunis who rely heavily on income from sale of arts and crafts to tourists to object, and it is possible the ban may be lifted or modified in the future. To learn the present status, contact the Pueblo of Zuni, P.O. Box 339, Zuni, NM 87327 (505/782-4481).

Dances removed from a religious context can, however, be seen during the annual Zuni tribal Fair held each August or September. Call the tribal office for particulars.

Tribal Museum: There is a modest Zuni Museum just east of the tribal office in Zuni Pueblo with exhibits concerning Zuni culture and history. It is open from 9:00 a.m. to 4:00 p.m. weekdays (505/782-4404).

Pueblo of Zuni
P.O. Box 339, Zuni, NM 87327
Phone 505/782-4481
Population: 8,996
Acreage: 421,481
(includes a religious site in Arizona)

PUEBLO OF ÁCOMA

Interstate 40 cuts across the northern edge of the Ácoma Indian Reservation between Grants and Albuquerque. Stretches of the reservation's eastern boundary abut portions of the western boundary of the Laguna Indian Reservation and, far to the south, the northwestern corner of the Alamo Navajo Reservation. It is forty miles from the northern boundary to the southern boundary along Chavez Canyon.

The Ácoma Reservation has become world renowned as the location of what during most of the twentieth century, at least, has been labeled "Sky City." This multi-storied pueblo, less romantically known as Old Ácoma, is one of three principal residential communities on the reservation. The others, originally farming settlements on the Rio San José dating from prehistoric times, are Acomita and McCartys. The name the Ácomas had for the farming community at McCarty's, "North Pass," was ignored when officials of the Atchison, Topeka, and Santa Fe Railroad christened what after 1879 had become a train stop near McCarty's Ranch, an 1870s ranch operated by an Irishman who had married a local Hispanic woman. Because of their proximity to the railroad and, more recently, to the main east and west highways across this part of New Mexico, Acomita and McCartys have become

BREEN

Ácoma Pueblo, New Mexico

Ácoma women walking in a parade in
Window Rock, Navajo Reservation, Arizona

BURKHALTER

the reservation's population centers. Ácoma Pueblo, the so-called Sky City, is now more of a ceremonial center, although nearly every family on the reservation keeps up an individual home or clan house there. A handful of families alternate residence on the mesa on a yearly basis and the village is never abandoned.

It is possible ancestors of today's Ácomas lived in the area of the modern reservation and in the surrounding region as early as sixteen hundred years ago. Some archaeologists believe Ácoma Pueblo was begun in the late thirteenth century, while others would push the date back to A.D. 1150. Ácoma remains in contention with the Hopi village of Oraibi as the oldest settlement in the United States continuously inhabited by people of one ethnic group. Ácoma participated in the successful Pueblo Revolt of 1680, and although New Mexico was

HOUSER

reconquered in 1692, it was 1699 before the Ácomas allowed missionaries to return. Subsequently, relations between Ácomas and Spaniards and, after 1821, between Ácomas and Mexicans were comparatively peaceful.

Acomita, where tribal headquarters are located, is reached from Interstate 40 at exit 102 going south via Indian Route 30. McCartys is south of Interstate 40 via Indian Route 33 from exit 96. Going south and east of the interstate from exit 89, six miles east of Grants, also takes the traveler to McCartys. Ácoma Pueblo (Sky City) is located southeast of Acomita via a spectacularly scenic drive on Indian Route 32. This approach provides a breathtaking overview of the Ácoma Valley from Seama Mesa, a landform referred to by Ácomas as Kuumi. Coming from the east on Interstate 40, a more direct approach to Ácoma Pueblo is via Indian Route 23 south of exit 108.

Recreational Opportunities

Not to be deprived of welcome income afforded through gambling, the Pueblo of Ácoma operates the Ácoma Sky City Casino immediately to the north of Interstate 40 at exit 102 seventeen miles east of Grants and fifty-six miles west of Albuquerque. There are slot and video machines, pull tabs, bingo, progressive jackpots, and live table games. The casino also houses the Cloud Nine Grille specializing in southwestern dishes. The casino is open daily from noon until 2:00 a.m. For further information, call 505/552-6017.

Southwest architect John Gaw Meem, a student of Frank Lloyd Wright, designed the white stone Catholic church dedicated to Santa María that was built in 1932-33 in McCartys and overlooks the railroad and the busy interstate highway. If the church appears old it is because it is essentially a half-size replica of seventeenth-century Mission San Esteban at Ácoma Pueblo. Wood carvings inside the church are works of art. Meem was also responsible for the design of St. Anne's church at Acomita, built in 1939-40.

By far the most important tourist attraction on the Ácoma Reservation is Ácoma Pueblo or, as signs now say, Sky City. This large adobe pueblo is laid out with three parallel rows of multi-storied contiguous houses, some of which contain windowless, aboveground chambers that serve as kivas. Entry into the kivas is by a ladder from the roof. The ceremonial plaza, which tour guides will point out, is in a divide separating the middle row of house blocks.

The pueblo lies north of the magnificent church of San Esteban del Rey with its twin bell towers, two-story convento (priests' living quarters) surrounding a patio, and a walled cemetery in front of its entrance. The church and, indeed, the entire pueblo are registered National Historic Landmarks. The stone-faced and dirt-floored church underwent extensive repairs and renovation beginning in the 1970s, and the walls are whitewashed each year before the village feast day in September.

Before ascending the paved road to the pueblo, it is necessary to stop at the visitor center at the junction of Indian Routes 32 and 23 near the west base of the mesa. Visitors must register, pay a fee, and wait for a guided tour of Sky City and Mission San Esteban del Rey. The village is closed from July 10 to 13 and on either the first or second weekend each October (call 505/470-4966 for information). Tourists are driven in a small bus to the village, and when the tour ends, those who wish can ride back

*Ácoma rainbow
dancer, Gallup,
New Mexico,
Inter-Tribal Indian
Ceremonial*

*Chilies and red
corn drying against
a wall, Ácoma Pueblo,
New Mexico*

PLACE

ROUSE

to the visitors center in a bus or, at times, walk down a steep trail, one with ancient steps carved into the sandstone, through fissures in the cliff on the northwest side of the village. This trail is called the Ladder Trail because of its combination of ladder and toe- and finger-holes cut in the solid rock and tortuous passages worn deep by years of use. It also appears on maps as the "Camino del Padre" for Father Juan Ramírez, builder of Mission San Esteban del Rey.

People wanting to use a still camera must pay an additional fee. Video cameras or movie cameras cannot be used on the reservation at any time. Anyone caught violating this strict prohibition is likely to have his or her videotapes or film confiscated. Still photography is not allowed inside the church or cemetery nor can still pictures be taken of religious celebrations such as those held on feast days.

Tourists at Sky City become sorely tempted to buy Ácoma pottery. Hundreds of Ácoma potters produce thousands of ceramic vessels for sale throughout the Southwest as well as for sightseers in the pueblo.

Pottery is sold by vendors who have their products laid out on tables alongside the streets and houses or, in some instances, in tiny stores in the house blocks. One such store is Bellaminos Second 500 Years with a colorful painted sign by the door announcing, "WELCOME COME IN WE'RE OPEN." There are also places along the tour route where one can buy food and soft drinks.

Northeast of Ácoma Pueblo there is another great sandstone butte that rises 430 feet above the valley floor: Kadzima, or, in English, Enchanted Mesa. Archaeological remains on the mesa's top give credence to Ácoma oral history that says Kadzima was once the home of ancestral Ácomas.

The visitor center, which also houses a museum and native food and crafts shops, is open daily from 8:00 a.m. to 4:30 p.m. November through March and from 8:00 a.m. to 7:00 p.m. April through October.

Festivals open to the public include those in Ácoma Pueblo in February when the Governor's Feast is held; the Harvest Dance and annual Feast of San Esteban on September 2 (the best time and place to see Ácoma dances); and Christmas celebrations from December 25-28. At Acomita, San Lorenzo's Day is celebrated on August 10. There are celebrations each Easter at Acomita and McCartys (Easter observances at Ácoma Pueblo are usually closed to the public), and McCartys hosts a feast in honor of Santa María the first Sunday of each May. There is an annual arts and crafts festival held at the visitor

center below Ácoma Pueblo, but the date is flexible. For information about all these events, call or write the Ácoma Tourist Visitor Center, P.O. Box 309, Ácoma, NM 87034 (800/747-0181 or 505/470-4966).

Camping and picnicking facilities are sometimes available at the Acomita Lake Recreation Site immediately south of Interstate 40 via exit 100. For the most recent information, call 505/552-6604.

Tribal Museum: There is no charge to visit a very good tribal museum in the visitor center at Ácoma Pueblo (Sky City). The permanent exhibit here, featuring photographs and artifacts, is entitled "One Thousand Years of Clay: Pottery, Environment and History."

Pueblo of Ácoma
P.O. Box 309, Acomita, NM 87034
Phone 505/552-6604
Population: 5,000
Acreage: 378,345

Mission San José, Laguna Pueblo, New Mexico

Laguna turkey dance

PUEBLO OF LAGUNA

Like that of the neighboring Ácomas, the language of the Laguna Puebloans is Keresan. This is no surprise given that Laguna Pueblo was apparently founded by some disgruntled Ácomas and by Eastern Keresans from Cochiti, Santo Domingo, and Zia who during the turmoil after the Pueblo Revolt of 1680 had first taken refuge in Ácoma. If historians are correct, their move from Ácoma fourteen miles northeast to where they began their own village took place in 1697. In 1699, New Mexico's governor conferred San José on the village as its patron saint and gave the community official recognition. In 1858, Congress confirmed a supposed 1689 Spanish land grant to the Lagunas. The reservation was created by executive order in 1910, and lands were added to it in 1938, 1939, and 1940-42.

In addition to Laguna Pueblo ("Old Laguna"), there are Laguna hamlets on the reservation at Casa Blanca, Encincal, Mesita, New Laguna, Paguate, Paraje, and Seama. Laguna Pueblo, where tribal headquarters are located, is reached from Interstate 40 at exit 114 via New Mexico State Highway 124.

Recreational Opportunities

There is fishing for bass and trout in Paguate Reservoir located north of Interstate 40 (exit 114) and east of New Mexico State Highway 279. The necessary tribal license—and directions to the reservoir—can be obtained at the Wildlife Conservation Office in Laguna or at the Paguate village offices.

The major attraction on the reservation is Laguna Pueblo and its San José church. The white-painted church, which crowns the hill on which the pueblo is built, can easily be seen from a nearby rest stop to the south on Interstate 40, and it tends to be a magnet for many people who might otherwise ignore the reservation altogether. Many of the publo's old buildings remain standing, and the setting remains a beautiful one.

The church of Mission San José was under construction by 1706, and the same building, made of field stones and mud mortar, has survived—thanks to repeated repairs and restorations—to the present. In the 1870s, thanks to the stubborn resistance of the Laguna sacristan of the church, the building was saved from demolition at the hands of Protestant reformers.

Decorating Laguna pottery

One of the artistic wonders inside the church is the altar screen and ceiling above the altar in the sanctuary. Sometime between 1800 and 1808, an unknown artist who has since been labeled "the Laguna santero" painted the sanctuary with bright colors in a kind of folk baroque symphony and fashioned an altar screen with spiralled salomonic columns so typical of baroque design.

The craft of pottery was revitalized at Laguna beginning in 1975, and Laguna pottery, which is similar to that of Ácoma, is available at the Casa Blanca Market Plaza off Interstate 40 at exit 108. It is also available in many stores throughout the Southwest that specialize in Indian arts and crafts.

The public may attend feast days celebrated in Laguna Pueblo on March 19 and September 19 as well as at Christmas. At Seama, the feast of Santa Ana is celebrated July 26; on August 15, Mesita, whose Sacred Heart church was built in 1935-36, observes the Feast of Our Lady of the Assumption; and Encinal celebrates the Nativity of the Blessed Virgin on September 8. Paguate's feast day is September 25 in honor of Saint Elisabeth, and Paraje, whose church was built in 1936, observes the Feast of Saint Margaret Mary on October 17. All these occasions feature Indian dances, and cameras, sketch pads, and tape recorders are prohibited at all of them. As always, it is wise to call or write ahead (see Tribal Address and Phone Number, below) to be sure the observances are going to occur and that visitors will be allowed.

Architect John Gaw Meem had a strong hand in the design of the churches at Paraje and Mesita as well as of those at McCartys and Acomita on the Ácoma Reservation.

Pueblo of Laguna
P.O. Box 194, Laguna, NM 87026
Phone 505/552-6654
Population: 7,300
Acreage: 528,684

Soaptree yucca
at White Sands
National Monument,
New Mexico

COLLIER

Starting in El Paso, Texas, and driving north on U.S. Interstate 10 to Las Cruces, New Mexico, and northeast on U.S. 70 takes one to the Mescalero Indian Reservation.

This day-long journey is an adventure in contrasts. To begin at the community of Ysleta del Sur in El Paso is to commence with a visit among descendants of Puebloan Indians, principally Tiguas, whose ancestors—some by choice and others by force—arrived at this place with Spaniards during the Spanish exodus from New Mexico brought on by the Pueblo Revolt of 1680. It is also to start from the broad valley of the Rio Grande, the tree-lined river whose water has been the vital lifeline of New Mexico and, since 1848, the liquid border separating Texas from Mexico.

The interstate highway leading to Las Cruces parallels the Rio Grande and passes the edge of the community of Tortugas, a place also settled by Tigua and other Indians after the Pueblo Revolt. Although they do not live on an Indian reservation, the people of Tortugas have stubbornly clung with pride to their sense of Indian identity and have managed to maintain a sense of community that distinguishes them from surrounding non-Indians.

From just north of Las Cruces on Interstate 25 (exit 6), U.S. Highway 70 crosses between the jagged Organ and San Andrés Mountains before dropping down to the Chihuahuan Desert and the level plain of the Tularosa Valley and continuing to the town of Tularosa. Tularosa, the western gateway to the Mescalero Indian Reservation, rests at the foot of the Sacramento Mountains. To climb from the valley at 4,500 feet above sea level to Mescalero, more than 6,000 feet high, is to go from desert to mountain forests and into the ancient heartland of the Mescalero Apaches. Although Apaches and Puebloans may have been enemies in the past, time has erased the animosities. Moreover, there was a curious link forged in modern times between Ysleta del Sur and Mescalero, as readers will soon see.

YSLETA DEL SUR PUEBLO

It would be impossible to overestimate the chaotic disruptions that took place in the lives of both New Mexican Spaniards and Indians as a result of the Pueblo Revolt of 1680. The Indians native to the El Paso/Juárez region when the Spaniards first arrived there in 1581 were variously labelled "Mansos" (Tame People) or "Sumas." Although it is not certain, it is likely Mansos and Sumas were, in fact, two distinct cultural groups rather than two labels for a single group. Descendants of these people were still in the El Paso/Juárez area a century later when Spaniards and many hundreds of Indians from the north crowded among them in the wake of the 1680 Pueblo Revolt.

The Indians suddenly settling around El Paso/ Juárez included Jumano, Piro, and Tompiro Indians who had earlier abandoned their pueblo settlements because of drought and pressure from Comanches and Apaches. They had first resettled along the Rio Grande at Socorro, Senecu, and other nearby locations. In 1680, when some 1,500 refugees from the north reached their towns, 317 of these displaced Puebloans abandoned their homes to join the Spaniards in the retreat southward to El Paso. Two years later, after an abortive

▼▼▼

attempt by the Spaniards to reconquer New Mexico, 385 Tiwa (Tigua) Indians of Isleta Pueblo were brought to El Paso as prisoners. These, too, were assigned new places to live.

In 1682, Piros and Tompiros became residents of the relocated pueblos of Senecu, on the south side of the Rio Grande, and of Socorro, on the north side. That same year, the Tiguas' pueblo was reconstituted as Ysleta del Sur (i.e., Isleta of the South), also on the north side of the river. By 1684, Ysleta was precisely in the location where it has remained to the present.

Washed over and eventually largely forgotten and ignored by successive governments of Spain, Mexico, the Republic of Texas, and the United States, by 1960 the remnant population of Tiguas at Ysleta had come to be identified by the outside world simply as "Mexicans" or "Mexican-Americans." Spanish had become their first language and English the second, with almost no words of Tigua surviving. Peoples' internal identification of themselves as Tiguas, however, had survived, as had their sense of a shared history, kinship, and social organization. There were also carefully sequestered symbols of group identity, like a tribal drum, articles of Indian clothing, pottery, and other artifacts that survived. Also enduring were songs and dances whose original significance had been lost but whose words and steps had been remembered, even as there were remnants of a tribal organization involving a native cacique, or leader, and a war chief.

El Paso extended its city limits to include the Ysleta neighborhood, and Tiguas who still owned their own homes became threatened with their loss because of increased property taxes. Their plight came to the attention of El Paso attorney Tom Diamond, and in the mid 1960s, Diamond orchestrated a successful effort to win for Tiguas federal recognition of their status as Indians. He was helped in this effort by Wendell Chino, Mescalero Apache Tribal Chairman. At Diamond's behest, it was Chino who arranged for a meeting in El Paso of the executive committee of the National Congress of American Indians. The resulting endorsement by the National Congress of American Indians of the Tiguas' cause went far toward its ultimate success.

On April 12, 1968, President Lyndon Johnson, himself a Texan, signed into law a bill extending federal recognition to the tribe. What formerly had simply been a barrio, or neighborhood, of El Paso became an Indian reservation whose lands were exempted from taxes.

The Tigua Indian Reservation is reached by taking Interstate 10 east from downtown El Paso to the Ysleta exit (Zaragosa Road, exit 32) to Alameda. Turn left one block, then turn right to the Tigua Indian Reservation and the Ysleta Mission (Our Lady of Mount Carmel Church). Tribal headquarters are located near the church at 119 South Old Pueblo.

Recreational Opportunities

The Tiguas operate the Speaking Rock Super Casino in a large building on South Old Pueblo across the street from tribal headquarters and next to the parking lot of the old mission church. Slot machines, bingo, and card games are available, and there is a restaurant in the casino. For further information, call 915/858-6934.

In 1682 or very soon afterward, a church was built for the Tiguas at Ysleta under Franciscan supervision and dedicated to Corpus Christi. The present mission church at Ysleta, part of whose walls are believed to date from 1744, underwent major repairs and remodeling about 1893 and again in 1897, 1901, and 1908.

The Tiguas celebrate St. Anthony's feast day at the church on June 13, an event at which Tiguas dance, the community also celebrates public festivals on the feast days of San Juan on June 24, of Saints Peter and Paul on June 29, and the Feast of the Three Kings, January 6. Further information is available by calling Our Lady of Mount Carmel Church (915/859-9848), or by calling the tribal culture center.

Tigua children perform traditional dances in the tribe's culture center each Saturday. Call 915/859-5287 for details, as well as for further information concerning feast day celebrations.

Individual families have arts and crafts booths in the culture center where wares are sold. The Cacique Restaurant is also located here.

Tribal Museum: The Ysleta del Sur culture center, located at 305 Yah Yah Lane (phone 915/859-5287), has on display a small collection of old Tigua artifacts. The center also sponsors Saturday tribal dances.

Ysleta del Sur Pueblo
P.O. Box 17679, El Paso, TX 79917
Phone 915/859-7913
Population: 1400
Acreage: 75

PLACE

TORTUGAS

Although not an Indian reservation, the community of Tortugas south of Las Cruces and adjacent to the University Park area of New Mexico State University, is, like Ysleta, home for descendants of Puebloan Indians as well as of other Indians who were in the El Paso area in 1680. Indeed, some of the people who call Tortugas home are on the tribal rolls of Ysleta del Sur Pueblo.

A great public fiesta is held at Tortugas every December 10-12 in honor of Our Lady of Guadalupe. mass, feasting, ceremonial processions, and costumed dancing to the accompaniment of drums and fiddles characterize the celebration, one attended by many hundreds, if not thousands, of people. There is also a San Juan's Day celebration in Tortugas on June 24.

The least confusing way to reach Tortugas if approaching from the south is by leaving Interstate 10 at exit 142 and going north to University Avenue. Take University west beneath the Interstate and go south on Main Street (New Mexico State Highway 478). Go south one mile to Tortugas Drive and turn east (left) into Tortugas. If approaching from the north on Interstate 10, take exit 142 to Conway Avenue. Go one block on Conway and turn south (left) on Main Street (State Highway 478). Drive a half mile to Tortugas Drive and turn left (east).

Manjeau Peak, New Mexico

THE MESCALERO APACHE TRIBE

High in the Sacramento and White Mountains lies the tree- and meadow-filled land of the Mescalero Apaches. It is a domain much reduced from the territory over which Mescaleros had freely ranged into the nineteenth century. Their former tribal territory had included virtually all of southwestern New Mexico from a line extending from just south of Socorro straight east into the Texas Panhandle. More than half their territory was once south of New Mexico in southwestern Texas, including the Big Bend, and in northern portions of the Mexican states of Chihuahua and Coahuila.

Precisely when Mescaleros, like other Athapaskan speakers, moved into the Southwest is unknown, but they were certainly in place by the early part of the seventeenth century. By that time, Spaniards were illegally trafficking in the slave trade, and Mescaleros were among their victims. The slave trade, added to the Mescaleros' propensity to help themselves to livestock and other goods in Spanish settlements, became a recipe for prolonged animosity between the two groups. Spanish and, later, Mexican policies toward Mescaleros vacillated between those of armed conflict and conciliation.

Although Mescaleros favored the United States in its 1846-48 war with Mexico, it wasn't long afterward that they found themselves at odds with the Americans who had taken over their lands north of the new international boundary. As non-Indian settlers moved into the region in larger numbers, the newcomers looked on Mescaleros as squatters who had no rights to the land and its resources. Fighting inevitably followed until finally, in 1863, the Mescaleros were militarily defeated. In 1873 their mountainous reservation was created by executive order.

Adjustments were made in the reservation's boundaries until 1883 when it assumed what is approximately its present shape. There was briefly an attempt to turn the reservation into a national park, but in 1922 Indian title to the land was confirmed by Congress.

Today's Mescalero Reservation enjoys a diversified economy, one that includes cattle raising, logging, and a fish hatchery. Ironically, high mountain country that in the nineteenth century seemed forbidding and inaccessible to outsiders and to the Mescaleros a poor place to eke out a living has become an enormous attraction for the general public. The White Mountains and their majestic Sierra Blanca (elevation 12,003 feet) provide some of the finest scenery in New Mexico, as well as skiing in the winter and an escape from heat in the summer. Tourism has become a major reservation industry and outsiders who obey the rules are warmly received.

Many Mescalero business ventures have proven highly successful. The tribal chairman jokingly told me in 1995, "Pueblos make pottery; Navajos make rugs; Apaches make money."

Mescalero tribal headquarters are in Mescalero, New Mexico, on U.S. Highway 70. Although people live at Whitetail and in a few other outlying areas, most Apaches live in Mescalero or its immediate vicinity. The west approach is from Tularosa at the junction of U.S. Highway 54 and U.S. 70. The approach from Roswell on the east is via U.S. 70/380 to Hondo and U.S. 70 through Ruidoso to Mescalero.

Recreational Opportunities

The centerpiece of the Apache recreational enterprise is the Inn of the Mountain Gods, "New Mexico's Most Distinguished Resort." Open all year round, it is located on Carrizo Canyon Road approximately eleven miles northeast of Mescalero on U.S. 70 and 3.5 miles southwest of Ruidoso. The mailing address is P.O. Box 269, Mescalero, NM 88340; the phone 800/545-9011.

In addition to its lodging facilities, the Inn boasts Casino Apache with its slot machines; the Ina Da Card Room (blackjack and craps); two cocktail lounges; a bar and grill; and the Dan Li Ka Dining Room where one can feast on such entrées as quail with sage cider cream, wild boar with piñons and merlot, salmon medallions, tournedos of beef, and lobster.

The Mescaleros' ancestors would surely be astonished as are all first-time visitors to this luxurious place.

Built in 1975 at a cost of some $20 million, the Inn is surrounded on all sides by a well-manicured lawn. The rustic-looking building spreads out over

▼▼

a considerable distance. It is adjacent to an 18-hole golf course designed by Ted Robinson that is touted as being among the best golf courses in the United States. The lodge—which has a convention center that can accommodate nine hundred people—overlooks the golf course as well as Lake Mescalero where boaters and anglers can enjoy themselves. There are volleyball, basketball, badminton, and six tennis courts as well as a heated swimming pool, whirlpool, and kiddies' pool, not to mention a trap and skeet shooting range. There is a tennis pro shop, and the outdoor tennis courts, weather permitting, are open between mid-May and mid-September. For people who are twenty years of age or younger and who therefore cannot gamble in the casino, as well as for others, there is the Tee Pee (video) Arcade.

ANNERINO

Saunas and electric golf carts are available at the golf/ski pro shop (phone 800/446-2963). Golfers be warned that deer, elk, bear, and mountain lions have the right of way on the golf course. Weather permitting, the golf course is open from April 1 through September 30 (phone 505/257-5141 ext. 7444).

Horseback riding is another option for visitors (phone 505/257-5141 ext. 7424). Stables, located one and half miles west of the Inn, are open daily from 8:30 a.m. to 3:00 p.m. in the spring, summer, and fall, weather permitting. A guide accompanies all rides. For those less adventurous, bicycles can be rented at the boat docks, as can rowboats, pedal boats, and aqua cycles (phone 505/257-5141 ext. 7439). Boat rentals are in the summer and fall only.

The Mescaleros' Sports Activities Department is headquartered at the trap and skeet facility at the Inn of the Mountain Gods (phone 505/257-9770). Here one can get all the necessary information, as well as permits, regarding both package hunts for bull elk (September) and regular hunts for bear (August), bull elk (September), cow elk (November), and turkey (April). The numbers of permits are limited and application deadlines for each year's hunts are strictly enforced.

Fishing permits are available at the bait and tackle shop (505/257-5141 ext. 7439) in the summer and fall and at the front desk in the main lobby in the winter and spring. Lake Mescalero is stocked with rainbow and cutthroat trout from the reservation's own hatchery. There is also fishing on the reservation in the Ruidoso Recreational Area, Silver Lake Recreational Area, Eagle Creek Lake Recreational Area, and at Ski Apache (call 505/671-4494 or 4427 for details).

Various Indian arts and crafts, including Apache pottery, bead work, cradleboards, and paintings, are for sale in gift shops at the Inn of the Mountain Gods. During spring and summer (and fall if the weather is nice) Apache Pride Arts and Crafts is open from 9:00 a.m. to 6:00 p.m. daily next to U.S. Highway 70 between Mescalero and Apache Summit (P.O. Box 818, Mescalero, NM 88340; phone 505/671-4823). Apache crafts, especially beaded goods, as well as jewelry and crafts of other Southwestern Tribes are sold here. Most of the items for sale are on consignment from their Indian makers.

Ski Apache is among the most popular ski resorts in the Southwest. Located on the Lincoln National Forest, the resort was built in 1962 and sold to the Mescalero Tribe in 1963. Originally called Sierra Blanca, the name was changed to Ski Apache in 1984. The facility is reached from Ruidoso by traveling north on State Highway 37 to Alto and by going west from Alto on State Highway 532. Snowfall here averages 180 inches a year. There are eight chair lifts, a surface lift, and a gondola servicing 40 runs and trails. Non-skiers can take a round trip ride in the gondola. Skis and snowboards are for rent and the tribe operates a ski school here including one, the Kiddie Korral, for four and five year olds. Write P.O. Box 220, Ruidoso, NM 88345; or call 800/545-9011 or 505/336-4356 for particulars). Ski Apache has its own site on the web: www.lookingglass.net/skiapach/

PLACE

The biggest public celebration on the reservation each year takes place over the long Fourth of July weekend. It is a combination observance of the coming of age ceremonies for young women, the arrival of the masked Mountain Spirits to protect the Mescaleros from hostile forces and epidemic disease, and the Fourth of July. There are cooking areas, booths, and tepees decorated with pine boughs, and women serve traditional Mescalero food, including dried agave hearts (mescal). There are dances during the daylight hours that are purely for entertainment, and at night the dances with religious significance take place when Mountain Spirits light the bonfires, dance, and indulge in ritual clowning. The girls whose puberty ceremonies are being observed are dressed in beaded buckskin, with sacred yellow pollen on their cheeks and foreheads as well as in their dark hair. They dance by their special tepee facing the rising sun.

Photography, sketching, and tape recording are not allowed at ceremonial events.

There is also a tribal rodeo in July and there are occasional powwows. For further information, call 505/671-4494 ext. 209.

Well worth a visit in Mescalero is the huge Catholic church built out of native stone over a thirty-year period before World War II by Franciscan friar Albert Braun and his Apache parishioners. It is on a hill at the east edge of Mescalero, near the fish hatchery, on the south side of the highway.

Tribal Museum: There is small but extremely tasteful and very well kept tribal museum in Mescalero (P.O. Box 176, Mescalero, NM 88340; phone 505/671-4494 ext. 254). Built in 1973, it has a good photographic exhibit and displays of selected Apache artifacts. The personnel in the museum are very helpful in answering visitors' questions.

The Mescalero Apache Tribe
P.O. Box 227, Mescalero, NM 88340
Phone 505/671-4494; Fax 505/671-9191
Population: 3,500
Acreage: 460,678

Sandia Mountain
Wilderness, New Mexico

HUEY

PUEBLOS OF THE LOWER RIO GRANDE

New Mexico's All Pueblo Indian Council divides its twenty members into the eight Northern Pueblos and the twelve Southern Pueblos. The latter include Zuni, Ácoma, Laguna, and Ysleta del Sur. The other Southern Pueblos, all of them along the Rio Grande or its Jémez River tributary, and beginning with Isleta Pueblo south of Albuquerque, include Sandia, Santa Ana, San Felipe, Santo Domingo, Cochiti, Zia, and Jémez. In New Mexico, this region is spoken of as the "Río Abajo," or Lower Rio Grande.

The language of Isleta and Sandia is Southern Tiwa; that of Jémez is Towa; and all the others speak Eastern Keresan. All are south of Santa Fe, while the eight Northern Pueblos lie to its north.

All of these peoples share a common history of Spanish incursion beginning with the 1540-42 expedition of Francisco Vásquez de Coronado followed by expeditions of other Spaniards until 1598 when Don Juan de Oñate arrived in New Mexico with a large colonizing expedition. Oñate succeeded in planting the beginnings of permanent non-Indian presence in the region. The Spaniards' presence remained uninterrupted until the Pueblo Revolt of 1680. The revolt was overcome in 1692 when Diego de Vargas led a successful campaign to reconquer New Mexico. Spain ruled until 1821 when the Mexican Revolution was crowned with success and New Mexico became a part of the Republic of Mexico.

In 1846, General Stephen Watts Kearny and his Army of the West invaded New Mexico and wrested it from Mexican control. The Puebloans swore their allegiance to the United States Government and have remained a part of the United States ever since.

The best place to begin to learn about New Mexico's Puebloan Indians, including aspects of their history, arts and crafts, and ceremonies is not on a reservation, but at the Indian Pueblo Cultural Center located at 2401 12th St., NW, Albuquerque, NM 87104 (phone 800/766-4405 or 505/843-7270). Open seven days a week (closed Thanksgiving, Christmas, New Years Day, and January 6 [Feast of the Three Kings]),

the Center offers visitors an unparalleled opportunity to achieve an overview of the nineteen distinct tribal units that comprise New Mexico's pueblos. The restaurant opens at 7:30 a.m. and the museum and gift shops open at 9:00 a.m. The restaurant closes at 3:30 p.m. while the rest of the facility remains open until 5:30 p.m.

The Center is located on the west side of 12th Street a block north of the 157 (12th Street) exit off of Interstate 40 west of Interstate 25. It is 1.75 miles east of the Rio Grande.

Owned and operated by the nineteen pueblos, there is a fee to visit the museum, one that displays photographs, traces Pueblo history in text, and exhibits premier arts and crafts most characteristic of each community. There is also the Pueblo House Children's Museum, a hands-on museum where children can learn about Pueblo history from the time of Puebloans' emergence into the present world to modern times. Each month, the Main Exhibit Gallery features the works of a Native American artist.

Traditional Indian dances and arts and crafts demonstrations are offered free to the public every weekend. The gift shops retail Indian-made products from throughout the Southwest, including pottery, paintings, sculpture, rugs, sandpaintings, kachinas, drums, and traditional as well as contemporary jewelry. There is a large selection of books about Indians in the book shop and the curio shop sells Southwestern-style clothing and souvenirs of the Southwest. The restaurant serves food, including desserts, that is traditional among Pueblo and Hispanic peoples of New Mexico.

There are special events held at the Center throughout the year, including Senior Citizens' Day when Pueblo elders display their arts and crafts for sale; a Veterans' Day arts and crafts fair; and the observance of American Indian Week when there are tours, dances, music, workshops, and lectures. A brochure listing these events, as well as a yearly calendar of public events in the various pueblos and on the Mescalero and Jicarilla reservations, can be obtained by visiting, calling, or writing the Indian Pueblo Cultural Center.

PUEBLO
OF ISLETA

Isleta, Spanish for "Little Island," is an acknowledgement of the fact that the pueblo is in a place that has periodically become an island when the Rio Grande has flooded. The water table under the village is quite high.

Isletans, whose language is Southern Tiwa, live in a village that appears to be an amalgamation of other settlements in the immediate vicinity that were there at least as early as seven hundred years ago. Franciscan missionaries supervised construction of a church in Isleta Pueblo between 1613 and 1617, a building that although much altered since, has remained standing to become what is almost certainly the oldest remaining church in the United States.

The Isleta Indian Reservation is on lands initially granted by the King of Spain, a grant that was confirmed by the U.S. Congress in 1858 and patented in 1864. Lands were added to the reservation either by Congress or by executive order in 1908, 1909, and between 1936 and 1938.

Farming and cattle raising continue to be important to the economy of Isleta. Many Isletans also work in nearby Albuquerque and commute on a daily basis. A tribal casino now brings much needed income to the tribe.

Although housing has sprawled away from the heart of the old pueblo center, largely along New Mexico State Highways 314 and 45 on the west side of the pueblo, Isleta remains compact and leaves the visitor no doubt of its cultural nature. Tribal headquarters are at the south end of the village.

Isleta Pueblo can be reached from Albuquerque on the north via Interstate 25 by taking exit 213 and following Isleta Boulevard directly south to the village. If coming from the south on Interstate 25, take exit 209, go east to Coors Boulevard (State Highway 14), take a short jog south (right) to Isleta Boulevard (State Highway 314), and turn sharply left (east) onto Isleta Boulevard (State Highway 314) and head north directly to the pueblo.

Recreational Opportunities

The Isleta Gaming Palace (phone 800/460-5686 or 505/869-2614), open twenty-four hours a day and seven days a week, features video slot machines, high stakes bingo, craps, and roulette as well as a card room where poker, seven-card stud, Texas Hold 'Em, Isleta 21, and Caribbean stud poker are available. The Palace, on the east side of State Highway 47, is reached by taking exit 215 off Interstate 25 south of Albuquerque. It is very near the junction of I-25 and Highway 47 and can easily be seen from the road. The casino's web address is http://www.com/isleta_gaming/newhome.html

Across from the Isleta Gaming Palace next to State Highway 47 is the Isleta Eagle Golf Course, a twenty-seven—hole facility of "high-desert chills and challenge designed around three lakes." Further amenities here include The Eagle's Nest Restaurant and the Isleta Eagle Golf Pro Shop. For information, call 505/869-0950.

For visitors who are interested in Indian communities, the visit to the pueblo itself will be the most rewarding experience. A broad plaza spreads out in the very center of the community, with the historic Saint Augustine church on the north side of the plaza. Originally dedicated to Saint Anthony when it

BURKHALTER

was built in 1613, in 1710 the patronage was changed to Saint Augustine. The church had been badly damaged in the revolt and had been used as a cow pen. The Franciscans made repairs, and the gabled bell towers were added between 1867 and 1881. For a while in the late nineteenth century and early twentieth century, the exterior of the church was remodeled with the addition of no fewer than eleven spires on the bell towers and a tower at the rear of the building. In 1962, it was remodeled again essentially to its present lovely appearance.

The church, which has many fine colonial-period religious paintings and statues inside of it, is generally open daily to visitors. There is an interesting museum in the convento wing extending east (right) of the church that is entered through a door in the nave. The museum is filled with photos and artifacts relating primarily to the history of the church.

Fronting on the plaza on the opposite side of the church are the Shirpoyo Art Gallery (P.O. Box 577, Isleta, NM 87022; phone 505/869-0449) and Margaret Jojola's arts and crafts shop (Box 28, Pueblo of Isleta, Isleta, NM 87022; phone 505/869-3290). Isleta arts and crafts are available in other places throughout the community as well, including private homes where people have put signs letting visitors know such items are available. The Isleta Pueblo Indian Market Center next to the tribal headquarters is another crafts market.

A few Isletans also carve figurines out of soft stone.

Some women in Isleta, especially when many visitors are likely to be present, use their beehive ovens (hornos) to bake delicious loaves of bread for sale.

The tribe operates Isleta Lakes and Recreation Area (P.O. Box 383, Isleta, NM 87022; phone 505/877-0370). Isleta Lakes, on the east side of the Rio Grande, is reached from State Highway 47 which, in turn, is reached by leaving Interstate 25 at exit 215. The recreation area is a short distance south of the Gaming Palace and Interstate 25, and a sign marks the turnoff to the west from Highway 47.

Situated among beautiful cottonwood trees near the Rio Grande, the twenty surface acres of Isleta Lakes provide good recreation for anglers. The lakes are regularly stocked with trout and channel catfish. Pay fees at the concession near the lakes that sells fishing equipment and supplies, soft drinks, cold beer, and light snacks. There are facilities for picnicking, a softball field, and a kiddie playground. There are also facilities for camping.

Isleta Pueblo celebrates an annual harvest dance on September 4 that is usually open to the public. Similarly, the feast celebration for Saint Augustine takes place August 28. Dances and other religious ceremonies are also held in January and April, although some may be closed to the public. Photography, sketching, and tape recording are not allowed at any of these observances. For further information, call the tribal office at 505/869-3111 or 6333.

Tribal Museum: There is no tribal museum, but there is a museum focusing largely on non-Indian historical themes in the convento attached to St. Augustine's church in the pueblo.

Isleta Pueblo
P.O. Box 1270, Isleta, NM 87022
Phone 505/869-3111 or 6333
Population: 4,000
Acreage: 211,103

North Sandia Peak, New Mexico

HUEY

PUEBLO OF SANDIA

Although ancestors of the Southern Tiwa-speaking people of Sandia Pueblo are likely to have been in the immediate vicinity for at least six hundred years, it does not appear in the written record by that name—which means "watermelon" in Spanish—until 1617. A Franciscan, Estevan de Perea, was at Sandia by 1610, and he built the first church, dedicating it to Saint Francis of Assisi. Before 1680, the Sandias added a chapel to the church, one dedicated to San Antonio de Padua.

The people of Sandia became active participants in the Pueblo Revolt and the church, but not the chapel, was destroyed in 1691. The pueblo was resettled in 1748 under the dual patronage of St. Anthony and Our Lady of Sorrows and the church was finally rebuilt in 1784. This structure eventually fell into ruin and a new one was built on higher ground at the north end of the pueblo in 1864. That building, the one now standing and dedicated solely to St. Anthony, was thoroughly renovated in 1976.

Tribal headquarters are located in Sandia Pueblo north of Albuquerque via New Mexico State Highway 313 (4th Street/Camino del Pueblo). From Albuquerque, Highway 313 is reached by leaving Interstate 25 at exit 234 and going west on Roy Avenue (State Highway 556) until reaching the intersection. Turn right (north) and continue about 4.3 miles to the junction with Indian Route 72. It is a little more than .2 mile east to the pueblo.

Approaching from the north on Interstate 25, go west from exit 240 to Bernalillo and go south from Bernalillo on State Highway 313 (Camino del Pueblo) just over three miles to the Indian Route 72 turnoff headed east.

Recreational Opportunities

Visitors who wish to walk in the pueblo should first obtain permission at the governor's office. Cameras, tape recorders, and sketch pads are not allowed.

The people of Sandia zealously protect their privacy. However, each June 13, the people observe the village feast day, St. Anthony's, with a celebration that includes a corn dance. This is normally open to the public.

Sandia Lakes Recreation Area is a fee area that provides day use fishing and picnicking. Drinking water is available and there are a playground and rest rooms. The lakes, stocked with rainbow trout, largemouth bass, and catfish, are located on State Highway 313 just north of Roy Avenue (take Interstate 25 exit 234). This popular recreation area, one with nature hiking trails, a barbecue pit, and volleyball court, is on the west side of the highway just north of Shady Lakes. The facility is open daily, although hours differ in summer and in winter. For details, call 505/897-3971.

Like most other Indian communities, Sandia has gotten into the gambling business. The tribe operates Sandia Indian Bingo in a large building just west off of Interstate 25's exit 234 on Roy Road (Tramway Road heads east from this same exit). Open seven days a week twenty-four hours a day, this gaming facility operates high stakes bingo games as well as video bingo, pick your numbers bingo, pull tabs, and speed bingo. For further

details, call 505/897-2173 or 898-0852. The tribe's boast is that players win more than $2 million each month.

What very few Sandia crafts continue to be made, such as necklaces of carved stones and other jewelry, are likely to be for sale at the Indian Pueblo Cultural Center in Albuquerque, 2401 12th St. NW. There is, however, an Indian arts and crafts store on reservation lands leased from the tribe. This is the Bien Mur Indian Market Center next to exit 234 off of Interstate 25 (Tramway exit). Possibly the largest reservation-based retail outlet for Indian arts and crafts in the Southwest, the store sells jewelry, kachinas, pottery, and textiles as well as other Indian-made products (phone 505/821-5400).

Equestrians will enjoy horseback riding on the Sandia Reservation. Sandia Trails (phone 505/898-6970) is just north of the intersection of 4th St. NW (State Highway 313) and 2nd St. NW (State Highway 47) at the far southwestern corner of the reservation. The quickest access is via Roy Avenue west from exit 234 on Interstate 25 to 4th Street (Highway 313), then south (left) to the stables. It takes 1.5 hours to ride the longest trail. Advance reservations are recommended.

Tribal Museum: There is no tribal museum, but there are some interesting historic photographs of Sandia on display in the governor's office.

**Pueblo of Sandia
Box 6008, Bernalillo, NM 87004
Phone 505/867-3317**

The Rio Grande

HUEY

SANTA ANA
INDIAN
PUEBLO

Just as the town of Bernalillo anchors the northern end of the Sandia Indian Reservation, so does it anchor the southern end of the San Felipe and Santa Ana Indian reservations. Bernalillo is also at the intersection of Interstate 25 and New Mexico State Highway 44, the latter running northwest to parallel the Jemez River tributary of the Rio Grande. In that direction lie three pueblos: Santa Ana, Zia, and Jémez.

The people of Santa Ana speak Eastern Keresan as do residents of four of their neighboring reservations along the lower Rio Grande: Zia, San Felipe, Santo Domingo, and Cochiti. Traditionally, Santa Ana puebloans have maintained close social, religious, and economic connections with residents of Zia, San Felipe, and Cochiti, ties that have included intermarriage, mutual aid with cleaning irrigation ditches, and attending one another's dances and ceremonies.

The Santa Ana Indian Reservation consists of lands presumably granted initially by the King of Spain, a 15,405-acre grant confirmed by the U.S. Congress in 1869 and patented in 1883. Court decisions and congressional legislation enlarged the reservation in 1897, 1909, 1938, and 1939. Tribal headquarters are located in Ranchitos or New Santa Ana, a suburb of Bernalillo, at 2 Dove Street (take I-25 exit 242 west).

Recreational Opportunities

Many Santa Anans have become employed by their gambling casino, the Santa Ana Star, located two miles west of I-25 on the north side of Highway 44 on Pueblo of Santa Ana lands (phone 505/867-0000). Owned and operated by S.A.N.E., Santa Ana Non-profit Enterprise, the casino features video slots and what their brochure advertises as "super high stakes Indian gaming."

The Santa Ana Star is near an enterprise located on tribal lands, the Santa Ana (or Valle Grande) Golf Course, 288 Prairie Star Road (P.O. Box 1736, Bernalillo, NM 87004; phone 505/867-9464; Fax 505/867-1964). This twenty-seven-hole championship public golf course, which affords golfers a spectacular view looking over the Rio Grande Valley toward the 10,780-foot high Sandia Mountains, was designed by Ken Killian. The pro shop, bar, and grill are housed in adobe-style architecture next to the Prairie Star Restaurant.

To reach the golf course, as well as the Prairie Star Restaurant, take Interstate 25 to exit 242 (Bernalillo); go west on State 44 two miles to Jemez Canyon Dam Road; and go north (right), following the signs to the course. Located north of Albuquerque about twenty miles, driving time from that city is about thirty minutes. It is about forty miles south of Santa Fe, with a fifty-minute driving time.

The Ta-Ma-Ya Cooperative Association sells pottery, woven belts, headbands, jewelry, and paintings in its facility in New Santa Ana two miles north of Highway 44 off Highway 313. It is open Tuesday and Thursday from 10:00 a.m. to 4:30 p.m. and from noon to 4:00 p.m. on Sunday.

Picnicking is available at the Jemez Canyon Reservoir five miles north of Highway 44 on Jemez Canyon Dam Road.

The original Santa Ana Pueblo is located on the Jemez River immediately north of Highway 44 ten miles west of its intersection with Interstate 25. The village, whose remaining structures are all one story, has a large ceremonial plaza, two kivas, and the church dedicated to St. Anne (Santa Ana) completed in 1750 and modified and repaired in 1927. It has been reasonably well cared for since.

Outsiders are allowed in the pueblo only on feast day celebrations, and that is a situation subject to change from year to year. One should call tribal headquarters in advance to learn the current status (505/867-3301, 3302, or 3303).

Santa Ana's most important celebration takes place on the feast day of its patron, July 26. There are also ceremonial dances held January 1 and 6, Easter, June 24 and 29, and December 25-28. Even when the public is allowed, there are strict prohibitions against photography of any kind, sketching, or tape recording.

Santa Ana Indian Pueblo
2 Dove Road, Bernalillo, NM 87004
Phone 505/867-3301, 3302, 3303
Population: 600
Acreage: 61,931

Zia pottery vessel

▼▼

PUEBLO OF ZIA

The Eastern Keresan Pueblo of Zia, like Santa Ana Pueblo, may ultimately have originated with peoples who lived in the Chaco Canyon area of New Mexico over sixteen hundred years ago. They had arrived in the general region of their present home by the end of the fourteenth century and possibly as early as the end of the twelfth. Among the half dozen pueblo archaeological sites in the Jémez River Valley almost certainly Zian in origin, five remained in use into the sixteenth century, and one of them, Zia Pueblo, to the present.

If it were known in New Mexico for nothing else, Zia would remain renowned as the pueblo from whom in 1925 the State of New Mexico borrowed its symbol of the sun as the state's emblem. The Zia sun symbol is on the state flag as well as on countless state road signs and documents. It has become the logo of New Mexico identity.

Zia's Spanish land grant of 1689 was confirmed by the U.S. Congress in 1858 and the lands were patented in 1864. Additional lands were acquired for the Zia Indian Reservation by executive order in 1938 and by Act of Congress in 1924. Tribal headquarters are just to the north of State Highway 44 in an office on the south side of the Jémez River below the hill on the river's north side where the pueblo stands. It is seventeen miles northwest of Bernalillo.

Recreational Opportunities

The pueblo is open to visitors during daylight hours, but one should register first at the tribal office. No photography is allowed in the village. The pueblo, which has a ceremonial plaza and two kivas, is today all one story. A great many, if not most, Zians now live in individual housing below the pueblo.

The village feast day, when visitors are normally welcomed and when traditional dances are held, is August 15 (the Feast of Our Lady of the Assumption). There are also public ceremonies at Easter and Christmas and there is a powwow on Memorial Day.

Protests from animal rights activists notwithstanding, rooster pulls, introduced to the region by Spaniards during the colonial period, remain a feature of some fiestas at Zia. A live rooster is buried neck-high in loose dirt and from fifteen to twenty horsemen ride by in an attempt to grab it out of the dirt. Should someone succeed, he has to defend it from the other riders who try to take it away from him. He does this by using the rooster as a club to hit the others over the head.

In 1996 community leaders revived the Zia Pueblo Crow Dance, a humorous dance invented by a group of Zians in 1920. The dance was performed occasionally after that, such as at the annual Gallup Inter-Tribal Ceremonial. The revival, which took place in early October, also featured the seldom seen buffalo dance. Money raised on that occasion was used for the Zia Pueblo Scholarship Trust Fund. To learn if the crow dance or similar fundraising events are to be held, call the tribal office at 505/867-3304.

During fiestas, Zia pottery, beadwork, clothing, buckskin items, woven belts, sculptures, and paintings are on sale as are traditional Zia foods.

Zia pottery continues to be made in a tradition unbroken since prehistoric times. Zia decorations on the well-made wares include the hallmark Zia long-necked and long-legged bird (a roadrunner?) as well as deer, flowering plants, and double rainbow bands. Zia artists also create fine paintings. Both pottery and paintings are for sale in the tribe's visitor center next to tribal headquarters.

Even on a slow summer day in Zia there is likely to be a vendor in the pueblo selling soft drinks, potato chips, and similar snacks. It gives visitors an excuse to stop to chat and absorb some of the local ambience. Some Zia craftspeople and artists sell from their homes. There are no signs, but local inquiry may bring directions.

Zia Lake, a fee area open all year round on the north side of the Jémez River about 2.5 miles west of the pueblo, offers fishing for trout and catfish. There is a picnic area here as well.

Tribal Museum: The Zia Cultural Center next to the tribal offices has a small display of Zia photographs, fine Zia pottery, traditional Indian dress, beadwork, and stone sculptures—some of which are for sale. Potters occasionally give pottery-making demonstrations here. The center is normally open from 8:00 a.m. to 5:00 p.m. weekdays.

Pueblo of Zia
General Delivery, San Ysidro, NM 87053
Phone 505/867-3304
Population: 740
Acreage: 121,600

PUEBLO OF JÉMEZ

Towa is the language of Jémez Pueblo. Although distantly related to Tiwa and Tewa, two other languages in the Kiowa-Tanoan family of languages, it is not mutually intelligible with them. And although at one time the language was widely used in New Mexico, having been spoken by people of many communities, including the once-populous but now-abandoned Pecos Pueblo, it now survives only at Jémez.

Archaeological evidence suggests the Towas of Jémez arrived in the area of their present homeland in the mountains and mesas along the Jémez River over six hundred years ago. They were also in the Pecos region south of Santa Fe by that time.

Spaniards who encountered the Towas along the Jémez River and its tributaries in the sixteenth century, starting with the Coronado expedition in 1541, counted as many as eight, and possibly eleven, Towa towns there. In 1598, when Juan de Oñate colonized New Mexico, the Franciscans sent Friar Alonso de Lugo to administer religious affairs among the Towas of the Jeméz River region. He left in 1601, but not before he founded Mission San José at Giusewa Pueblo.

Giusewa was abandoned in the late 1630s and its impressive ruins, about twelve miles north of Jémez Pueblo on State Highway 4, are now administered as Jémez State Monument by the Museum of New Mexico. This is a fee area with a visitor center, drinking water, restrooms, picnic area, and a self-guided tour opportunity. There are interpretive exhibits in the visitor center (phone 505/829-3530).Between 1621 and 1623, another Franciscan founded the Mission of San Diego de la Congregación in Jémez Pueblo. Spanish policy was to congregate, hence Congregación, as many people as possible who were living in scattered settlements into one or two large towns where they would become more susceptible to a program of forced assimilation under the watchful eye of a missionary. Many Towas, either by persuasion or by force, were added to the population of Walatowa in the early seventeenth century. Their church was accordingly christened San Diego (Saint Didacus) of the Congregation.

Glorietta Mesa

In 1838, the population of Walatowa grew by another seventeen to twenty persons when Towas who had been living as the last Puebloan residents of Pecos Pueblo moved in with their linguistic cousins on the Jémez River. The abandoned ruins of Pecos Pueblo are today administered by the National Park Service as Pecos National Historical Park (Drawer 11, Pecos, NM 87552; phone 505/757-6414). The Pecos people were readily accepted by the people of Jémez, and to the present the Pueblo of Jémez recognizes a Governor of Pecos in its midst.

The Jémez Indian Reservation began with a Spanish land grant in 1689 that was confirmed by the U.S. Congress in 1858 and a patent for which was issued in 1864. Lands were added either by executive order or by congressional action in 1906, 1915, 1938, 1941, and 1942.

Jémez tribal headquarters are located in Jémez Pueblo. The pueblo is on New Mexico State Highway 4 six miles north of the community of San Ysidro which, in turn, is reached via State Highway 44 from exit 242 on Interstate 25 north of Albuquerque.

Recreational Opportunities

Because the pueblo is fairly small and the number of visitors is large, especially during summer months, the Jémez people have found it necessary to close most of the village to outsiders. Even casual strolling through the pueblo's streets is no longer allowed. This ameliorates the feeling many residents doubtless had that they were living in a kind of human zoo. As a brochure distributed by the village says, "The Pueblos are not 'living museums' or theme parks, but are regular communities. Like any village, these Pueblos are homes for those who live here and should be respected as such."

This is not to say, however, that a visit to Jémez Pueblo is no longer worthwhile. Far from it. The tribe has erected the Walatowa Visitor Center on the east edge of the village next to Highway 4 on Trading Post Road. The visitor center, which allows photography within its fenced enclosure, has beehive ovens where bread-making demonstrations are held; a nature walk, with plants traditionally used by Jémez people identified; a display of a reconstructed traditional Towa "field house," the kind that was used near communal fields, springs, or hunting and gathering areas (perhaps the cultural equivalent of an isolated log cabin or sod house in non-Indian society); a display of photographs; and a gift shop. There are occasional artists' demonstrations and studio tours, and traditional dances are sometimes performed here. By advance arrangement, there are limited opportunities for village tours conducted by Pueblo staff. One should contact the Pueblo of Jémez, Department of Tourism, P.O. Box 100, Jémez Pueblo, NM 87024 (phone 505/834-7235; Fax 505/834-7331).

The visitor center, west of the trading post on State Highway 4, is open seven days a week from 8:00 a.m. to 5:00 p.m. all year round.

Jémez is known for its pottery and plaited willow baskets. Their pottery consists of a wide variety of forms, including such figurines as storyteller figures, owls, and people in everyday scenes; bowls and jars; and double-spouted wedding vases. The revival in Jémez pottery is one that has been going on since the 1940s. Jémez craftspeople also make silver and turquoise jewelry, sculptures, and embroidered textiles. These and arts and crafts of other Southwest Indians are available in the visitor center gift shop as well as in shops and stores alongside Highway 4. One of these is Sal and Flo Yepa's Sun & Fire Pottery House, P.O. Box 112, Jémez Pueblo, NM 87024 (phone 505/834-7717). Here the specialty is pottery from Jémez and Laguna.

Annual events in Jémez normally open to the public are those observed on New Year's Day, animal dances or matachine dances; January 6-7, buffalo and animal dances; Easter, corn dances; August 2, feast day of Our Lady of the Angels of Porciúncula (patroness of Pecos Pueblo), Pecos Bull ceremony, corn dances; November 12, San Diego Feast Day, Corn dances; and December 12, matachine dances.

The first weekend in December there is an arts and crafts show in the Jémez Pueblo Civic Center.

North of Jémez Pueblo about three miles on Highway 4 is the Jémez Red Rocks Scenic Area where on the first weekend in June there is the annual Jémez Red Rocks Arts & Crafts Show. This is followed on the first and second weekends in October by the Fall Art Fiesta. Permanent booths are set up here, and on weekends from April 1 to October 15 there is the Jémez Pueblo Open Air Market featuring arts and crafts, demonstrations, and traditional foods.

Far from Jémez Pueblo, on a completely different part of the Jémez Indian Reservation, are two clusters of ponds that offer great weekend opportunities for anglers. These are the Holy Ghost and Dragonfly recreation areas northwest of San Ysidro on State Highway 44 leading to Cuba and to Bloomfield, New Mexico. The well-marked turnoff to Dragonfly Recreation Area—which is west of the highway—is fifteen miles southeast of Cuba on Highway 44 or about twenty-five miles northwest of San Ysidro. The turnoff east to the Holy Ghost Recreation Area, also well marked, is twenty-two miles southeast of Cuba or eighteen miles northwest of San Ysidro. Interestingly enough, State Highway 44 crosses a large detached portion of the Zia Indian Reservation before one reaches the Jémez Reservation and these two recreation areas—a reminder that in the Southwest one is often in seemingly endless Indian Country.

These two fee areas are open only on weekends between April 1 and October 15 from sunup to sundown. The Holy Ghost area boasts three large ponds, one of which, as purists will appreciate, is restricted to flies or lures only. The middle pond has a platform for handicapped anglers. Restrooms and picnic areas are available in both places but there is no fresh drinking water nor are any other facilities available.

To inquire further about the recreation areas, or about hunting and horseback riding possibilities on the reservation, call the Department of Tourism at 505/834-7235.

Tribal Museum: There is a display of historic photographs and artifacts in the Walatowa Visitor Center west of the trading post on State Highway 4 on the eastern edge of Jémez Pueblo.

Pueblo of Jémez
P.O. Box 100, Jemez, NM 87024
Phone 505/834-7359
Population: 2,580
Acreage: 89,624

PUEBLO OF SAN FELIPE

Having made a westward side excursion into the mountains up the Jémez River from Bernalillo, the traveler continuing north along the Rio Grande next comes to the San Felipe Indian Reservation and, to the west of the highway, the Pueblo of San Felipe.

San Felipe is another of the five Eastern Keresan pueblos. Only twenty-five miles north of Albuquerque, the village rests at the foot of Santa Ana Mesa on the west bank of the Rio Grande six miles north of its junction with the Jémez River. The ancestors of San Felipe's people, like those of neighboring Keresans, were in the Rio Grande Valley no later than the fourteenth century.

A pueblo in the location of San Felipe was apparently already in existence when the Coronado expedition passed by in 1540. A Spanish expedition of 1581-82 reported two pueblos here, one on either bank of the Rio Grande. The village on the west bank had some two hundred houses arranged in blocks from two to three stories high. When colonizer Juan de Oñate took over New Mexico in 1598 on behalf of Spain, the pair of pueblos on opposite sides of the river were still there. San Felipe Apóstol (St. Philip the Apostle) was the patronage bestowed on the community by the Franciscan missionaries, and before 1607 a church was built in the settlement on the west side of the river.

San Felipe was issued a Spanish land grant in 1689 that was confirmed by the U.S. Congress in 1858 and patented in 1864. A second Spanish land grant made in 1770 was confirmed by Congress in 1898 and patented in 1905. Other lands were added to the reservation in 1902 by executive order and in 1937 by Act of Congress.

The modern San Felipe is located on both sides of the river, with scattered individual homes and agricultural fields on the east bank and the pueblo on the west bank. The pueblo, in addition to its eighteenth-century church, has a pair of kivas as well as a few dwellings that are two stories high. Lying as it does against the east flank of Santa Ana Mesa and approachable only by a bridge over the Rio Grande, it is in a very protected and picturesque setting.

Tribal headquarters are located in the pueblo. The village is three miles west of exit 252 on Interstate 25.

Recreational Opportunities
On the east side of Interstate 25 at exit 252 the San Felipeans have constructed San Felipe's Casino Hollywood (phone 505/867-6700). It boasts all the usual amenities of such establishments, including video slots, craps tables, roulette, blackjack tables, a restaurant, and a buffet. It is open twenty-four hours a day seven days a week.

San Felipe does not promote its pueblo as a tourist attraction, but quite the opposite. Cameras, tape recorders, and sketch pads are strictly banned, and anyone wanting simply to walk around the village needs first to get permission at the tribal offices. Even with permission, sightseers might meet with less than a warm welcome from some residents. However, there are individuals who sell Indian arts and crafts from their homes, and these are indicated by signs posted at those dwellings. There are a few San Felipeans who make silver and turquoise jewelry as well as heishe, necklaces of shell or turquoise carved in the shapes of round discs, plus some modern, innovative forms of pottery.

Non-Indians are not allowed inside the church except when services are being held there.

The one time of the year when outsiders are invariably welcomed into the pueblo is on the village feast day, May 1. Cars, buses, pickups, and vans crowd into the community and their drivers and passengers pour out to see the colorful green corn dance. Dancing starts about noon and proceeds with rows of costumed dancers filing into the plaza to dance before a statue of San Felipe, their patron saint. After dark, dancing ceases and feasting begins, lasting far into the night.

San Felipe is further renowned for its Christmas celebration that starts with a Christmas Eve mass in the eighteenth century dirt-floored church. The arrival of Christ, usually around midnight, is announced by a chorus of bird warbles and whistles produced by youngsters in the choir loft—reminding listeners that when Christ was born all the birds of the earth began to sing. The celebration continues with the arrival at the church of costumed figures who dance to the beat of a drum. Included among the dancers are those who wear antlers in imitation of deer. The ceremony ends before dawn, but on Christmas Day and for a few days following various festivities continue.

San Felipe also holds a buffalo dance on February 2, a corn dance the last weekend in June, and other dances on short notice at other times of the year. For all ceremonies that take place at San Felipe, outsiders should always call ahead to see if they will be admitted to the pueblo (phone 505/867-3381, 3382, or 3383).

Pueblo of San Felipe
P.O. Box 4339, San Felipe, NM 87001
Phone 505/867-3381, 3382, or 3383
Population: 2,500
Acreage: 48,930

SANTO DOMINGO PUEBLO

Whether or not Santo Domingo is, as has been asserted by at least one anthropologist, "the most important of the Keresan pueblos," the assessment is one with which most Santo Domingos would probably agree. The pueblo, as a village, is by far the largest among all of today's Puebloan settlements and its inhabitants are among some of the most culturally conservative.

Santo Domingo is one of the towns that provided Puebloan leadership for the 1680 Pueblo Revolt. In 1681, however, a Spanish punitive expedition sacked the pueblo and Santo Domingos took refuge with other Puebloans on Horn Mesa near Cochiti Pueblo. In 1692 and '93, "persuaded" by Diego de Vargas, some Santo Domingos returned to their pueblo to begin life anew under Spanish sway. Their re-constructed village included a new church, one that fell into such disrepair that a second church was built in the mid-eighteenth century. Both structures, as well as a cemetery, were completely washed away by the Rio Grande in a great flood in 1886. There was no church for a decade, but about 1895 a young secular priest, one of many French clerics who had come to serve in New Mexico, oversaw construction of a new one. Located on high ground east of the pueblo, it looked a great deal like the mid-eighteenth century structure that had been washed downstream. He had, in effect, built a brand new old church. It is the one visitors to the pueblo see today.

Tribal headquarters are in Santo Domingo Pueblo. The pueblo, which is about midway between Albuquerque and Santa Fe, is reached by leaving Interstate 25 at exit 259 and driving six miles northwest on New Mexico State Highway 22. The pueblo consists of eight long rows of contiguous dwellings and other rooms and of intervening streets. Some of the structures are two stories high, and there are two kivas in addition to the church at the far east end of town at the village's entrance.

Recreational Opportunities

Almost as if to "head 'em off at the pass," the Santo Domingo tribal government has built a modern cultural center (phone 505/465-2625) and a tribal gift shop (P.O. Box 159, Santo Domingo Pueblo, NM 87052; phone 505/465-0030) at the southern edge of the reservation on the west side of Interstate 25 at exit 259. There are also booths here where each Thursday and Sunday from late spring until early fall Santo Domingo artists and craftspeople sell their wares. A small convenience market and service station round out the complex—one intended to invite travelers to see and appreciate the artistry and craftsmanship of Santo Domingos and, at the same time, hopefully to relieve unwanted tourist pressure in the pueblo itself. The Tribal Gift Shop has an extraordinarily fine stock of Santo Domingo jewelry and pottery.

Santo Domingos fashion both silver and turquoise jewelry as well as fine heishe necklaces and bracelets. Some of Santo Domingo's potters are among the best of Puebloan potters. Woven belts, and leather moccasins and leggings are also counted among their crafts.

For whatever reason, Santo Domingos have long been itinerant peddlers of their wares as well as traders of goods, such as Navajo rugs, made by other Indians. They appear at arts and crafts shows and bazaars all over the Southwest and as far away as California and Oklahoma. Their own products are widely traded among other Indians. As a gift, in 1995 I bought a pair of Santo Domingo earrings from an Apache at Mescalero who, in turn, had traded them from a Cochiti woman who was selling on the plaza in Santa Fe under the portico of the Palace of the Governors.

Although the traditional leadership in the pueblo, as well as many residents, discourage visitors who simply walk and stare throughout the community, many individual Santo Domingo entrepreneurs rely heavily on walk-through traffic to sell arts and crafts as well as food. Signs make it clear where these things can be purchased. Photography, recording, and sketching are absolutely forbidden, and anyone caught with a camera, sketch pad, or tape recorder is liable to have them confiscated.

One day during the year when everyone is welcome to visit Santo Domingo Pueblo is August 4, the traditional Feast of St. Dominic. Even then, however, the Pueblo's regulations regarding visiting the village must be carefully adhered to. The feast day is celebrated with a corn dance, one with hundreds of costumed participants. In the streets Indian vendors sells arts and crafts, food, soft drinks, and souvenirs. There is also a carnival complete with Ferris wheel and similar rides, some of them being enjoyed by dancers in ceremonial dress.

On Labor Day, there is normally a special arts and crafts market held in the pueblo.

Tribal Museum: The Santo Domingo Cultural Center by exit 259 off Interstate 25 has a museum with displays of photographs and Santo Domingo arts and crafts (phone 505/465-2625).

Pueblo of Santo Domingo
P.O. Box 99, Santo Domingo, NM 87052
Phone 505/465-2214
Population: 5,000
Acreage: 71,093

PUEBLO DE COCHITI

The northernmost of the Keresan Pueblos on the Rio Grande and the nearest to Santa Fe is that of Cochiti. While the prehistory of the Cochitis is uncertain, it is likely their ancestors were among those of other Keresans who arrived on the Rio Grande no later than the 1300s. Cochiti Pueblo, while not specifically mentioned in the chronicles of the 1540-42 Coronado expedition, was almost certainly in existence at the time. It was there in 1581 and in 1582 when other Spaniards came into the region, and it was among the pueblos whose members swore allegiance to the Spanish Crown in 1598 when Juan de Oñate established the first permanent Spanish colony in the Southwest.

Cochiti, somewhat off the beaten path, was administered by Franciscan missionaries as a visita, a mission visiting station without a resident priest, for much of the seventeenth century. The first reference to Cochiti mission as "San Buenaventura," its patronage today, dates from 1667.

Cochitis were willing participants in the 1680 Pueblo Revolt, and from then until 1692-93, they lived in a settlement they established on Potrero Viejo, above Cañada, about five miles northwest of today's community of Cochiti Lake. The Cochitis participated with other Puebloans in the unsuccessful revolt against Spaniards that took place in 1696. The Franciscan priest at Cochiti in 1696 saved his life by fleeing south to San Felipe Pueblo whose people were more sympathetic to Spaniards and Christians.

Whatever church may have existed in the pueblo before the revolt was ruined, and by 1706, even its successor was in sorry repair. There was a church at Cochiti in 1776, whether a newer one or a reconstructed version of the 1706 building is unclear. The church underwent major repairs and alterations in 1819, 1900, and in the mid-1960s.

Cochiti's Spanish land grant of 1689 was confirmed by the U.S. Congress in 1858 and the land was patented in 1864. The Indian Lands Commission added acreage to the reservation in 1938.

By far the greatest twentieth-century upheaval on the Cochiti Reservation took place between 1965 and 1975 when the U.S. Army Corps of Engineers,

HUCKO

after several years of negotiations with the Cochitis, constructed one of the eleven largest earthfill dams in the world across the Rio Grande upstream from Cochiti Pueblo. This rock and earth dam, 251 feet high and a little more than five miles long, created 1,200-acre Cochiti Lake and caused downstream seepage problems that ruined most lands Cochitis had used for agriculture. In 1993, the tribe negotiated a cash settlement with the federal government for damage to downstream farm lands on the reservation.

When the dam was completed in 1975, the tribe negotiated a ninety-nine-year lease with a firm to develop 7,500 acres of reservation land overlooking Cochiti Lake from its west side as a retirement or leisure community. An entire subdivision was constructed, but in 1985 the developer backed out and the project was taken over by the tribe. The present result is Cochiti Lake, a community with a small shopping center and various other facilities.

Tribal headquarters are located in Cochiti Pueblo. The pueblo is thirty miles southwest of Santa Fe. From Santa Fe, take Interstate 25 to exit 264 and follow State Highway 16 and follow the signs 12.5 miles to the pueblo. If approaching from Albuquerque, use exit 259 and take State Highway 22 to the village. The road into the pueblo, Indian Route 84, cuts back sharply southwest soon after going past Cochiti Dam.

Recreational Opportunities
Cochiti is a small pueblo graced with two kivas, San Buenaventura church, and dwellings and other rooms placed around a central plaza. Many Cochitis today do not live in the pueblo proper but in single unit houses within fairly close proximity to the settlement's ancient heart. There are ample

signs as one approaches and enters the village that there is to be no photography, tape recording, or sketching. But so are there signs on individual homes that jewelry is for sale within.

To tour the pueblo on foot, one should first get permission at the tribal office.

Although Cochiti pottery appears in many forms, the best known Cochiti pottery styles are the so-called storyteller figurines invented by potter Helen Cordero in 1964. These figurines are doll-like figures, usually of a mother or other adult female and children, either singly or attached to the female figure, who are the intended audience for her stories. Storyteller figurines have become so popular that they are now made by other Puebloan potters as well, such as those at Jemez.

Cochiti Pueblo is also the drum manufacturing center of the Southwest. Drums with two hide heads have become one of the universal symbols of the American Indian, but ironically enough, they are a musical instrument introduced into the New World by Europeans. New World aboriginal drums were, as among the Eskimos, made of a single piece of hide stretched on a hoop; foot drums, made of wooden planks set on the ground; basket drums; pottery drums; and, in Mexico, the teponaztli, a wooden drum made from a hollowed out log and played with the log horizontal. These fine pieces of craftsmanship are used in religious dances and in kiva ceremonies, but so are they sold in large numbers to non-Indians wanting a decorative piece of Puebloan craftsmanship.

The Feast of San Buenaventura, Cochiti's patron saint, is celebrated on July 14, and the public is welcome in the Pueblo on that day to enjoy good Cochiti foods (including bread fresh baked in hornos) and to witness a corn dance. The public may also be allowed at dances and feasting at Easter, Christmas, and New Year's Day, but as always, one should call the tribal office in advance to be sure.

Cochiti Lake, both the community and reservoir, afford reservation visitors additional recreational opportunities. The lake has recreation areas managed by the Army Corps of Engineers on both its east and west sides: the Cochiti Lake Recreation Area on the west, near the town of Cochiti Lake, and Tetilla Peak Recreation Area on the east. The latter is reached by taking a road north of State Highway 16 before reaching the eastern side of the dam. Both areas have restrooms, boat ramps,

drinking water, picnic facilities, group shelters, scenic trails, and a courtesy dock. Cochiti Lake Recreation area also has a fishing dock, nature trail, and visitor center. The visitor center has displays acquainting viewers with the need and purpose for the dam, the history of the area, recreational opportunities, local plants and animals, the U.S. Army Corps of Engineers, and archaeological resources—including examples of prehistoric pottery excavated in areas inundated by the lake's waters.

Picnicking; fishing for rainbow trout, walleye, catfish, bluegill, crappie, and largemouth bass; boating and water recreation; and swimming, including scuba diving and snorkeling, are available in the lake. There are no fees except for camping and electrical hookups for RVs. Fishers must have a valid New Mexico fishing license.

There are also overlook sites in both recreation areas that have restrooms, picnic facilities, drinking water, and scenic trails. And there is a picnic facility with restrooms on the east side of the Rio Grande where it emerges below the dam in the stilling basin.

The growing non-Indian community of Cochiti Lake, now being developed under tribal auspices, is north of the dam and Cochiti Pueblo on State Highway 22. The eighteen-hole Cochiti Lake Golf Course (phone 505/465-2230), designed by Robert Trent Jones II, has been ranked in the first twenty-five of America's seventy-five best gold courses by Golf Digest. The course is a par seventy-two and plays to 6,500 yards. Open all year round, weather permitting, there are a pro shop, snack bar offering breakfast and lunch, and professional golfers who offer lessons by appointment. The course is located at 6515-B Hoochaneetsa Blvd., Cochiti Lake, NM 87083.

The Cochiti Recreation Center (505/465-2239) in Cochiti Lakes includes a swimming pool, playground, tennis courts, and bingo parlor. The pool is closed in the winter.

Pueblo de Cochiti
P.O. Box 70, Cochiti, NM 87072
Phone 505/465-2245 or local 867-3211
Acreage: 50,681
Population: 1,057

The Nambé Badlands in the Sangre de Christo Mountains, New Mexico

HOPKINS

Six of New Mexico's eight northern Indian Pueblos are towns of Tewa-speaking peoples, while at two, Taos and Picuris, the language is Northern Tiwa. All of them are located north of Santa Fe, New Mexico's capital city, and since 1965 they have been cooperatively organized under the Eight Northern Indian Pueblos Council with headquarters in San Juan Pueblo (phone 800/793-4955 or 505/852-4265).

These pueblos share the same general history as that of the southern towns. They began to feel the direct impact of Spain with the coming of the Coronado expedition of 1540-42; they became a part of the colony of New Mexico in 1598 with the arrival of Don Juan de Oñate; they were subjected to efforts of Franciscan missionaries to assimilate them into Spanish culture; they joined in the Pueblo Revolt of 1680; they were a part of Mexico between 1821 and 1846; and since 1846 they have been a part of the United States. These eight pueblos, moreover, represent the survivors of eleven Tewa communities that were present in 1540. The others, lasting into the seventeenth century, were Yunge (which Oñate called San Gabriel), Cuyamungue, and Jacona.

Each summer, usually about the third week in July, one of the northern pueblos hosts the Eight Northern Indian Pueblos Artist and Craftsman Show, a gathering featuring more than 1,500 Native American artists, traditional dances and music, native foods, and a traditional foot race. It was held in the Pueblo de San Ildefonso in 1997. For dates and details concerning each year's show, phone 800/793-4955 ext. 31 or 505/852-4265 ext. 31.

PUEBLO OF TESUQUE

Although only eight miles north of Santa Fe, and with the southern edge of the Tesuque Indian Reservation abutting the open air facility for the famed Santa Fe Opera, in many respects the people of Tesuque have remained among the more culturally conservative of all the Tewa Puebloans. The members of this small community have maintained an active ceremonial life, have maintained their pueblo, and have found ways to adapt to the world around them without surrendering their distinctive identity.

Archaeologists believe the ancestors of the Tesuques arrived in the Tesuque Valley about the middle of the ninth century, possibly from the Chaco Canyon area, mixing with whatever peoples were already present. During a population explosion in the thirteenth century, small villages became consolidated into larger pueblos, and Tesuque appears to have been one of them, although located about three miles east of the present town. In 1541, when the Coronado expedition came by, it was at this more easterly location and remained there until after 1692.

The Pueblo Revolt, although planned elsewhere, actually began in Tesuque when the natives killed their Franciscan missionary, Fray Juan Bautista Pío, destroyed the church, and helped lay siege to Santa Fe. In 1694, after the 1692 re-conquest of New Mexico by Diego de Vargas, the Tesuques moved their pueblo to its present location. A new church was built in 1695 only to be replaced by another in 1745. The 1745 construction, rebuilt to shorter dimensions in 1880 and altered many times since, is apparently in the same location as today's church facing south on the northeast corner of the plaza, it includes some of the eighteenth-century foundations.

The Tesuque Indian Reservation owes its original land base to a Spanish land grant confirmed by the U.S. Congress in 1858. The lands were patented in 1864 and further additions to the reservation were made in 1937.

Until the 1990s, the economy of Tesuque was among the more depressed of New Mexico's Puebloan communities. A gambling casino, RV park, and other attractions for visitors, however, have greatly improved the tribe's economic posture, as has the tribe's close proximity to a rapidly expanding urban area where there are more employment possibilities.

Recreational Opportunities

The pueblo's greatest income provider is the Camel Rock Resort Casino (phone 800/462-2635, or 800/852-4646, or 505/984-8414). It is about ten miles north of Santa Fe on U.S. Highway 84/285 and features high stakes bingo, live action games, and video slot machines. The casino, which never closes, has a restaurant.

Also important to the pueblo's financial well-being are the RV parks, gift shops, and, one of Tesuque's unique enterprises, Tesuque Natural Farms. Organically grown crops, principally alfalfa, lettuce, and herbs, are raised for pueblo consumption and for sale in area markets.

Tesuque Pueblo itself is on the New Mexico State Register of Historic Places and has been well cared for. Visitors should register at the governor's office

in the pueblo and, if desired, obtain photography permits (no photos allowed without a permit). One can take a walking tour of the pueblo and visit with local artisans, especially with those making and selling Tesuque pottery, a craft revived in very recent years. Potter Teresa Tapia models small animals and paints them with intricate geometric designs in black and red. Potters have also revived the famous Tesuque "rain gods," which are not rain gods at all, but are a form that was commissioned in the 1890s by a Santa Fe curio dealer for the Gunther Candy Company of Chicago who used them as a promotion. The Gunther Candy Company has long since ceased to exist, but the popular "rain gods," small seated figures holding a bowl in their laps, have been revived at Tesuque—and they are usually of far better quality than the originals.

There are many local shops and galleries in Tesuque that one can easily visit on a walking tour of the pueblo. One of these, for example, is in the heart of the pueblo: Tewa Tioux Gallery, P.O. Box 652, Tesuque, NM 87574 (phone 505/989-9564).

A flea market is operated on land leased from the tribe at its southern perimeter on the west side of U.S. Highway 84/285 practically adjacent to the Santa Fe Opera. The market is open only on weekends, Friday through Sunday, although vendors can bring their wares starting on Thursday.

Ceremonial dances normally open to the public take place in the pueblo on its feast day (the Feast of San Diego de Alcalá), November 12; on New Year's Day; on January 6 (Feast of the Three Kings, or Epiphany); and on an unspecified day in June, when there is a corn dance. The November 12 observance consists of dancing only. There are no food booths on that occasion.

As always, call the tribal office in advance.

Fishing and picnicking are additional options for visitors to the Tesuque Reservation. Aspen Ranch and the Vigil Grant, both wooded areas surrounded by the Santa Fe National Forest, afford fishing and camping. For details, call the tribal office.

Pueblo of Tesuque
Route 5, Box 360-T, Santa Fe, NM 87501
Phone 505/983-2667
Population: 400
Acreage: 16,811

PUEBLO OF POJOAQUE

Pojoaque Pueblo, should it want to, could borrow a slogan from Tombstone, Arizona: "The town too tough to die." Not that the Tewa-speaking people of Pojoaque are tough in the image of western gunfighters, but they have surely been persistent. The place was all but deserted in the early twentieth century, but in the 1930s it was reborn, made a community once more when a few people who had left earlier and some of their descendants moved back onto reservation lands. The changes in growth and prosperity since then have been truly dramatic.

At least some Pojoaque ancestors were in the upper Rio Grande Valley by the tenth century. Their more immediate Tewa ancestors arrived in the late thirteenth and early fourteenth centuries. When Coronado and other Spaniards made their exploring and failed colonization efforts in New Mexico in the sixteenth century, it may have been among the larger Tewa settlements in the valley.

Encroachment by non-Indians, lethal epidemics, economic difficulties, and all manner of social discord reduced the size of Pojoaque's population until finally it became no longer possible to carry out normal Tewa social and religious life. In 1909 the pueblo was described as abandoned, although its former residents, living in nearby Nambé and Santa Clara pueblos as well as in other places, continued to check on their agricultural fields on the reservation. In 1934, fourteen Pojoaques, including children, reclaimed their reservation from squatters who had taken up residence there and who had been pasturing and grazing their livestock on Pojoaque lands. The reservation's Tewa population has grown steadily since then. The basis of the Pojoaque Reservation is a Spanish land grant confirmed by the U.S. Congress in 1858 and patented in 1864. It is strategically located on either side of U.S. Highway 84/285, the major link between Santa Fe and Taos, and traffic between the two places must cross the reservation.

Tribal headquarters are located in Pojoaque next to the main highway about twelve miles north of Santa Fe. Nothing remains of original Puebloan architecture, and today's community has a thoroughly modern and non-Indian appearance except for the multi-story Poeh Cultural Center and Museum built as a replica of a prehistoric Anasazi pueblo. A new kiva, the only one on the reservation, has also been built at Pojoaque, an indication of the cultural revitalization that is taking place.

Nambé Falls, Nambé Pueblo, New Mexico

HOPKINS

Recreational Opportunities

Dining and gambling are available at Pojoaque's forty thousand square-foot Cities of Gold Casino, which fronts on U.S. Highway 84/285. Opened in July 1995, both restaurant and casino are available twenty-four hours a day seven days a week. High stakes bingo, poker, live 21, and various kinds of video machines are the featured games. For further information, call 800/455-3313 or 505/455-7425.

The Pojoaque Pueblo visitors center is located in the Pojoaque Pueblo Plaza just off the highway to the west (Route 11, Box 21B, Santa Fe, NM 87501). The Visitors Center, which serves as a tourist information center, offers for sale the works of some eight hundred Tewa artists and craftspeople, including the best of Tewa pottery (phone 505/455-3460; Fax 505/455-7128).

The people of Pojoaque celebrate the feast day of Our Lady of Guadalupe, December 12, with a morning mass and vespers at the church and with various costumed dances. Food booths and arts and crafts booths are a further feature of the fiesta. Thanks to Pojoaque potters like Cordi Gomez, who at age two was one of the fourteen people who helped reclaim the pueblo's lands in 1934, the ancient craft of Pojoaque pottery has been revitalized. It is a strong, thin-walled ware made of clay flecked with mica. Pojoaque potters, some of whom have connections with potters at Santa Clara and San Ildefonso pueblos, continue to make handsome undecorated utility wares like bean pots, salt dishes, small pitchers, and sugar bowls. These are sought after by Puebloans as well as by non-Indians. There are also Pojoaque painters and silversmiths now at work on the reservation.

Tribal Museum: The spectacular Poeh Cultural Center and Museum at Pojoaque is a replica of a prehistoric Anasazi village, one complete with a multi-storied Sun Tower that tends to dominate the landscape. Intended primarily for Pojoaques and other Tewas, the building is used as a school in which established Tewa artists teach others the crafts of pottery making, sculpture, textile crafts, and art business management. The museum houses a permanent collection and also has temporary displays of the work of its students. Tours of the teaching facility are available by appointment. The museum is open weekdays from 8:00 a.m. to 4:00 p.m. and Saturday from 9:30 a.m. to 1:30 p.m. Traditional dances are also held here on some weekends and there are bread-making demonstrations as well (phone 505/455-3334 or 2489 for details).

Pueblo of Pojoaque
Route 11, Box 71, Santa Fe, NM 87501
Phone 505/455-2278
Population: 285
Acreage: 11,601

NAMBÉ PUEBLO

The general outlines of the prehistory of the Tewa-speaking people of Nambé Pueblo are doubtless no different than those for Tesuque, Pojoaque, and the other three Tewa towns of the northern Rio Grande. References to Nambé in sixteenth-century Spanish documents are equivocal, but the village was almost certainly visited by a Spanish expedition in 1591. The first mention of a mission here dates from 1613, and a church was built in 1617. It was dedicated to San Francisco de Asís, the founder of the Franciscan Order. The mission seems to have had resident priests until 1680 when its minister, Fray Tomás de Torres, was killed at the onset of the Pueblo Revolt. The Nambé people also participated in the abortive 1696 uprising against the Spaniards.

A new church was built in Nambé Pueblo in 1725. It lasted until 1908 when it collapsed into ruin. A new church was built in 1910 to replace the one that had collapsed, and it lasted until 1960 when it was condemned as unsafe and torn down. In 1974, the present church, designed by architect Allen L. McNown, took its place in the pueblo about thirty yards east of where the old ones had stood. Its physical link to the past hangs from a horizontal beam above the doorway, the bell from the 1725 church.

By the early 1960s, Tewa culture at Nambé had become so weakened that visitors were allowed to descend into the village kiva to look around. In recent years, however, there has been a revival in ceremonialism and the kiva is again closed to sightseers.

The Nambé Indian reservation's land base dates from a Spanish land grant that was confirmed by the U.S. Congress in 1858 and patented in 1864. Further lands were added in 1902 by executive order.

Tribal headquarters are in Nambé Pueblo. The pueblo is reached by taking U.S. Highway 84/285 north of Santa Fe about fifteen miles to its junction with New Mexico State Highway 503 about one mile

▼▼▼

north of Pojoaque. Follow Highway 503 west about three miles until coming to a sign that indicates a road going south (right) to Nambé Falls. Follow this road two miles to the pueblo.

Recreational Opportunities

Nambé Pueblo is in picturesque surroundings in the foothills of the Sangre de Cristo Mountains. Enough of the original pueblo remains, including a kiva, to make a stroll through the pueblo a pleasant experience. Visitors should register at the tribal office where brochures and photography permits are available.

The new church in the village, while modern, has architecture in keeping with a general pueblo style. In the 1950s, except for a few woven belts, native crafts had become all but extinct in the village. Today a small amount of weaving continues, and Nambé potters are making vessels either of micaceous clay or of black-and-red polished ware. They also fashion some jewelry. These and other Southwest Indian arts and crafts are available along the road leading to Nambé as well as in the community in several individually owned shops and stores, one of them a gallery displaying sculpture and traditional and contemporary art. The latter, Cloud Eagle Studios-Gallery, is on the right 1.4 miles south of State Highway 503 on the Nambé Waterfalls Road (phone 505/455-2662).

A popular reservation site is Nambé Falls, a picnicking and recreation area five miles beyond the pueblo on the same road. From the end of the road, there is a trail to the base of the falls where both picnicking and camping are allowed.

Nambé Falls is a series of three falls on Nambé Creek. The tallest has a drop of a hundred feet, and during times of heavy upstream rain or during snow melt, the falls are a spectacular sight. The Nambé Indian Reservation and the Havasupai Indian Reservation are the only reservations in the Southwest with waterfalls that have become visitor attractions.

Near the falls, at the headwaters of Nambé Creek, is Nambé Lake. Here there are RV sites, barbecue grills, restrooms, and drinking water. Non-motorized boating and fishing for cutthroat and rainbow trout are the main attractions at the lake. Permits for various activities, including hiking, are available either at the tribal office or on site (phone 505/455-2304 for particulars).

The recreation area is closed from November through March.

Nambé Pueblo owns and operates a tour company, Nambé Pueblo Tours, Route 1, Box 117-BB, Santa Fe, NM 87501 (phone 800/946-2623 or 505/455-2036). Native American guides take tourists to the eight Northern Pueblos as well as to Taos, Bandelier National Monument, and other places in northern New Mexico.

Visitors to the Nambé Indian reservation also have the opportunity to view buffalo. This majestic animal, once so important in the economy and ritual lives of many northern Puebloan groups, has been re-introduced to the reservation in a small herd. Directions on viewing the herd can be obtained at the tribal office.

Nambé Pueblo observes its feast day, that of San Francisco de Asís (St. Francis of Assisi), on October 4 with tribal dances that are open to the public. There is also a kind of public fiesta held at Nambé Falls on the Fourth of July, one at which the sale of native arts and crafts is an important feature.

Nambé Pueblo
Route 1, Box 117-BB, Santa Fe, NM 87501
Phone 505/455-2036
Population: 630
Acreage: 19,124

PUEBLO DE SAN ILDEFONSO

Archaeological evidence suggests that the Tewa-speaking people of San Ildefonso arrived near their present location over six hundred years ago. The chronicles of the Vásquez de Coronado expedition of 1540-42 are silent on the subject of San Ildefonso, a village called Po-woh-ge-oweenge ("Where the Water Cuts Down Through") in the Tewas' language. The community became temporary headquarters for a Spanish expedition in 1593 and it was among the Puebloan communities whose leaders swore allegiance to the Spanish crown in 1598 when Juan de Oñate laid the foundations for what was to become a Spanish colony and, eventually, a Mexican territory and then a state of the United States of America.

Franciscans established a residence in San Ildefonso as early as 1601. The friars came to stay in 1610 and continued their presence in the town until 1680 and the outbreak of the Pueblo Revolt when the two resident missionaries—one a priest and the other a lay brother—were killed and the church was destroyed.

After 1696, peace between Spaniards and San Ildefonsans became permanent, and in 1711 a new house of Christian worship was erected in the pueblo. An appended chapel was added between 1717 and 1722, and that, with the church, lasted until 1905 when the entire structure was razed and replaced by a simple barn-like building with a pitched roof. In 1969, this undistinguished edifice gave way to the one now standing, an imposing temple that evokes the appearance of the eighteenth-century mission.

The San Ildefonso Indian Reservation, whose northern boundary abuts the southern boundary of the Santa Clara Indian Reservation, is founded on a Spanish land grant confirmed by the U.S. Congress in 1858, patented in 1864. Further lands were added by and Act of Congress in 1929 and by an executive order in 1939.

Tribal headquarters and the Pueblo de San Ildefonso are reached from Santa Fe by driving nineteen miles north to Pojoaque on U.S. 84/284; turning west (left) onto New Mexico State Highway

Vessel made by San Ildefonso potter Maria Martinez

502 (the highway to Los Alamos); and going five miles to the turnoff to the north (right) and following the road about a mile into the pueblo.

Recreational Opportunities

Tourists visiting San Ildefonso should stop at the visitor center at the village's south entrance to register, pay a small admittance fee, obtain information, and, if desired, to purchase a permit to take photographs. There is a small museum across the plaza by the church. The self-guided walking tour of the village includes visits to locally owned arts and crafts shops and views of the plaza area with its kiva, historic pueblo structures, and the modern church built in Spanish mission style. The San Ildefonso Visitor Center (phone 505/455-3549) is open daily from 8:00 a.m. to 5:00 p.m. and on weekends during the summer.

Thanks largely to the efforts begun about 1919 by potters Maria Martinez and her husband, Julian Martinez, San Ildefonso has become justly famous for its beautiful pottery. The Martinezes developed a matte-painted, black-on-black ware, a style that has been carried on and is now made by other Puebloan potters as well, most notably at Santa Clara. San Ildefonso potters, like those at Santa Clara, also carve black and red wares with a technique developed about 1930. These beautiful vessels are in demand throughout the world.

San Ildefonso is also known for its painters, some of whom, in the early 1900s, were among the first Puebloans to use commercial watercolors. There are also a few craftspeople who make moccasins, who are jewelers, and who fashion embroidered textiles.

One of the locally owned retail outlets in the pueblo is Sunbeam Indian Arts, San Ildefonso Pueblo, Route 5, Box 304-A, Santa Fe, NM 87501 (phone 505/455-7132). Featured is the pottery of Barbara Gonzales, a direct descendant of Maria Martinez, and of her husband and sons. The Popovi Da Studio of Indian Arts, begun by Maria and Julian Martinez's son, features fine pottery and is operated by Anita Da (phone 505/455-3332). Another pottery outlet is Juan Tafoya Pottery, Route 5, Box 306-A, San Ildefonso Pueblo, NM 87501 (phone 505/455-2649). The specialty here is black-on-black ware.

The largest stock of local Indian pottery, including historic pieces by Maria and Julian Martinez, is in Babbitt's Cottonwood Trading Post, San Ildefonso Pueblo, Route 5, Box 320, Santa Fe, NM 87501 (phone 800/766-6864 or 505/455-7596). This store, owned by a non-Indian family whose members have traded on Southwest Indian reservations for generations, also sells Hopi kachina dolls, Navajo rugs, Zuni fetishes, baskets, cradleboards, and Indian-crafted gold and silver jewelry.

There are no food booths or arts and crafts booths at San Ildefonso's feast day observance that starts in the evening of January 22 and continues on January 23. This religious celebration includes deer dances and, in alternate years, Comanche and buffalo dances; evening vespers in the church; and a morning mass followed by dancing in the plaza until noon on the 23rd. No photographs are allowed.

With the other pueblos, San Ildefonso observes New Year's Day as well as the Feast of the Three Kings on January 6. There are corn dances in June and in late August/early September. Matachine dances and other dances are included in the Christmas celebration on December 25.

As always, phone the tribal office in advance to confirm that the observances are occurring and are open to the public.

Picnicking and fishing are offered from April through October at a 4.5-acre trout and catfish pond a mile southwest of the pueblo. Information and permits for anglers are available in visitor center.

Tribal Museum: The San Ildefonso Pueblo Museum is across the plaza by the church. Historical and cultural exhibits include one that explains the process of making black-on-black pottery. The Popovi Da Studio of Indian Arts has a private museum that features the works of potters Maria and Julian Martinez. It is open by appointment only (phone 505/455-3332).

Pueblo de San Ildefonso
Route 5, Box 315-A, Santa Fe, NM 87501
Phone 505/455-2273
Population: 575
Acreage: 26,191

SANTA CLARA INDIAN PUEBLO

The Tewa-speaking Santa Clara peoples have a tradition that they came into the world from beneath a lake in southern Colorado. They migrated southward, and both they and archaeologists agree that their ancestors once occupied a series of cave dwellings in mesa cliffs at a place called Puye. Archaeologists tell us this was in the fourteenth and early fifteenth centuries. The Tewas abandoned the place in the 1400s and moved down into the Rio Grande Valley to their present village—or quite nearby—where Spaniards found them in 1540-41.

Santa Clara Pueblo was a part of the New Mexico colonized by Juan de Oñate in 1598, and between 1622, when he arrived there, and 1634 when he wrote a lengthy report, Franciscan missionary Alonso de Benavides built a church in the pueblo. This structure was apparently still standing when Santa Clarans joined in the Pueblo Revolt of 1680, but it was probably destroyed during the uprising. A second church was built in 1706, but it collapsed and a third was constructed in 1758. That building lasted until 1909 when, just as people in the pueblo

were trying to put on a new roof, a great storm moved in and destroyed the church. There was no church for about nine years, but in 1918 what was described as "a partial replica of this old church, but on a smaller and simpler scale," came into being. It is that edifice, somewhat expanded and remodeled, visitors see today.

Like many other New Mexico Puebloan communities, it was a Spanish land grant confirmed by the U.S. Congress in 1858 and patented in 1864 that became the basis of the Santa Clara Indian Reservation. A second grant of 1763, confirmed by Congress in 1894 and patented in 1909, as well as an executive order addition of lands in 1905

77

enlarged the original grant by more than thirty-three thousand acres.

Tribal headquarters are located just outside of the pueblo proper on the north side. Santa Clara Pueblo can be reached from San Ildefonso Pueblo to the south by driving north on State Highway 30. It is about eight miles north of the junction of State Highways 30 and 502. From Española on U.S. Highway 84, the pueblo is about 1.5 miles to the south. Much of Española, the bustling urban center of Rio Arriba County, is actually on the Santa Clara Indian Reservation. Commercial properties here are leased from the tribe.

Recreational Opportunities

The tribal tourism office is located in the governor's office that one sees on the right as one enters the pueblo coming from Española. Visitors are asked to register here and, if they wish to take pictures, get a photography permit as well. Strolling around the village, including the outlying area of modern homes, the main plaza, and the church will bring one past many homes and business that display a sign reading, "Pottery for Sale." Many of these same places, as well as others, also sell paintings, sculpture, beadwork, and embroidery by native artists.

Like San Ildefonso, Santa Clara is renowned for its highly polished black pottery, much of it carved. More than two hundred potters fashion full-size bowls, jars, figurines, and plates as well as miniatures, all generally of exceptional quality. There are also highly polished redwares and polychrome pieces. Santa Clara potters are extremely innovative, and new styles continue to evolve. For many visitors, the most rewarding times to visit the pueblo are when there are public dances on religious feast days. At Santa Clara these are on August 12, the Feast of Santa Clara de Asís, the village patron, and on June 13, St. Anthony's feast day. Various dances are held on August 12 and Comanche Dancers take center stage in the plaza on June 13. As with other Northern Pueblos, there are observances on Christmas, New Year's Day, and on January 6 for the Feast of the Three Kings. Santa Clara also celebrates the Holy Innocents Day on December 28 with children's dances. Call first to see if they are open to the public.

The Puye Cliff Ruins, a National Historic Landmark, are owned by Santa Clara Pueblo and are on the Santa Clara Indian Reservation. A fee, payable at the entrance, is charged for access to the site, a complex of stone walled rooms both cliffside and on top of the cliff, including a kiva. From here there are fine views of Santa Clara Canyon, the Española Valley, and the distant Sangre de Cristo Mountains.

To reach the ruins, go south from the pueblo three miles on State Highway 30 and turn west (right) onto Indian Route 601 and follow it eleven miles. The ancient cliff dwellings lie on three levels and are connected by stone stairways and ladders. On top of the cliff are the ruins of what was once a 740-room pueblo.

Visitors can tour the Puye Cliffs unattended or with a guide. The three trails are open seven days a week all year long, from 8:00 a.m. to 8:00 p.m. in the summer and from 8:00 a.m. to 4:00 p.m. in the winter. Guided tours and public feast packages are available from April through September (reserve five days in advance by calling the Santa Clara Tourism Office at 505/753-7326 or sending a Fax to 505/753-8988). The Puye Cafe and Gift Shop is open from 10:00 a.m. to 4:30 p.m. Monday through Friday. The gift shops sells Santa Clara arts and crafts as well as pueblo souvenirs. There is also a conference center here available for small group and corporate functions (check with the tourism office).

A popular recreation area on the reservation is at Santa Clara Canyon, a deep ravine cut by the waters of Santa Clara Creek at 7,350-feet elevation. It is open seven days a week April through October and requires an entry fee.

The canyon is reached by continuing west of Indian Route 601 past the cliff ruins to the end of the road. Spruce, piñon, and aspen enclose the beautiful canyon, and anglers will find not only good fishing along miles of streams, but in any one of four ponds well-stocked with trout and catfish. Picnickers, hikers, and sightseers will also enjoy themselves here. Restrooms and drinking water are available, and there are sites for camping and RVs.

Special tourism packages are available that include a traditional feast meal, pottery demonstrations, tours, and dances. Arrangements for these, which must be made two weeks in advance, are handled by the Tourism Office, P.O. Box 580, Española, NM 87532 (phone 505/753-7326; Fax 753-8988).

Santa Clara Indian Pueblo
P.O. Box 580, Española, NM 87532
Phone 505/753-7330 or 7326
Population: 1,742
Acreage: 45,965

ANNERINO

SAN JUAN PUEBLO

The first time I visited San Juan Pueblo was in 1965. I had been propelled there in part because a friend, Florence Hawley Ellis, had excavated part of the ruins of the town established on the west side of the Rio Grande in 1598 by colonizer Juan de Oñate, and I wanted to see the site. As I crossed the river from the pueblo on U.S. Highway 285, a sign on a street corner said, "See the oldest capital in the United States," a slight exaggeration given that Saint Augustine, Florida, not only remained extant, but was founded thirty-three years earlier, in 1565.

When I got to the fenced area where the ruins lay, another sign said, "KEEP OUT, SEE LEE MONTOYA." Mr. Montoya, it happened, was plowing an adjacent field seated on a plow pulled by a pair of horses. Oñate's capital, San Gabriel del Yunge as the conqueror had named it, was on the Montoyas' traditional farm lands.

We had a pleasant conversation. I learned that one of Lee Montoya's daughters was Anita Da, the wife of Popovi Da, the artist son of famed San Ildefonso potters Maria and Julian Martinez. And he gave us permission to visit the ruins of the first capital city in the American Southwest. All we could see were outlines of shallow foundations spread out over what, considering the historical significance of the place, seemed to be a very small area. One could stroll around its outer perimeter in fewer than twenty minutes.

Reports suggest that the people of Yungue willingly relinquished their site to the Spaniards and that they moved across the river to live with relatives in the other pueblo. It was then that Oñate christened the other pueblo San Juan [Bautista] de los Caballeros (St. John [the Baptist] of the Warrior Knights).

All did not go well for the founder of Spanish New Mexico. Oñate fell into disgrace among Spanish authorities and no later than 1610 the capital was moved from San Gabriel del Yunge to Santa Fe where it has remained ever since.

Whatever church was at San Juan in 1680 was destroyed during the Pueblo Revolt. By the time Spaniards returned to New Mexico in 1692, resistance on the part of San Juan's people had ended. A new church was built before 1710. It suffered the

damage of time and was replaced between 1746 and 1763 by a long, narrow, and quite substantial building. It was re-roofed in 1865 and severely remodeled many times before it was replaced on the same site with a new brick building in 1912-13. This church, decidedly French in architectural conception in keeping with the nationality of its builder, Father Camilo Seux, shares the visual scene along State Highway 74 a road that passes through San Juan Pueblo with an equally French-appearing Chapel of Our Lady of Lourdes that Father Seux built in 1890.

San Juan's Spanish land grant, confirmed by the U.S. Congress in 1858 and patented in 1864, dates from 1689. Only twenty-three acres have been added to the original grant since then.

Tribal headquarters are located among the U.S. Post Office, Bureau of Indian Affairs day school, and the Chapel of Our Lady of Lourdes on the east side of State Highway 74 in San Juan Pueblo. The pueblo is located about five miles north of Española just to the west of State Highway 68 on State Highway 74. It is also immediately south of U.S. Highway 285 on the east side of the Rio Grande. Because of its location at the junction of major highways, and especially because of the many buildings along State Highway 74 through the town, the sense of San Juan's being a pueblo is not immediately felt. However, just to the east of the highway there remain two plazas and two kivas and contiguous rooms built in typical pueblo fashion.

Recreational Opportunities

Tribal leaders have organized the TSAY Corporation of San Juan Pueblo to manage a wide variety of tribal enterprises, including those involved directly with recreation.

TSAY's address is Route 74, P.O. Box 1270, San Juan Pueblo, NM 87566 (phone 505/852-4431; Fax 505/852-4026).

Leading the list of income earners for TSAY is the Ohkay Casino on the east side of State Highway 68 just north of Española at San Juan Pueblo (phone

800/PLAY-AT-OK or 505/747-1668). Open twenty-four hours a day all year round, the casino has slot machines and high stakes card tables (poker and blackjack). The casino's patrons are invited to eat in its Ohkay Café.

Fishing and picnicking are provided by TSAY either along the Rio Grande at sites reached by dirt roads or at three tribal fishing lakes next to the east bank of the Rio Grande on the southern part of the reservation just north of Española and west of State Highway 68 (phone 505/753-5067). The lakes, resting serenely among large cottonwood groves, are stocked with trout and bass. Boat rentals are available. This is also an RV and camping site, one with a swimming pool, restrooms, showers, laundry, and a mini-market that has a few slot machines in it. There is even a buffalo herd here for viewing.

The Ohkay T'owa Gardens Cooperative on the San Juan Indian Reservation, which processes and grows dried New Mexico traditional native food products, provides an enjoyable visit. For information, call 505/747-3147.

Visitors wanting to take pictures in San Juan Pueblo will need to get a photography permit at the tribal offices.

The wonderful facility for the Oke Oweenge Crafts Cooperative is in the pueblo on the west side of Highway 74 south of the St. John Baptist Catholic Church. Begun in 1968 by the craftspeople of San Juan Pueblo, the cooperative has continued throughout its existence to foster and support handmade crafts through education and training, gallery displays, and direct sales. The crafts—all of high quality—include jewelry, pottery, weaving, sewing, basketry, painting, beadwork, and woodworking, all of them combining contemporary and traditional San Juan motifs.

The building housing the training center, gallery, and sales area was built in 1973 in modern pueblo

▼▼

style. Its staff and craftspeople are on hand to answer questions and to be of service during hours the facility is open, Monday through Saturday from 9:00 a.m. to 5:00 p.m. Its mailing address is simply San Juan Pueblo, NM 87566 (phone 505/852-2372).

San Juan Pueblo boasts an excellent place to eat lunch (or a late breakfast), the Tewa Indian Restaurant, on its main thoroughfare near the heart of the village. Indian herbal teas, frybread, blue corn products, fruit pies, bread pudding, red or green chili stews, and other traditional fares are on the menu. Hours are weekdays from 9:00 a.m. to 2:30 p.m.

Yearly events to which the public is welcome are those observed on New Year's Day, when new pueblo officers are installed in their positions; January 6, when there are dances in honor of the new officers; Easter Sunday, when there are dances; and the last week of September when harvest dances are held. There are a San Antonio's Day Dance on June 13, matachines dances and a religious procession on December 24-25, and a Turtle Dance on December 26. The most important celebration of the year is that on June 23-24 when the village observes its feast day, that of San Juan Bautista (St. John the Baptist), with dances and food. Other events, including a deer dance in February and cloud or basket dances at other times, are scheduled on short notice. One should call the tribal office for details.

San Juan Pueblo
P.O. Box 1099, San Juan, NM 87566
Phone 505/852-4400 or 4210
Population: 2,358
Acreage: 12,236

PUEBLO OF PICURIS

At some point in the prehistoric past, Tiwa-speaking peoples who had arrived in New Mexico as early as the twelfth century, divided into two segments, one of them moving south where some of their descendants continue to live at Sandia, Isleta, and Ysleta del Sur pueblos, and the others remaining in the north at Taos and Picuris pueblos. The division, whenever it occurred, brought about sufficient change in the common language spoken by the two segments that in historic times a Southern Tiwa and Northern Tiwa became distinct, but mutually intelligible, dialects.

The people of Picuris were in place by the late 1100s. Their simple pithouse structures gave way less than a century later to buildings of coursed adobe and, by the end of the fourteenth century, to the kinds of multi-storied structures we now associate with pueblo architecture. Construction reached a peak early in the sixteenth century when some of the buildings were described by Spaniards as being from seven to eight stories tall—a remarkable achievement if true.

In the 1740s, Fray Fernando Duque de Estrada thoroughly renovated whatever church it was that had been built in the pueblo earlier in the century. His efforts were short-lived, partly due to the fact that raids by Comanche Indians forced the temporary abandonment of the town. The church was torn down and a new one was under construction

BURKHALTER

in 1776. The Indians managed to keep this structure more or less in repair via a series of alterations until, finally, in 1986 a whole section of the nave wall collapsed and the adobe church had to be rebuilt anew. The eight-year project, which involved both labor and funds contributed by neighboring communities, was completed in 1997. Tom Martinez, a village elder, led a group of laborers who re-created the church brick by brick, by hand, just as their ancestors had done.

The Spanish land grant for Picuris Pueblo—the basis of today's Picuris Indian Reservation—dates from 1689. Congress confirmed the grant in 1858 and it was patented in 1864.

Tribal headquarters are located in Picuris Pueblo. The village can be reached either by taking New Mexico State Highway 76 northeast from Española; Highway 75 east from its junction with Highway 68 north of Española and south of Ranchos de Taos; or Highway 518 south from Ranchos de Taos to Highway 75, then five miles west to the town. The pueblo is in the northernmost valley through which the Rio Pueblo flows. It is in the high country on the western slope of the Sangre de Cristo Mountains and is surrounded by the Carson National Forest. The pueblo is twenty-three miles south of Taos and fifty-five miles north of Santa Fe.

Recreational Opportunities

Because of its somewhat remote location from heavily traveled highways, a sojourn to Picuris Pueblo is likely to be a very pleasant and relaxed one. Visitors should register at the visitor center found to the right as one enters the pueblo from the south (phone 505/587-2957). Photography permits are available here, and visitors will get a brochure concerning the self-guided tour of the community. The visitor center also has a gift shop, museum, and the Hidden Valley Restaurant. The center overlooks Tutah Lake, a small pond where, with a permit, trout fishing is available. Puna Lake, a second trout fishing pond, is on the reservation as well.

A small amount of jewelry is made by a few Picuris people, but the principal craft item of Picuris is pottery. Local potters produce a much sought after unpainted ware made from micaceous clay. These vessels, usually in traditional utilitarian shapes, are occasionally decorated by the application of thick ropes, beads, or small animals made from clay. In response to buyers' demands, some pottery is also painted.

With a permit in hand, visitors who follow the posted tour route through the pueblo are allowed to photograph areas along the route, always

respecting the privacy of individuals. Past archaeological investigations in Picuris Pueblo have exposed many sites and have added considerably to information about the town's history.

Those who take the walking tour will visit the site of the earliest Catholic churches in the community, those in use before 1776. They will also visit the present church, the one whose construction was completed in 1997 on the site of the older one. It includes lumber, doors, balustrades, and other elements salvaged from the eighteenth-century building.

Also on the tour are remains of the older parts of the pueblo, many that were prehistoric. Here one will see a standing block of rooms; kivas, including a seven-hundred-year-old kiva with a round tower above it; and a modern kiva that remains in use. It is a quiet walk that joins the harmony between past and present.

Like the other Northern Pueblos, Picuris celebrates New Year's Day and the Feast of the Three Kings (January 6). There are also celebrations in honor of San Pablo (St. Paul) on January 25; San Antonio (St. Anthony) on June 13; and the village patron, San Lorenzo (St. Lawrence), on August 9-10. The latter features a sunset dance on the evening of the 9th and a mass on the morning of the 10th followed by a procession, traditional foot races, and traditional pole climbing contests. Food booths are open and there are arts and crafts vendors.

The first weekend of July Picuris comes alive with the High Country Arts and Crafts Festival, one attended by Indian artists and craftspeople from throughout the region. There are dances held in the pueblo on Christmas Day, and children dance on December 28 in honor of Holy Innocents Day. Various dances are likely to be held in February that are open to the public, but, as ever, it pays to first call ahead for information (505/587-2957).

Tribal Museum: There is a very nice, if small, museum in the visitor center at the pueblo. A selection of artifacts that were recovered during archaeological excavations in the village in the 1960s is on display here.

Pueblo of Picuris
P.O. Box 127, Peñasco, NM 87533
Phone 505/587-2519
Population: 339
Acreage: 14,980

TAOS PUEBLO

Like the people of Picuris Pueblo, those of Taos Pueblo speak Northern Tiwa. Despite enormous changes that have occurred over the centuries, and despite their intimate involvement with outsiders, Taos Indians have managed to maintain a strong sense of their unique cultural identity and to persevere as a people.

Taos Pueblo, more, perhaps, than any of the other New Mexican and Arizona Puebloan communities, has opened at least its outer doors wide to a never-ending flood of visitors. The Rio Pueblo de Taos that divides the community into northside and southside house blocks may never have threatened the village by rushing out of control beyond its banks, but in modern times swarms of sightseers, photographers, film makers, writers, artists, and curiosity seekers have motivated the majority of Taos Indians to find housing beyond the pueblo's boundaries. The comparatively small percentage of people, about 7 percent of Taos Indians, who choose to remain within the pueblo's confines find themselves during daylight hours throughout much of the year participating in a kind of living museum.

The pithouse-dwelling ancestors of the Taos people were in the general region of the west side of the Sangre de Cristo Mountains between 1000 and 1200. During the thirteenth century, larger, multi-family surface dwellings appeared. Settlement in the immediate vicinity of today's Taos Pueblo began about 1350, and Tiwas have remained here ever since. By the time members of the Vásquez de Coronado expedition came north in 1540, spectacular mud-plastered multi-storied structures on the north and south sides of the Rìo Pueblo de Taos stood on or very near where such structures stand today.

After a series of churches were built and destroyed, a new San Jerónimo church went up around 1850, this one located where it stands today. Fronting on the plaza, it is about a hundred yards southeast of the ruins of the eighteenth-century structure. This present church has undergone numerous alterations since it was built.

By the mid-eighteenth century Taos Pueblo had become a great trading center, a place where Plains Indians—even those who were often enemies—and Puebloans along with Hispanos, Utes, Apaches, and Navajos gathered each year for a week-long

Taos bread ovens

trade fair. Women and children captives were sold as slaves; vendors sold their agricultural produce; craftsmen sold their various products; and everyone enjoyed a week of partying and brawling. Later in the eighteenth century, the trade fair was moved out of the pueblo to the nearby and much larger Hispanic settlement of Fernández de Taos, the place today known simply as Taos.

The Taos Indian Reservation owes its beginning to a Spanish land grant confirmed by Congress in 1858 and patented in 1864. Taoseños received another Spanish grant in 1818 that was officially recognized

The 1850s church of San Jerónimo, Taos Pueblo, New Mexico

by the United States in the early part of the twentieth century. Further additions to the Taos Indian Reservation were made in 1940 and in 1970, the latter when the sacred site of Blue Lake and some forty-eight thousand surrounding acres in the Carson National Forest were returned to the tribe by an Act of Congress.

Taos Pueblo, seventy miles north of Santa Fe, is three miles north of the town of Taos. Leaving central Taos, drive north on U.S. Highway 64 (Paseo del Pueblo Norte) until coming to a well-marked sign just beyond the Van Vechten Lineberry Museum indicating the road on the right that leads across the southwestern corner of the reservation to the pueblo, where the road ends. Tribal administrative offices are two miles from the main village on the Taos and Taos Pueblo road.

Recreational Opportunities

The United Nations has designated Taos Pueblo as a "World Heritage Site," virtually assuring, if such assurance were needed, that the pueblo is destined to play host to visitors from all over the world. The village is divided into two halves, the North House and South House, and its multi-roomed, contiguous structures have been maintained with loving care. North House has a room five stories in the air, and the buildings' setting, with the Sangre de Cristo Mountains rising in the background and a clear stream separating the pueblo's halves, make this a dream come true for artists and photographers. Bread continues to be baked in hornos, the beehive-shaped ovens introduced by Spaniards in the sixteenth century, and craftspeople have their wares, as well as products of other Puebloan and Southwest Indians, available for sale. There are kivas, livestock corrals, the San Jerónimo church,

and a pair of foot bridges over the stream. There are no power poles, TV aerials, or telephone poles because the pueblo has chosen to remain without electricity, telephones, and—except for the stream—running water. Water is carried into homes from the stream in buckets.

There are, however, usually many cars, vans, trucks, and buses, these being the conveyances used by most visitors to reach the pueblo.

As one approaches the entrance to the pueblo, attendants indicate where to park. Visitors pay an entrance fee and appropriate camera fees at the Guide House Booth set up for that purpose. One can either walk around the pueblo unattended or with a group escorted, at no extra charge, by a Taos guide. People are asked not to wade in the stream, the village's source of drinking water; to respect "restricted area" signs; not to take pictures inside the San Jerónimo church; not to enter the walled compound and cemetery around the ruins of the eighteenth-century church; and not to enter homes that lack signs indicating they are stores or food concessions. As always, no pictures of people should be taken without their permission.

The pueblo is open to visitors daily from 8:00 a.m. until 5:30 p.m. unless there are private Indian rituals, including funerals, in progress. There are nine yearly occasions when the public is invited, without bringing cameras, to enjoy tribal ceremonies and celebrations. These are New Year's Day (turtle dance); January 6, Feast of the Three Kings (buffalo or deer dance); May 3, Feast of Santa Cruz (foot race and corn dance); June 13, Feast of San Antonio (corn dance); 2nd weekend in July, Taos Pueblo Powwow; July 25-26, Feast of Santa Ana and Santiago (corn dance); September 29-30, patronal Feast of San Jerónimo (sunset dance, foot race, pole climbing, social dances, and trade fair);

December 24, Christmas Eve (procession); and December 25, Christmas Day (deer dance or matachines dancers).

Taos artisans are known for their micaceous pottery, silver and turquoise jewelry, flutes, beadwork, tanned buckskin moccasins, and drums. There are more than thirty arts and crafts shops either in the pueblo or along the approach to it that sell these and other Indian wares.

In addition to being able to buy food in the pueblo, traditional feast day foods are regularly served for lunch at the Tiwa Kitchen on the left hand side of the road leading to the pueblo (phone 505/751-1020).

The tribe also operates the Taos Mountain Casino (P.O. Box 1477, Taos, NM 87571; phone 800/946-8267 or 505/758-4460). Advertising itself as "New Mexico's only non-smoking Indian gaming establishment," it has a full complement of slot machines, video games, and table games like poker and blackjack as well as food service. It is on the left hand side of the road a mile from the entrance to the reservation.

Horseback tours are available through the Taos Indian Horse Ranch. To make reservations, contact Cesario Stormstar Gomez at P.O. Box 3019, Taos, NM 87571 (phone 800/659-3210 or 505/758-3212).

For further details, one can write or phone the Tribal Tourism Department, P.O. Box 1846, Taos, NM 87571; 505/758-8626.

Taos Pueblo
P.O. Box 1846, Taos, NM 87571
Phone 505/758-9593
Population: 2,170
Acreage: 95,341

Taos Canyon

HUEY

Jicarilla Apaches and Utes share neighboring reservations in a region of high plateaus, mesas, mountains, and intermontane basins of northern New Mexico and southern Colorado. And while it is a little known fact, the Ute Mountain Indian Reservation extends southward from Colorado into north-western New Mexico where its western boundary abuts the eastern boundary of the Navajo Indian Reservation. The Jicarillas, like other Apache groups, speak an Athapaskan language, while the Utes speak what linguists have labeled the Southern Numic branch of the Uto-Aztecan language phylum. Language and other traditional cultural differences aside, Utes and Jicarillas find themselves at the end of the twentieth century sharing a similar environment as well as similar kinds of developments and prospects for the future. They are, in a sense, facing their destinies in a world high above sea level apart from the rest of the American Southwest.

JICARILLA APACHE TRIBE

The Jicarillas, along with the Navajos, Mescaleros, Lipans, Chiricahuas, and Western Apaches, were one of the Athapaskan groups who migrated into the Southwest from the Great Plains between the fourteenth and sixteenth centuries. The Jicarillas' early historic aboriginal hunting, gathering, farming, and camping territory, virtually all of it east of their present-day reservation, extended equally on both sides of today's New Mexico and Colorado boundary. At a minimum, it stretched from Chama, New Mexico, in the west to the boundary between New Mexico and the Oklahoma Panhandle in the east and from Mora, New Mexico, in the south to near the Arkansas River in Colorado in the north. This range of more than nine million acres put them in regular contact with the Northern Tiwas of Picuris and Taos as well as with the Tewas of San Juan Pueblo.

The Spanish government, followed by that of Mexico after 1821, made large grants of Jicarilla lands to Spanish and Mexican settlers without consulting with Jicarillas. These land grants were later recognized by the U.S. Government, a recognition that ultimately forced the United States to create a reservation on which to settle the displaced people.

Soon after the U.S. takeover of New Mexico in 1846, many conflicts arose between Americans and Jicarillas, and the Indians began carrying out raids against wagon trains and smaller settlements. Finally, in 1855, both Jicarillas and Utes, tired of warfare with Americans, signed a treaty. It was, however, not ratified by the U.S. Senate and never

enjoyed the force of law. Even so, Jicarillas maintained the peace. A reservation was set aside for them in northern New Mexico by executive order in 1874, only to be abrogated by another executive order in 1876 because Jicarillas had not moved onto it. In 1880 another reservation, the basis of the present one, was set aside, but three years later all the Jicarillas were rounded up and forced to move to the Mescalero Reservation. They remained at Mescalero only three years before they abandoned the place to return to the north. This time, in 1887, their 1880 reservation—that lay entirely within New Mexico and straddled the Continental Divide from 6,000 to 8,000 feet above sea level—was made permanent. In 1907 and 1908, lands at a somewhat lower elevation were added to the south, a place where livestock could be grazed during the winter. Allotments of reservation lands to individual Apache families took place in 1887 and again in 1909 when areas were resurveyed and earlier confusions were straightened out. The government permitted sales of timber from both allotted and tribal lands, and timber sales, combined with the cattle industry, should have led Jicarillas out of the dire poverty from which they had been suffering. Government policies frustrated these efforts, however, and it was only in the 1920s after families were given sheep to raise that the economy began to improve.

By the 1970s, Jicarillas were earning substantial sums of money from livestock, both cattle and sheep, as well as from sales of timber, natural gas, and oil. Money from leases of natural resources was distributed to individuals on a per capita basis, as is the case today. Additionally, in 1970 the tribe was paid more than $8 million dollars by the U.S. government as compensation for lands they had lost beyond the boundaries of their nineteenth- and early twentieth-century reservation.

People who once lived in widely scattered communities on the reservation began after World War II to move to Dulce and its immediate vicinity. Old ways of life that involved traditional hunting, gathering, and small-scale farming gave way—as it has among all Indians—to the demands of a cash economy, and the "urban center" of Dulce is one result.

By the 1960s, tribal leaders had recognized the potential for community betterment through development of tourism and recreational facilities on their uniformly beautiful reservation. In cooperation with the New Mexico Department of Game and Fish, wildlife resources were developed, including camping facilities, guide services, and related activities

Tribal headquarters are located in Dulce on U.S. Highway 64 twenty-five miles west of Chama, New Mexico. Dulce is about seventy-five miles east of Farmington, New Mexico, via the same highway. A scenic approach to the Jicarillas' headquarters, but one not particularly recommended during the winter, is from the south via State Highway 537 that leaves State Highway 44 at Tancosa Junction twenty miles west of Cuba, New Mexico. Highway 537 runs most of the length of the Jicarilla Indian Reservation, taking the sightseer through virtually all of its environmental zones. Highway 537 intersects U.S. 64 nine miles south of Dulce.

Visitors coming to Dulce from the north take U.S. 84 from Pagosa Springs, Colorado, to U.S. 64, then west on Highway 64 twelve miles.

Recreational Opportunities

Dulce is not a town filled with tourist attractions, but it is nonetheless the population hub of the Jicarilla Indian Reservation and where people stay overnight while visiting either for pleasure or business. In addition to having an airport that can accommodate small-to medium-size planes, there are service stations, a grocery and dry goods store, restaurants, motels, and, not surprisingly, the Apache Nugget gaming casino (phone 505/759-3777). The latter, located about a mile west of the Jicarilla Inn on U.S. 64, offers a full complement of slot machines, video slots, and such table games as poker and blackjack (no bingo).

Over a weekend each mid-July, the town and rodeo grounds at Dulce come alive when Jicarillas hold their Little Beaver Powwow and Round-up, a three-day rodeo that includes a cross country pony express race. The affair also features a Rodeo Queen contest, parade, carnival, and various kinds of crafts demonstrations and Apache dances (call 505/759-3242 for details).

In 1964 the tribal council established the Jicarilla Arts and Crafts Industry to foster preservation of traditional beadwork, coiled basketry, buckskin tanning, and leatherwork. These crafts workers, principally older Apache women, demonstrate their abilities at the Jicarilla Arts and Crafts Museum in Dulce. Their products can often be found on sale in the Apache Mesa Gallery and Gift Shop in the nearby Jicarilla Inn.

An important celebration open to the public takes place in mid-September at Stone Lake just south of the junctions of Indian Routes 8 and 15 about twenty miles south of Dulce on Indian Route 8. This Go-Gee-Ya Feast, as Jicarillas call it, is chiefly the occasion for Jicarilla family reunions, but others are equally welcome. Amateur contestants compete in rodeo events and there are traditional dancing; food; various games; and a ceremonial relay race. For information, call tribal headquarters at 505/759-3242.

The reservation's principal summer attractions are those involving outdoor activities: fishing, hiking, horseback riding, and visiting archaeological ruins. Various kinds of reservation hunts take place in January, April, and September through December, while winter sports include snowshoeing, snowmobiling, or cross-country skiing. The nearest downhill skiing, and it is off-reservation in southern Colorado twenty miles north of Pagosa Springs on U.S. Highway 160, is at the Wolf Creek Ski Area.

Fishing and hunting permits are available from the Jicarilla Apache Tribe, Department of Game and Fish, P.O. Box 313, Dulce, NM 87528 (phone 505/759-3255, 3442, or 3513; Fax 505/759-3457). Fishing licenses are available on either a daily or yearly basis. With the exception of Stone Lake, which is open only April 1 through November 30, all other waters are open for fishing all year round. These include Dulce Lake, La Jara Lake, Enbom Lake, Mundo Lake, Hayden Lake, Horse Lake, and Navajo River. Anglers fishing Willow Creek and Horse Lake Creek must be accompanied by a tribal member.

The reservation's cold water lakes produce rainbow, cutthroat, and brown trout. Redwood docks are provided at some lakes for shore fishers, while boats (trolling speeds are the maximum allowed) and floating tubes are also popular. All seven lakes are accessible by vehicle; all but Horse Lake, where no overnight camping is allowed, have restrooms; and all lakes have picnic areas.

Stinking Lake, a fourteen hundred-acre marsh, in addition to some fourteen hundred ponds on the reservation have made it a magnet for migrating ducks. Duck hunting season is in the early fall before the freeze. In addition to a reservation permit, duck hunters must have a Federal Duck Stamp and use steel shot.

As with hunting waterfowl, no guide is needed to accompany hunters wanting to bag a Merriam turkey. One does, however, need a valid permit to go after one of these birds in the spring season. The permits, like those for big game, are limited and are available by a drawing.

Jicarilla tribal member guides are required for all big game hunts. Most guides use four-wheel drive vehicles, but some lead foot or horseback hunts. There are more than eighty such guides available and the tribe's Game and Fish Department issues a list of names and phone numbers. All permits, except those for bear, mountain lion, and cow elk, which are given out first-come first-served, are issued on a drawing basis. The cow elk season is in November, December, and January; bear season is in April into June and late September through October; and mountain lion from mid-November through March.

Cliff Palace at Mesa Verde National Park, Colorado

HUEY

Drawings are held for permits to hunt bull elk (parts of September [archery], October, and November); mule deer (December); and trophy bull elk (September through November).

For complete details for each year's hunts, with dates and updated regulations, contact the Department of Game and Fish.

Two prehistoric ruins can be reached by vehicle on the reservation's back roads. These are Honolulu Ruin (take Indian Route 6 west from the Counting Pens on State Highway 537 to its junction with Indian Route 63, and follow 63 to the end of the road), and Cordova Canyon Ruins (follow Indian Route 13 south six miles from its junction with State Highway 537 a half mile south of Dulce Lake).

Prehistoric ruins are strictly protected by federal law and should be left absolutely undisturbed. Visitors should take nothing but pictures and leave nothing but footprints. To remove even a single artifact or to disturb the smallest wall is forever to destroy a page from an irreplaceable history book.

Tribal Museum: The Jicarilla Arts and Crafts Museum is within easy walking distance west of the Jicarilla Inn on the same (north) side of Highway 64. It has excellent displays of high quality Jicarilla coiled baskets, beadwork, sewing (so-called Apache "squaw dresses"), pottery, and paintings. There are also historical black-and-white photographs of Jicarillas and of scenes on the reservation from earlier times

The museum building also provides space for the Jicarilla Arts and Crafts Industry where one can see Jicarilla basket makers and other craftspeople at work.

The Jicarilla Apache Tribe
P.O. Box 507, Dulce, NM 87528
Phone 505/759-3242
Population: 2,764
Acreage: 823,580

UTE MOUNTAIN UTE TRIBE

The Utes, like Southern Paiutes (including Chemehuevis), are traditionally speakers of a language group referred to by linguists as "Numic." Numic, in turn, is related to, although not mutually intelligible with, Northern Paiute, Shoshone, Hopi, and other Uto-Aztecan languages. At present, as is true for many Southwest and other Indian groups in the United States, the first language for the majority of Utes has become English, and there are tribal members who no longer have a fluent grasp of their native language.

Before the 1830s and before non-Indians began to arrive in their territory in significant numbers, bands of Ute Indians ranged over about 130,000 square miles of today's western Colorado and eastern Utah, 87,500 of them in Colorado. Among these were members of the Weeminuche band whose descendants are the majority of today's residents of the Ute Mountain Indian Reservation of southwestern Colorado and northwestern New Mexico.

The Weeminuche's range, on the western side of the Continental Divide, once extended from the Dolores River in western Colorado through the Blue Mountains to the edge of eastern Utah's canyonlands mesas and plateaus. They were no doubt involved with other Utes in periodic raids against Pueblo, Apache, Hopi, and Navajo settlements, actions that led to enmities lasting as late as the end of the nineteenth century.

As late as the middle of the nineteenth century, Ute territory covered 56 million acres, or about 85 percent, of Colorado. In 1868, the territory was reduced by a ratified treaty between the United States and several bands of Utes to the 14,730,000-acre Consolidated Ute Reservation covering some 40 percent of Colorado in its western half. In 1873-74 these same Utes were forced to relinquish a

HUCKO

Ute beaded cradleboard

▼▼

3,450,000-acre parcel in the south for mining, except that a narrow band along Colorado's southern border—today's Ute Mountain and Southern Ute reservations—was spared from the cession. In 1880, however, Utes were forced to cede all the Colorado lands north and west of the 1874 cession. The bands whose descendants now live on the Ute Mountain and Southern Ute reservations were already in place and were allowed to remain, sparing these comparatively few square miles of land from further alienation. In 1915, the Ute Mountain Reservation, where members of the Weeminuche band lived, was separated from the Southern Ute Reservation to become its own legal entity.

In the mid-1920s, a small number of Southern Paiutes moved from Arizona to Allen Canyon. They became known as the Allen Canyon Paiute or Ute and in 1925 they agreed officially to join the Ute Mountain band. The Ute Mountain Utes used to refer to them—and some still may—as the "White Mesa" people or simply as "Paiutes." Their descendants are now integrated into the tribe.

The New Mexico portion of the Ute Mountain Indian Reservation is a desolate, largely roadless and uninhabited region that happens to contain natural gas and oil fields. A few Utes go there occasionally to tend livestock. The principal access roads to this part of the reservation, north of U.S. Highway 64 between Farmington and Shiprock, are barred by locked gates.

Tribal headquarters are located in Towaoc, Colorado, about eleven miles south of Cortez, Colorado, or about twenty-two miles north of Shiprock, New Mexico, to the west off U.S. Highway 160/666. Parts of the reservation abut the western and southern boundaries of Mesa Verde National Park.

Recreational Opportunities

The Ute Mountain Casino (phone 800/258-8007 or 970/565-8800) is located eleven miles south of Cortez, Colorado, on U.S. Highway 160/666 in Towaoc. It offers bingo, slots, live 21 and poker, video poker and keno, and live keno. Because the Navajo Nation has not gotten into the gaming business, the Ute Mountain Casino is "the largest in the Four Corners." The casino has a full service restaurant, Kuchu's, that specializes in regional dishes.

Opposite the casino, on the road north to Cortez, is the Ute Mountain Pottery plant, a tribal enterprise begun in 1970. This is a thoroughly modern industrial pottery manufacturing facility, one that involves the use of commercial clays, paints, and glazes and mold casting of such popular forms as pitchers and mugs. Designs, including some carved into the vessels after they have been fired (sgraffito), are applied by hand and very often the wares go out containing a card with the decorator's name. Ceramics from this pottery are shipped to gift shops throughout the world.

The Ute Mountain Pottery is open to the public for walking tours Monday through Saturday from 9:00 a.m. to 6:00 p.m. In the summer, it is open on Sunday from noon to 6:00 p.m. For details, phone 970/565-8548.

An important attraction on the reservation is the 125,000-acre Ute Mountain Tribal Park. It has been set aside to preserve hundreds of prehistoric Anasazi ruins, both cliff dwellings and surface structures, some of them partially reconstructed. Because of its comparative isolation, the ruins here—some of which match those at nearby Mesa Verde National Park—receive few visitors.

Reservations need to be made at least twenty-four hours in advance to take one of the half-day or full-day guided tours. Visitors drive their own vehicles and provide their own drinking water, lunches, and fuel (best to arrive with a full gas tank). The assigned guide elaborates on both Anasazi and Ute cultures.

Horseback tours can also be arranged.

Visitors to the park also have the option of hiking, backpacking, mountain biking, and primitive camping.

Tours start from the Ute Mountain Visitor Center on U.S. Highway 666 twenty-two miles south of Cortez or twenty-one miles north of Shiprock. To make reservations, or for information concerning hours and fees, write the Ute Mountain Tribal Park, Towaoc, CO 81334; phone 800/847-5485 or 970/565-3751.

The Ute Mountain Round-up Rodeo is held each June at the Legion Arena in Towaoc. It features a rodeo, parade, carnival, barbecue, and social dancing. For details, phone 970/565-8151.

Towaoc has a library in which tribal archives and published material about Utes are kept. The library can be visited by appointment (phone 970/565-3751).

The bear dance, which spread among the Paiutes, Walapais, Havasupais, and Mohaves in the late nineteenth century, appears to have been a Ute invention. It was originally performed in late winter or early spring to coincide with the time bears were coming out of hibernation. It was, among other things, a time for festivities that afforded people the chance to renew social ties or to make new ones.

Utes continue to hold a bear dance, and the people on the Ute Mountain Indian Reservation hold theirs a mile east of Towaoc for five days over the first weekend of each June. In addition to traditional dancing and singing, there are food, games, and displays and sales of arts and crafts. A few Ute craftspeople still make beaded moccasins, belts, and buckskin bags as well as baskets.

**Ute Mountain Ute Tribe
Box 52, Towaoc, CO 81344
Phone 970/565-3751
Population: 1,911
Acreage: 555,000**

SOUTHERN UTE TRIBE

The Indian residents of today's Southern Ute Indian Reservation in southern Colorado are descendants of the Muache and Capote bands of Ute. At one time, the Muache lived from north of Trinidad, Colorado, to the vicinity of Denver and on the east side of the Culebra and Sangre de Cristo mountains as far south as Santa Fe. After they acquired the horse from Europeans in the late seventeenth century, they and the Jicarilla Apaches extended their ranges all the way east into the Texas panhandle.

Utes of the Capote band ranged east of the Continental Divide south of the Conejos River and east of the Rio Grande to the west side of the Sangre de Cristo Mountains. They lived in areas in the San Luis Valley of southern Colorado as well as around where Chama and Tierra Amarilla are located in New Mexico.

In 1880, the Muache and Capote bands ended up with the Weeminuche band on a single reservation in southernmost Colorado. In 1915, the reservation was divided into the Ute Mountain and Southern Ute reservations, with Weeminuche peoples being assigned the former. Ironically enough, Ignacio, the Ute from whom the tribal capital of the Southern Ute Reservation takes its name, was a Weeminuche chief.

The portion of the 1880 reservation occupied by Muache and Capote band members was allotted to individual Utes under terms of the 1887 General Land Allotment (Dawes) Act. Before allotting was stopped by a federal law passed in 1934, they had lost nearly thirty-five thousand acres of their lands through sales (allottees considered competent to manage their own business affairs were given clear title to their lands, and many of those persons subsequently sold their property). The mix of tribal and allotted lands on the Southern Ute Reservation continues to impose its special problems as it does on all reservations where the situation continues to exist.

The headquarters of the Southern Ute Tribe are located in Ignacio, Colorado, twenty-two miles southeast of Durango, Colorado. To reach Ignacio, take U.S. Highway 160 six miles southeast of Durango to its junction with Colorado State Highway 172. Continue southeast on Highway 172 sixteen miles to Ignacio. If coming from Pagosa Springs, take U.S. HIghway 160 west to its junction with Highway 521, and follow 521 south to Ignacio.

Recreational Opportunities

The Southern Ute Tribe makes an all out effort to attract visitors to the reservation. The centerpiece in this enterprise is the Sky Ute Casino, Lodge, and Museum, a facility that also houses a conference center, the Pino Nuche Restaurant, the Sky Ute Casino Restaurant, and the Rolling Thunder Café (phone 1/800/876-7017 or 970/563-3000). A free shuttle service carries passengers from the surrounding Durango, Pagosa Springs, Farmington, and Purgatory areas.

The Sky Ute Casino, which never closes and which has a non-smoking area, features poker tournaments, blackjack, video poker, slots, keno, and bingo. There are nine blackjack tables, more than three hundred slots, and a glass-enclosed poker room.

Ute crafts, including beaded products, baskets, and buckskin goods, are available for sale in the facility's gift shop.

The Southern Ute Heritage Dancers perform every Wednesday evening from June through September in the Sky Ute Lodge. This program, for which a fee is charged, also features a barbecue and tour of the Cultural Center.

Sky Ute Downs, a few minutes away from the casino and lodge, is an equestrian center and race track in Ignacio that is open all year around. It hosts a variety of horse shows, rodeos, and Indian powwows. Included among the many events held here are exciting games of polocrosse, a team game played on horseback with a rubber ball and a stick with a head like that of a lacrosse-stick (hence polo + lacrosse). Phone 970/563-4502 for the Sky Ute Downs yearly schedule.

Like the Ute Mountain Utes, the Southern Utes hold an annual bear dance that is open to the public. The dance among the Southern Utes is held over Memorial Day weekend (phone 800/772-1236 ext. 300 for details). The Southern Utes also hold a Sun Dance twice each year (phone 800/772-1236 ext. 300). The sun dance, which originated among Plains Indians, was borrowed by Utes during the nineteenth century. The sun dance is aimed at curing illness, restoring harmony, and promoting spiritual and physical well being. It is a formal confirmation of religious faith and a promise of hope for the future, and while outsiders are normally allowed to attend, it is a religious rather than a social occasion.

The second weekend of each September, the tribe holds the Southern Ute Fair and Powwow, one complete with a parade, foot races, dancing, and various games. Vendors sell food as well as Indian arts and crafts during the fair and powwow.

For information concerning hunting and fishing on the reservation, call the tribal Fish and Game Department at 970/563-0130.

Although not on the reservation, there are nearby recreation areas that are popular with anglers and campers and that the tribe promotes in its tourism literature. The first of these are the Chimney Rock and Lake Capote areas east of Ignacio near the junction of U.S. Highway 160 and State Highway 151. Lake Capote is stocked with trout and has an adjacent general store that sells camping and fishing permits and that rents rowboats and fishing equipment. Tent spaces and spaces for RVs with hookups are in the campground. It is open from April through September (phone 970/731-5256 for details).

Operated by the State of Colorado on state-owned land, Navajo State Recreation Area is sixteen miles southeast of Ignacio on State Highway 151 at the head of the Navajo Reservoir near where the Piedra River flows into it. The lake is touted as one of Colorado's best fishing sites.

The Navajo State Recreation Area is two miles from the town of Arboles, Colorado. It includes a nature trail, marina, restaurant, picnic areas, campgrounds, store, and boat rentals (phone 970/883-2208 for details). Part of the upper end of the Navajo Reservoir is on the Southern Ute Indian Reservation.

Tribal Museum: The Southern Ute Cultural Center and Gallery is located inside the Sky Ute Lodge. Its museum features Ute bead and leatherwork as well as a traditional tepee and sweat lodge. There are many interesting historical photographs and an audiovisual program acquainting viewers with Ute history. The museum's hours are from 10:00 a.m. to 6:00 p.m. weekdays and from 11:00 a.m. to 3:00 p.m. on weekends. It is closed Sundays in the winter. For details, call 970/563-4531.

Southern Ute Tribe
P.O. Box 737, Ignacio, CO 81137
Phone 970/563-4525
Population: 1,316
Acreage: 302,000

▼▼▼

Off-Reservation Gatherings

There are four annual occasions, one in Arizona and three in New Mexico, that bring significantly large numbers of Southwestern and other Indians together in off-reservation and non-museum settings. One of these is the Indian Market held each August in downtown Santa Fe, New Mexico. Some of the Southwest's finest potters, jewelry makers, clothing makers, painters, sculptors, drum makers, basket weavers, rug weavers, and beadworkers crowd the Santa Fe Plaza area from 8:00 a.m. to 6:00 p.m. for two days. For details, call 505/622-8581.

For more than 75 years, Gallup, New Mexico, has played host to the Inter-Tribal Indian Ceremonial. Held over six days each August in the nearby Red Rock State Park, this is probably the largest yearly gathering of Indians in the Southwest. Featured are parades, rodeos, Indian ceremonial dances, a juried arts and crafts show, sales of native foods, indoor/outdoor marketplaces, and races. The event is sponsored by the Inter-Tribal Indian Ceremonial Association, P.O. Box 1, Church Rock, NM 87311 (phone 800/233-4528 or 505/863-3896).

The Totah Festival in Farmington, New Mexico (phone 800/448-1240) takes place over a weekend late in August or early in September and features a Navajo rug auction, a contest powwow, and a juried exhibition and sale of Native American arts and crafts.

Three days over a weekend in February is when the O'odham Tash Indian Festival takes place in southern Arizona at the city of Casa Grande, a location central to the Tohono O'odham, Gila River, Salt River, Ft. McDowell, and Ak Chin reservations. A parade, powwow, juried arts and crafts exhibits and sales, and sales of traditional foods are on the agenda for this favorite wintertime gathering of Indians from many tribes. For further information, write the O'odham Tash Indian Festival, P.O. Box 11165, Casa Grande, AZ 85230-1165, or call 520/836-4723.

Off-Reservation Museums in Arizona and New Mexico with Significant Displays Relating to Indians of the Southwest

There are several outstanding museums in Arizona and New Mexico not on reservations that feature the histories and cultures of various contemporary Southwest Indian groups. They are the following:

ARIZONA:

The Amerind Foundation, Inc.
P.O. Box 400, Dragoon, AZ 85609
(phone 520/586-3666; Fax 520/586-4679)

Arizona State Museum
The University of Arizona,
Tucson, AZ 85721
(phone 520/621-6281; Fax 520/621-2975)

Heard Museum
22 E. Monte Vista Road,
Phoenix, AZ 85004-1480
phone 602/252-8840)

Pueblo Grande
4619 W. Washington Street,
Phoenix, AZ 85034
(phone 602/495-0901)

Museum of Northern Arizona
3101 Fort Valley Road,
Flagstaff, AZ 86001
(phone 520/774-5213; Fax 520/779-1527)

NEW MEXICO:

Indian Pueblo Cultural Center
2401 12th Street NW,
Albuquerque, NM 87102
phone 800/766-4405 or 505/843-7270)

Millicent Rogers Museum
P.O. Box A, Taos, NM 87571
(phone 505/758-2462; Fax 505/758-5751)

Museum of Indian Arts and Culture
Museum of New Mexico, Camino Lejo,
P.O. Box 2087, Santa Fe, NM 87504-2087
(phone 505/827-6344; Fax 505/827-6497)

Wheelwright Museum of the American Indian
704 Camino Lejo, P.O. Box 5153,
Santa Fe, NM 87502
(phone 800/607-4636 or 505/982-4636)

Pronouncing Indian Tribal Names

Ácoma: AHK-oma
Ak-Chin: AHK-chin
Chemehuevi: Chem-eh-WHAY-vee
Cochiti: CO-cheat-ee
Cocopah: CO-co-pah
Gila River: HEE-la
Havasupai: ha-va-SUE-pie
Hopi: HO-pee
Hualapai: WAL-eh-pie
Kaibab Paiute: KIE-bab PIE-yoot
Jémez: HEM-ez
Jicarilla: hic-eh-REE-ya
Laguna: lah-GOO-nah
Mescalero: mess-cal-AIR-o
Mojave: mo-HAV-ee
Nambé: nam-BAY
Navajo: NAV-eh-ho
Pascua Yaqui: PA-skwa YAH-kee
Picuris: pee-kur-EES
Pima-Maricopa: PEE ma-mar-i-CO-pah
Pojoaque: po-WAH-kay
Quechan: kay-CHAHN
Sandia: san-DEE-a
San Felipe: san fell-EE-pay
San Ildefonso: san ill-de-FON-so
Santo Domingo: SAN-toe doe-MIN-go
Taos: TA-os
Tesuque: tess-OO-kee
Tohono O'odham: TOE-ho-no AW-aw-dahm
Tonto: TAWN-to
Tortugas: tor-TWO-gahs
Utes: YOOTS
Yavapai: YA-va-pie
Ysleta: is-LET-a
Zia: ZEE-a
Zuni: ZOO-nee